GREAT DRAWINGS OF ALL TIME **II**

GREAT DRAWINGS OF ALL TIME

VOLUME **II**

German, Flemish
and Dutch
Thirteenth through
Nineteenth Century

SELECTED AND EDITED BY **IRA MOSKOWITZ**

SHOREWOOD PUBLISHERS INC. NEW YORK

Copyright © 1962 by Shorewood Publishers Inc.

Library of Congress Catalog Card Number: 62-19989

All rights reserved. No part of the contents of this book
may be reproduced without the written permission of the
publishers, Shorewood Publishers Inc., New York

Designed by Peter Oldenburg

Printed by Shorewood Press Inc., New York

GREAT DRAWINGS OF ALL TIME

VOLUME **I** *Italian*

TEXT BY

WINSLOW AMES, Art Historian

VOLUME **II** *German, Flemish and Dutch*

TEXT BY

OTTO BENESCH, Director, Albertina, Vienna

J. G. VAN GELDER, University of Utrecht, Netherlands

EGBERT HAVERKAMP-BEGEMANN, Curator, Department of Prints,
   Yale University Art Gallery

FRITS LUGT, Institut Néerlandais, Paris

VOLUME **III** *French*

TEXT BY

AGNES MONGAN, Assistant Director, Fogg Art Museum, Harvard University

VOLUME **IV** *Oriental, Spanish, English, American,
Contemporary*

TEXT BY

JOHN I. H. BAUR, Associate Director, Whitney Museum of American Art, New York

JAMES CAHILL, Assistant Curator, Chinese Art, Freer Gallery, Washington, D.C.

RICHARD ETTINGHAUSEN, Curator, Near Eastern Art, Freer Gallery, Washington, D.C.

JUSTINO FERNÁNDEZ, Art Historian

JOHN DAVIS HATCH, JR., Museum Consultant

THEODORE A. HEINRICH, Director, Royal Ontario Museum, Toronto

ELAINE JOHNSON, Assistant Curator, Department of Prints and Drawings,
   Museum of Modern Art, New York

PERRY T. RATHBONE, Director, Museum of Fine Arts, Boston

F. J. SÁNCHEZ-CANTÓN, Director, Prado, Madrid

JANÓS SCHOLZ, Collector and Historian

HAROLD P. STERN, Curator, Japanese Art, Freer Gallery, Washington, D.C.

A Shorewood Fine Arts Edition

Contents

ARTISTS AND PLATES   ix

GERMAN DRAWINGS   preceding Plate 304
    Introduction by Otto Benesch
    Comments on drawings by Otto Benesch

FLEMISH AND DUTCH DRAWINGS   preceding Plate 453
    Introduction by Frits Lugt
    Comments on Flemish drawings by Egbert Haverkamp-Begemann
    Comments on Dutch drawings by J. G. van Gelder

NOTE: A glossary of media and bibliography will be found at the end of Volume IV.

ARTISTS AND PLATES

PLATE

446 Aachen, Hans von, "The Baptism of Christ"
     Cambridge, Fitzwilliam Museum

447 Aachen, "Portrait of Giovanni da Bologna"
     New York, Dr. Julius Held

444 Aldegrever, Heinrich, "Portrait of a Man in a Flat Hat"
     Paris, Louvre, Cabinet des Dessins

417 Altdorfer, Albrecht, "St. Nicholas of Bari Rebuking
     the Tempest"
     Oxford, Ashmolean Museum

418 Altdorfer, "A Pair of Lovers Seated in a Corn Field"
     Basel, Kupferstichkabinett

419 Altdorfer, "The Agony in the Garden"
     Berlin, Kupferstichkabinett

420 Altdorfer, "St. Andrew Enthroned"
     Berlin, Kupferstichkabinett

421 Altdorfer, "Samson Rending the Lion"
     Berlin, Kupferstichkabinett

422 Altdorfer, "Sheet of Studies with Five Heads and a
     Castle in the Background"
     Vienna, Albertina

423 Altdorfer, "Salome with the Head of St. John the Baptist"
     Cleveland, Ohio, The Cleveland Museum of Art

449 Asam, Cosmas Damian, "The Coronation of the Virgin"
     Vienna, Albertina

435 Augsburg Draughtsman, Ca. 1515, "Reading of a
     Letter of Foundation by a Bishop in the Presence
     of Emperor Henry and Empress Kunigunde"
     Munich, Staatliche Graphische Sammlung

305 Austrian Master, Ca. 1320, "The Flight into Egypt
     and the Baptism of Christ"
     Vienna, Albertina

306 Austrian Master, Ca. 1400, "St. Margaret and the Dragon"
     Budapest, Museum of Fine Arts

308 Austrian Master, Ca. 1415, "The Mocking of Christ"
     Copenhagen, Royal Museum of Fine Arts

309 Austrian Master of 1424, "Emperor Sigismund with the
     Kings of Bohemia and Poland"
     Paris, Louvre, Collection Rothschild

373 Baldung, Hans (called Grien), "St. Jude Thaddeus"
     Lille, Palais des Beaux-Arts, Musée Wicar

374 Baldung, "Portrait Study of an Old Woman (half-length)"
     Jenkintown, Pennsylvania, Mrs. Lessing J. Rosenwald

PLATE

375 Baldung, "The Lamentation over the Body of Christ"
     Basel, Kupferstichkabinett

376 Baldung, "Two Nude Men, Fighting"
     Venice, Accademia

377 Baldung, "Head of 'Saturn' "
     Vienna, Albertina

378 Baldung, "The Virgin and Child with Angels and the Dove
     of the Holy Ghost"
     London, British Museum

379 Baldung, "Shooting at the Dead Father"
     Berlin, Kupferstichkabinett

380 Baldung, "Venus with the Apple of Paris(?)"
     Berlin, Kupferstichkabinett

381 Baldung, "Portrait of a Young Woman in Profile to Right"
     Berlin, Kupferstichkabinett

382 Baldung, "Lucretia"
     Frankfort-on-Main, Staedel Art Institute

383 Baldung, "Portrait of a Man Praying with a Rosary"
     Berlin, Kupferstichkabinett

482 Beer, Jan de, "Aristotle and Phyllis"
     London, British Museum

443 Beham, Barthel, "Portrait of a Bearded Man in a Flat Cap
     (J. Jost?)"
     Berlin, Kupferstichkabinett

472 Bosch, Hieronymus, "Merry Company in a Giant Egg"
     Berlin, Kupferstichkabinett

473 Bosch, "Two Pharisees"
     New York, Robert Lehman

474 Bosch, "Two Witches"
     Rotterdam, Museum Boymans-van Beuningen

475 Bosch, "The Owls' Nest"
     Rotterdam, Museum Boymans-van Beuningen

476 Bosch, "Tree-Man in a Landscape"
     Vienna, Albertina

477 Bosch, "St. Anthony"
     Berlin, Kupferstichkabinett

478 Bosch, "The Entombment"
     London, British Museum

465 Bouts, Dirk, "Portrait of a Young Man"
     Northampton, Massachusetts, Smith College Museum

397 Breu, Joerg the Elder, "The Crowning with Thorns"
     Munich, Staatliche Graphische Sammlung

PLATE

398   Breu, "Portrait of a Young Woman"
Berlin, Kupferstichkabinett

519   Brouwer, Adriaen, "Studies of Peasants"
Berlin, Kupferstichkabinett

511   Brueghel, Jan the Elder, "Stormy Sea"
Berlin, Kupferstichkabinett

491   Bruegel, Pieter the Elder (attributed to), "The Lamentation"
Vienna, Albertina

492   Bruegel, "Studies of Crippled Men and Women"
Vienna, Albertina

493   Bruegel, "The Painter and the Connoisseur"
Vienna, Albertina

494   Bruegel, "Ripa Grande, Rome"
Chatsworth, Devonshire Collections

495   Bruegel, "Landscape with Monastery at the Foot of a Mountain"
Berlin, Kupferstichkabinett

496   Bruegel, "Landscape with Rest on the Flight into Egypt"
Berlin, Kupferstichkabinett

497   Bruegel, "Alpine Landscape"
Brunswick, Maine, Bowdoin College, Walker Art Museum

498   Bruegel, "Alpine Landscape"
Cambridge, Massachusetts, Fogg Art Museum

499   Bruegel, "Alpine Landscape with a River, Village, and a Castle"
New York, The Pierpont Morgan Library

500   Bruegel, "Spes (Hope)"
Berlin, Kupferstichkabinett

501   Bruegel, "The Temptation of St. Anthony"
Oxford, Ashmolean Museum

502   Bruegel, "Rider and Two Horses"
Vienna, Albertina

503   Bruegel, "Peasant Seated, Holding a Basket"
Vienna, Albertina

504   Bruegel, "Crippled Beggar"
Amsterdam, Rijksmuseum

505   Bruegel, "Three Peasants"
Rotterdam, Museum Boymans-van Beuningen

506   Bruegel, "Peasant Woman Seated"
Berlin, Kupferstichkabinett

507   Bruegel, "Studies of Three Peasants"
Berlin, Kupferstichkabinett

508   Bruegel, "The Horse-Dealer"
Frankfort-on-Main, Staedel Art Institute

509   Bruegel, "Two Seated Peasant Women Seen from the Back"
Dresden, Staatliche Kunstsammlungen

510   Bruegel, "Two Rabbis"
Frankfort-on-Main, Staedel Art Institute

469   Bruges, School of, Ca. 1490, "Lady Kneeling in a Landscape"
Rotterdam, Museum Boymans-van Beuningen

PLATE

470   Bruges, School of, Ca. 1490, "Female Saint Standing in a Landscape"
Copenhagen, Royal Museum of Fine Arts

395   Burgkmair, Hans the Elder, "Portrait of Wolfgang von Maen"
Chatsworth, Devonshire Collections

396   Burgkmair, "The Virgin and Child"
Paris, Louvre, Cabinet des Dessins

454   Campin, Robert (attributed to), "Thief on the Cross"
Cambridge, Massachusetts, Fogg Art Museum

462   Christus, Petrus (after), "Portrait of a Man with a Falcon"
Frankfort-on-Main, Staedel Art Institute

463   Christus, Petrus (after), "Portrait of a Man"
Vienna, Albertina

384   Cranach, Lucas the Elder, "A Thief on the Cross, Turned to Right"
Berlin, Kupferstichkabinett

385   Cranach, "A Thief on the Cross, Turned to Left"
Berlin, Kupferstichkabinett

386   Cranach, "The Crucifixion"
Cambridge, Fitzwilliam Museum

387   Cranach, "St. Eustace Kneeling in a Landscape"
Boston, Massachusetts, Museum of Fine Arts

388   Cranach, "The Death of the Virgin"
Berlin, Kupferstichkabinett

389   Cranach, "Portrait of a Man in a Wide-Brimmed Hat"
London, British Museum

390   Cranach, "Portrait of a Man in a Fur Hat"
London, British Museum

604   Cuyp, Albert, "Study of Trees"
New York, The Metropolitan Museum of Art

479   David, Gerard, "Studies of Four Heads"
Ottawa, National Gallery of Canada

480   David, "Studies of a Young Woman's and of a Man's Head"
Frankfort-on-Main, Staedel Art Institute

428   Deutsch, Niklaus Manuel, "The Unequal Couple"
Basel, Kupferstichkabinett

429   Deutsch, "Lucretia (Bust)"
Basel, Kupferstichkabinett

330   Dürer, Albrecht, "Self-Portrait at the Age of Thirteen"
Vienna, Albertina

331   Dürer, "Albrecht Dürer the Elder"
Vienna, Albertina

332   Dürer, "Soldiers beneath the Cross"
Frankfort-on-Main, Staedel Art Institute

333   Dürer, "Young Couple"
Hamburg, Kunsthalle

334   Dürer, "Female Nude, Seen from the Back, Holding a Staff and a Drapery"
Paris, Louvre, Cabinet des Dessins

335   Dürer, "View of Arco"
Paris, Louvre, Cabinet des Dessins

[x]

336   Dürer, "Studies of Two Horsemen"
      London, Count Antoine Seilern

337   Dürer, "Christ Taken into Captivity"
      Basel, Kupferstichkabinett

338   Dürer, "A Lady of Nuremberg in Church Dress"
      London, British Museum

339   Dürer, "Head of a Roebuck"
      Bayonne, Musée Bonnat

340   Dürer, "Head of the Virgin"
      Berlin, Kupferstichkabinett

341   Dürer, "Head of the Dead Christ Crowned with Thorns"
      London, British Museum

342   Dürer, "Standing Female Nude, A Staff in Her Right Hand"
      Ottawa, National Gallery of Canada

343   Dürer, "The Dead Christ, Lying on a Pall"
      Cleveland, Ohio, The Cleveland Museum of Art

344   Dürer, "The Mantle of the Pope"
      Vienna, Albertina

345   Dürer, "Donor with Rosary Kneeling in Prayer"
      New York, The Pierpont Morgan Library

346   Dürer, "Portrait of an Architect"
      Berlin, Kupferstichkabinett

347   Dürer, "Head of an Apostle"
      Vienna, Albertina

348   Dürer, "The Virgin with the Child and Little St. John"
      Bayonne, Musée Bonnat

349   Dürer, "The Virgin Suckling the Child"
      Vienna, Albertina

350   Dürer, "Two Versions of the Virgin and Child"
      Frankfort-on-Main, Staedel Art Institute

351   Dürer, "The Virgin Seated on a Chair,
      Offering an Apple to the Child"
      Venice, Accademia

352   Dürer, "Portrait of the Artist's Mother"
      Berlin, Kupferstichkabinett

353   Dürer, "The Holy Trinity"
      Boston, Massachusetts, Museum of Fine Arts

354   Dürer, "Sheet of Studies with Six Nude Figures,
      the Main Figure Tied to the Trunk of a Tree"
      Frankfort-on-Main, Staedel Art Institute

355   Dürer, "Portrait of Hans Burgkmair the Elder"
      Oxford, Ashmolean Museum

356   Dürer, "Portrait of Emperor Maximilian I"
      Vienna, Albertina

357   Dürer, "The Lamentation for Christ"
      Vienna, Albertina

358   Dürer, "St. Anne (Portrait of Agnes Dürer)"
      Vienna, Albertina

359   Dürer, "Head of a Young Woman with Her Eyes Closed"
      London, British Museum

360   Dürer, "Heads of a Young Woman and of an
      Old Woman from Bergen"
      Chantilly, Musée Condé

361   Dürer, "Portrait of a Ninety-Three-Year-Old Man"
      Vienna, Albertina

362   Dürer, "Madonna and Child Enthroned with
      Saints and Angels"
      Bayonne, Musée Bonnat

363   Dürer, "Study for St. Barbara (Bust)"
      Paris, Louvre, Cabinet des Dessins

364   Dürer, "Study for St. Apollonia (Bust)"
      Berlin, Kupferstichkabinett

365   Dürer, "The Agony in the Garden"
      Frankfort-on-Main, Staedel Art Institute

457   Dutch or Flemish, Ca. 1420-1450, "Mary and St. John"
      Dresden, Staatliche Kunstsammlungen

543   Dyck, Anthony van, "The Entombment"
      Chatsworth, Devonshire Collections

544   Dyck, "Christ Falling under the Cross"
      Turin, Biblioteca Reale

545   Dyck, "Christ Falling under the Cross"
      Lille, Palais des Beaux-Arts, Musée Wicar

546   Dyck, "The Mystic Marriage of St. Catherine"
      New York, The Pierpont Morgan Library

547   Dyck, "The Descent of the Holy Ghost"
      Paris, Louvre, Cabinet des Dessins

548   Dyck, "Diana and Endymion"
      New York, The Pierpont Morgan Library

549   Dyck, "The Martyrdom of St. Catherine"
      Paris, Ecole National Supérieure des Beaux-Arts

550   Dyck, "Study for Christ Crowned with Thorns"
      Oxford, Ashmolean Museum

551   Dyck, "Studies for Sleeping Disciples"
      Berlin, Kupferstichkabinett

552   Dyck, "The Betrayal of Christ"
      Hamburg, Kunsthalle

553   Dyck, "Studies of a Woman Sleeping"
      Madrid, Biblioteca Nacional

554   Dyck, "Studies of the Head of a Horse and of a
      Man on Horseback"
      Amsterdam, Rijksmuseum

555   Dyck, "Portrait of Hendrik van Balen"
      Chatsworth, Devonshire Collections

556   Dyck, "View of Rye"
      New York, The Pierpont Morgan Library

448   Elsheimer, Adam, "Classical Landscape"
      Basel, Dr. Robert von Hirsch

481   Engelbrechtsen, Cornelis, "Heads of Men,
      Women, and Children"
      Amsterdam, Rijksmuseum

PLATE

455 Eyck, Jan van, "Portrait of Cardinal Albergati"
Dresden, Staatliche Kunstsammlungen

456 Eyck, Jan van (?), "Portrait of a Man"
Rotterdam, Museum Boymans-van Beuningen

457 Flemish or Dutch, Ca. 1420-1450, "Mary and St. John"
Dresden, Staatliche Kunstsammlungen

453 Flemish, Early, or Franco-Flemish, Ca. 1420,
"The Betrayal of Christ"
London, British Museum

461 Flemish, Ca. 1450, "Men Shoveling Chairs"
New York, Robert Lehman

471 Flemish, Late XV Century, "Scribe Writing,
the Author Presenting His Book"
*Washington, D. C., National Gallery of Art,
Rosenwald Collection*

453 Franco-Flemish, or Early Flemish, Ca. 1420,
"The Betrayal of Christ"
London, British Museum

615 Furnerius, Abraham, "Landscape with a Bridge"
Leningrad, Hermitage

320 German (Suabian?) Artist, Ca. 1470,
"Mary with the Body of Christ at the Foot of the Cross"
Vienna, Albertina

514 Gheyn, Jacques de, "Pietà"
Amsterdam, Rijksmuseum

515 Gheyn, "Woman on Her Death-Bed"
Amsterdam, Rijksmuseum

516 Gheyn, "The Birdcatcher"
Rotterdam, Museum Boymans-van Beuningen

517 Gheyn, "Four Heads of a Horse"
Berlin, Kupferstichkabinett

466 Goes, Hugo van der, "The Meeting of Jacob and Rachel"
Oxford, Christ Church

467 Goes (school of), "Kneeling Woman"
New York, The Pierpont Morgan Library

468 Goes (school of), "Virgin and Child"
New York, Robert Lehman

623 Gogh, Vincent van, "Weeping Woman"
Chicago, Illinois, The Art Institute

624 Gogh, "View of Arles"
*Providence, Rhode Island, Rhode Island
School of Design*

625 Gogh, "The Blue Cart"
Cambridge, Massachusetts, Fogg Art Museum

626 Gogh, "Peasant of the Camargue"
Cambridge, Massachusetts, Fogg Art Museum

627 Gogh, "Bridge at Arles"
Los Angeles, California, Los Angeles County Museum

628 Gogh, "The Iron Bridge at Trinquetaille on the Rhône"
New York, Robert Lehman

629 Gogh, "Tree in a Meadow"
Chicago, Illinois, The Art Institute

PLATE

630 Gogh, "A Grove of Cypresses"
Chicago, Illinois, The Art Institute

512 Goltzius, Hendrick, "Portrait of a Man"
Berlin, Kupferstichkabinett

513 Goltzius, "Group of Trees in a Wood"
Hamburg, Kunsthalle

Gossaert, Jan Gossaert van Mabuse, see Mabuse

602 Goyen, Jan van, "Landscape near a River"
Berlin, Kupferstichkabinett

603 Goyen, "River Bank"
Paris, Louvre, Cabinet des Dessins

432 Graf, Urs, "Place of Execution"
Vienna, Albertina

433 Graf, "St. Sebastian Tied to a Tree"
Basel, Kupferstichkabinett

434 Graf, "The Beheading of St. Barbara"
Basel, Kupferstichkabinett

Grien, see Baldung

399 Grünewald, Matthias, "Kneeling Man with Raised Hands"
Berlin, Kupferstichkabinett

400 Grünewald, "The Virgin Kneeling with Folded Hands"
Basel, Kupferstichkabinett

401 Grünewald, "An Elderly Woman with Clasped Hands"
Oxford, Ashmolean Museum

402 Grünewald, "The Virgin and Child with Little St. John"
Berlin, Kupferstichkabinett

403 Grünewald, "A Saint with a Staff Standing in the Forest"
Vienna, Albertina

404 Grünewald, "Christ the King, Whose Train Is Carried
by Two Angels"
Berlin, Kupferstichkabinett

405 Grünewald, "The Virgin and Child Seated by a Tree"
Berlin, Kupferstichkabinett

406 Grünewald, "The Virgin Kneeling and Turning a Leaf
of the Bible"
Berlin, Kupferstichkabinett

407 Grünewald, "St. Dorothy and the Christ Child"
Berlin, Kupferstichkabinett

408 Grünewald, "St. Catherine"
Berlin, Kupferstichkabinett

409 Grünewald, "Portrait of an Ecclesiastic"
Stockholm, Nationalmuseum

410 Grünewald, "Head of a Screaming Angel"
Berlin, Kupferstichkabinett

411 Grünewald, "Head of a Weeping Angel"
Berlin, Kupferstichkabinett

412 Grünewald, "Trinity"
Berlin, Kupferstichkabinett

413 Grünewald, "Man with Moustache and Clasped
Hands (Bust)"
Berlin, Kupferstichkabinett

PLATE

414   Grünewald, "Head of a Smiling Woman"
      Paris, Louvre, Cabinet des Dessins

415   Grünewald, "Head of a Young Woman"
      Berlin, Kupferstichkabinett

416   Grünewald, "Margaret Prellwitz, Mother of Hans Schoenitz"
      Paris, Louvre, Cabinet des Dessins

436   Holbein, Ambrosius, "The Astrologer and the Theologian"
      Basel, Kupferstichkabinett

393   Holbein, Hans the Elder, "Seated Woman with Long
      Loose Hair"
      Copenhagen, Royal Museum of Fine Arts

394   Holbein, Hans the Elder, "The Virgin Offering Her
      Breast to the Sleeping Child"
      Basel, Kupferstichkabinett

436   Holbein, Hans the Younger, "The Astrologer and
      the Theologian"
      Basel, Kupferstichkabinett

437   Holbein, Hans the Younger, "Portrait of a Leper (so-called)"
      Cambridge, Massachusetts, Fogg Art Museum

438   Holbein, Hans the Younger, "Portrait of the Mayor
      Jakob Meyer (Bust)"
      Basel, Kupferstichkabinett

439   Holbein, Hans the Younger, "Portrait of Anna, the Daughter
      of Jakob Meyer (In Profile to the Left)"
      Basel, Kupferstichkabinett

440   Holbein, Hans the Younger, "Portrait of an English
      Lady in Hat and Coif"
      London, British Museum

441   Holbein, Hans the Younger, "Cardinal John Fisher,
      Bishop of Rochester"
      Windsor Castle, Royal Collection

442   Holbein, Hans the Younger, "Portrait of
      Sir Charles Wingfield"
      Windsor Castle, Royal Collection

424   Huber, Wolf, "Portrait of a Man in a Cap (Bust)"
      Berlin, Kupferstichkabinett

425   Huber, "Head of a Young Man"
      New York, The Metropolitan Museum of Art

426   Huber, "View of Feldkirch"
      London, British Museum

427   Huber, "The Rapids of the Danube near Grien"
      *Washington, D. C., National Gallery of Art,
      Rosenwald Collection*

621   Huysum, Jan van, "Flower Piece"
      *Shawnee Mission, Kansas, Mr. and Mrs.
      Milton McGreevy*

622   Jongkind, Johan Barthold, "Windmills"
      Cambridge, Massachusetts, Fogg Art Museum

557   Jordaens, Jacob, "The Entombment of Christ"
      Antwerp, Stedelyk Prentenkabinet

558   Jordaens, "Head of an Old Man Drinking (Portrait
      of Adam van Noort)"
      Cambridge, Fitzwilliam Museum

PLATE

559   Jordaens, "Venus Sleeping"
      Lille, Palais des Beaux-Arts, Musée Wicar

560   Jordaens, "A Study of a Seated Man"
      Los Angeles, California, Los Angeles County Museum

613   Koninck, Philips, "Landscape with Houses amidst Trees"
      Leningrad, Hermitage

614   Konick, "Landscape with Boathouse"
      New York, Harry G. Sperling

366   Kulmbach, Hans Suess von, "Two Pairs of Lovers
      and an Old Woman"
      Munich, Staatliche Graphische Sammlung

367   Kulmbach, "The Holy Virgin and Child with Angels Making
      Music, St. Jerome and St. Anthony." On the Wings:
      "St. Sebastian, St. Roch"
      Vienna, Albertina

368   Kulmbach, "The Nativity"
      Frankfort-on-Main, Staedel Art Institute

430   Leu, Hans the Younger, "St. Jerome Repentant in
      a Mountainous Landscape"
      Frankfort-on-Main, Staedel Art Institute

431   Leu, Hans the Younger, "Pietà"
      Cambridge, Massachusetts, Fogg Art Museum

483   Leyden, Lucas van, "Study for David Victorious over Goliath"
      Amsterdam, Rijksmuseum

484   Leyden, "An Old Man Drawing"
      London, British Museum

485   Leyden, "Girl Reading"
      Vienna, Albertina

486   Leyden, "Bust of a Young Man in a Fur Hat"
      London, British Museum

487   Leyden, "A Mother Offering the Breast to a Child"
      London, British Museum

601   Lievens, Jan, "Portrait of the Clergyman Caspar
      Streso (1603-1644)"
      Paris, Frits Lugt

319   Lochner, Stephan, "The Virgin Seated, Presenting
      an Apple to the Child"
      Paris, Louvre, Cabinet des Dessins

488   Mabuse, Jan Gossaert van, "The Judgment of Paris"
      Edinburgh, The National Gallery of Scotland

489   Mabuse, "Portrait of Christian II, King of Denmark"
      Paris, Frits Lugt

490   Mabuse, "Adam and Eve"
      Providence, Rhode Island, Rhode Island School of Design

452   Marées, Hans von, "Ancient Chariot with a Pair of
      Horses and Several Female Figures"
      Munich, Staatliche Graphische Sammlung

307   Master of the Utrecht Life of the Virgin, Ca. 1410-1415,
      "A Courtly Company"
      Uppsala, Royal University Library

PLATE

311-312   Master of the Votive Panel of St. Lambrecht, Ca. 1430, "The Lamentation for Christ" (Recto); "The Entombment of Christ" (Verso)
London, British Museum

313   Master of King Albert, Ca. 1440, "The Virgin of the Annunciation"
Cambridge, Fitzwilliam Museum

315   Master of the Worcester Carrying of the Cross, Ca. 1440-1450, "Group at Calvary"
Frankfort-on-Main, Staedel Art Institute

318   Master E. S., "The Baptism of Christ"
Paris, Louvre, Cabinet des Dessins

324   Master of the Housebook, "Maximilian I at the Peace Banquet at Bruges in 1488"
Berlin, Kupferstichkabinett

326   Master of the Altarpiece of Aix-la-Chapelle, Ca. 1500, "The Resurrection of Lazarus"
Berlin, Kupferstichkabinett

450   Maulbertsch, Franz Anton, "Fides, Justitia, and Pictura"
Vienna, Albertina

Nithart, Mathis Gothart, see Grünewald

327   Nuremberg Artist, Ca. 1480, "Calvary"
Budapest, Museum of Fine Arts

451   Olivier, Ferdinand, "Landscape of Aigen near Salzburg"
Vienna, Albertina

605   Ostade, Adriaen van, "Peasants Dancing"
Haarlem, Teyler Museum

606   Ostade, "Group of People Leaning over a Rail"
Frankfort-on-Main, Staedel Art Institute

607   Ostade, "The Letter (Les Harangueurs)"
Berlin, Kupferstichkabinett

608   Ostade, "Study for the van Ostade Family Portrait"
Paris, Frits Lugt

609   Ostade, "Seated Man Seen from the Back"
Frankfort-on-Main, Staedel Art Museum

610   Ostade, "Study of a Pig"
Rotterdam, Museum Boymans-van Beuningen

616   Potter, Paulus, "Two Pigs"
Paris, Louvre, Cabinet des Dessins

617   Potter, "Study of a Bull"
Turin, Biblioteca Reale

566   Rembrandt (Rembrandt Harmensz. van Rijn), "The Reading"
Bayonne, Musée Bonnat

567   Rembrandt, "Self-Portrait"
London, British Museum

568   Rembrandt, "Old Man Seated in an Armchair"
Haarlem, Teyler Museum

569   Rembrandt, "The Lamentation for Christ"
Berlin, Kupferstichkabinett

570   Rembrandt, "Study for Jacob Lamenting"
Berlin, Kupferstichkabinett

PLATE

571   Rembrandt, "Self-Portrait"
Washington, D. C., National Gallery of Art, Rosenwald Collection

572   Rembrandt, "The Crucifixion"
Frankfort-on-Main, Staedel Art Institute

573   Rembrandt, "Saskia Seated by a Window"
Paris, Frits Lugt

574   Rembrandt, "Study of Two Women, Each with a Baby"
Stockholm, Nationalmuseum

575   Rembrandt, "Woman Carrying a Child Downstairs"
New York, The Pierpont Morgan Library

576   Rembrandt, "Woman in North-Holland Costume, Seen from the Back"
Haarlem, Teyler Museum

577   Rembrandt, "The Naughty Boy"
Berlin, Kupferstichkabinett

578   Rembrandt, "An Elephant"
Vienna, Albertina

579   Rembrandt, "Portrait of Saskia in a Turban"
Bayonne, Musée Bonnat

580   Rembrandt, "Two Studies of Saskia Asleep"
New York, The Pierpont Morgan Library

581   Rembrandt, "Panorama of London, with Old St. Paul's (Seen from the North)"
Berlin, Kupferstichkabinett

582   Rembrandt, "Lion Resting"
Paris, Louvre, Cabinet des Dessins

583   Rembrandt, "Study in Reverse for the 'Hundred Guilder Print'"
Berlin, Kupferstichkabinett

584   Rembrandt, "The Return of the Prodigal Son"
Haarlem, Teyler Museum

585   Rembrandt, "Cottage near the Entrance of a Wood"
New York, Robert Lehman

586   Rembrandt, "The Death of Jacob"
Montreal, The Montreal Museum of Fine Arts

587   Rembrandt, "Standing Male Nude"
London, British Museum

588   Rembrandt, "The Liberation of St. Peter from Prison"
Frankfort-on-Main, Staedel Art Institute

589   Rembrandt, "Nurse and Eating Child"
Vienna, Albertina

590   Rembrandt, "A Farm on a Country Road"
Chatsworth, Devonshire Collections

591   Rembrandt, "A Farm on the Waterfront"
Chatsworth, Devonshire Collections

592   Rembrandt, "Cottage beside a Canal"
Chicago, Illinois, The Art Institute

593   Rembrandt, "The Prodigal Son among the Swine"
London, British Museum

PLATE

594 Rembrandt, "The Raising of the Daughter of Jairus"
Copenhagen, Royal Museum of Fine Arts

595 Rembrandt, "The Baptism of Christ"
Dresden, Staatliche Kunstsammlungen

596 Rembrandt, "The Carrying of the Cross"
Haarlem, Teyler Museum

597 Rembrandt, "Noah's Ark"
Chicago, Illinois, The Art Institute

598 Rembrandt, "Christ Walking on the Waves"
London, British Museum

599 Rembrandt, "Female Nude Sitting on a Stool"
Chicago, Illinois, The Art Institute

600 Rembrandt, "Parable of the Wicked Servant"
Leningrad, Hermitage

Rijn, Rembrandt Harmensz. van, see Rembrandt

520 Rubens, Peter Paul, "Three Caryatids, after Primaticcio"
Rotterdam, Museum Boymans-van Beuningen

521 Rubens, "Study for the Figure of Christ"
Cambridge, Massachusetts, Fogg Art Museum

522 Rubens, "Study of a Nude Male Torso"
Oxford, Ashmolean Museum

523 Rubens, "Study of a Male Figure, Seen from behind"
Cambridge, Fitzwilliam Museum

524 Rubens, "The Death of Adonis"
London, British Museum

525 Rubens, "Studies for Apostles"
Cambridge, Massachusetts, Fogg Art Museum

526 Rubens, "Study for a St. Mary Magdalen"
London, British Museum

527 Rubens, "Study for Daniel in the Lion's Den"
New York, The Pierpont Morgan Library

528 Rubens, "Study of a Lion"
London, British Museum

529 Rubens, "Study of a River God"
London, Victoria and Albert Museum

530 Rubens, "Three Robed Men"
Copenhagen, Royal Museum of Fine Arts

531 Rubens, "Study for a St. Mary Magdalen"
Cambridge, Fitzwilliam Museum

532 Rubens, "Studies of Cows"
London, British Museum

533 Rubens, "Two Farm Wagons"
Berlin, Kupferstichkabinett

534 Rubens, "Portrait of Isabella Brant"
London, British Museum

535 Rubens, "Portrait of Marie de' Medici"
Paris, Louvre, Cabinet des Dessins

536 Rubens, "Young Woman with an Ostrich Fan"
Paris, Louvre, Cabinet des Dessins

PLATE

537 Rubens, "Young Woman with Crossed Hands"
Rotterdam, Museum Boymans-van Beuningen

538 Rubens, "Portrait of Thomas Howard, Earl of Arundel"
*Williamstown, Massachusetts, Sterling and
Francine Clark Art Institute*

539 Rubens, "The Feast of Herod"
Cleveland, Ohio, The Cleveland Museum of Art

540 Rubens, "A Country Lane"
Cambridge, Fitzwilliam Museum

541 Rubens, "Tree with Brambles"
Chatsworth, Devonshire Collections

542 Rubens, "Woodland Scene"
Oxford, Ashmolean Museum

611 Ruisdael, Jacob van, "Landscape with a Stone Bridge"
Leningrad, Hermitage

612 Ruisdael, "View of Haarlem"
Paris, Louvre, Cabinet des Dessins

564 Saenredam, Pieter Janszoon, "The Nave and Side Aisles
of the Cathedral at Utrecht"
Utrecht, Gemeente Archief

565 Saenredam, "Interior of St. Catherine's Church at Utrecht"
Utrecht, Gemeente Archief

304 Salzburg, School of, Ca. 1230, "The Glory of the
Almighty with Scenes from the Book of Daniel
and from the Revelation of St. John"
Salzburg, Treasury of the Monastery of St. Peter

518 Savery, Roelandt, "A Young Monkey"
Amsterdam, Rijksmuseum

369 Schaeufelein, Hans Leonhard, "The Last Supper"
London, British Museum

370 Schaeufelein, "Head of the Apostle St. James the Greater"
Stockholm, Nationalmuseum

371 Schaeufelein, "Portrait of an Old Woman in Head Cloth"
Copenhagen, Royal Museum of Fine Arts

321 Schongauer, Martin, "The Angel Gabriel for an
Annunciation (half-length)"
Berlin, Kupferstichkabinett

322 Schongauer, "The Virgin and Child on a Grassy
Seat, with a Carnation Plant"
Berlin, Kupferstichkabinett

323 Schongauer (follower of), Ca. 1490, "St. Dorothy
Holding out a Basket to the Christ Child"
London, British Museum

562-563 Snyders, Frans, "Studies of a Boar's Head"
London, British Museum

372 Springinklee, Hans, "The Rest of the Holy Family
on the Flight into Egypt"
London, British Museum

445 Stimmer, Tobias, "The Painter and His Muse"
Basel, Kupferstichkabinett

329 Stoss, Veit, "The Presentation in the Temple"
Berlin, Kupferstichkabinett

PLATE

391 Strigel, Bernhard, "The Holy Family, 1491"
London, British Museum

392 Strigel, "A Pair of Unequal Lovers with the Devil and Cupid"
Berlin, Kupferstichkabinett

325 Suabian Artist of the Circle of Bartholomaeus Zeitblom,
Ca. 1490-1500, "The Genealogical Tree of Jesse"
Stuttgart, Graphische Sammlung

618 Ter Borch, Gerard, "Two Men on Horseback"
Amsterdam, Rijksmuseum

619 Ter Borch, Gerard the Elder, "Young Girl Reading a Book"
Amsterdam, Rijksmuseum

561 Uden, Lucas van, "Woodland with Monastic Buildings"
New York, The Pierpont Morgan Library

620 Velde, Willem van de, "Ships Saluting in a Calm"
Lille, Palais des Beaux-Arts, Musée Wicar

310 Viennese Master, 1425-1430, "The Annunciation"
Vienna, Albertina

314 Viennese Master of 1441-1442, "St. Catherine"
Vienna, Albertina

PLATE

458 Weyden, Rogier van der, "Virgin and Child"
Rotterdam, Museum Boymans-van Beuningen

459 Weyden, "St. Mary Magdalen"
London, British Museum

460 Weyden (after), "Portrait of a Young Woman"
London, British Museum

464 Weyden (school of), "Portrait of a Man"
Berlin, Kupferstichkabinett

316 Witz, Konrad, "The Virgin and Child in a Chamber"
Berlin, Kupferstichkabinett

317 Witz (Master of the Circle of, Ca. 1440-1450),
"The Virgin and Child with St. Paul,
Seated in a Landscape"
Budapest, Museum of Fine Arts

328 Wolgemut, Michael, "God the Father Enthroned"
London, British Museum

325 Zeitblom (Suabian Artist of the Circle of, Ca. 1490-1500),
"The Genealogical Tree of Jesse"
Stuttgart, Graphische Sammlung

German Drawings

German Drawings

THE DRAWINGS reproduced here originated in the large territory inhabited by German-speaking peoples, an area that includes Switzerland and Austria and extends to the borders of the former Austro-Hungarian monarchy. Not identical with the Holy Roman Empire, this region nevertheless corresponds more closely to it than to present-day Germany. In other words, the coherence is cultural rather than political.

The art of this area is that of Central Europe, powerful in its consolidation of widespread—even conflicting—forces, an art which assimilates and transforms influences from neighboring regions and gives them stimulation in return. Richness of imagination and strength of expression are its predominant characteristics. Its deeply probing, earnestly pondering, even brooding spirit does not abhor disharmony or reject crudeness if expression so demands. The humanistic discipline of form inherent in the art of the Romance nations is also to be found, but rather as a result of conscious labor than as a natural element. Ever alive to the personality behind the appearance and to the spell of nature, German art attaches special importance to portraits and landscape.

Drawing, with its necessary metamorphosis of representational elements into lines and tones, is a particularly appropriate medium for German art, rich as it is with imaginative components and a creative transformation of the outer world. Drawing therefore played a foremost role in German art at a time when the creative forces were still mainly concerned with sculpture and painting but were limited to the architecturally bound techniques of wall painting and stained glass or to book illumination. At that time, drawing served only the purpose of design or illustration in outline on vellum (Nos. 304 and 305). Drawing on paper in its own right did not emerge before the development of panel painting (No. 310) and the graphic arts of printing with wood blocks and copper plates. The latter were invented in Southern Germany; this region and that of the Rhine were also most prolific in early drawing.

This development coincides with the climax of the "International style" at the beginning of the fifteenth century, called *der weiche Stil* in German because of the lyrical flow of its soft forms, in which the eloquent cascades of drapery play an important part. Nourished by sources from the South and West, this highly refined art centered mainly at the secular and ecclesiastical courts and is a typical expression of their culture. Such courts were established at Prague, Vienna, and the seats of powerful archbishop-electors on the Rhine and elsewhere. They maintained close contact with court art of all other European countries. Continual interchange of artists and their production made this in actuality an international style. As in the era of the late Renaissance, because of this interdependence it is sometimes not easy accurately to establish the national origin of a work of art. German drawings, however, have an unmistakable and particular character. Most of the extant early works originated in the southeast—Austria, Bohemia, and the neighboring regions of Franconia and Bavaria—less because these countries were more prolific but than because chance has preserved more of their production, either in entire stocks or pasted as decorations on the inside covers of books stored in monastic libraries. Most of the early woodcut examples, originating in the southeast, have been similarly preserved for posterity.

With the growing political and economic importance of cities, the International style soon took on the distinctive features of the individual provinces, inhabited as they were by different racial stocks, and developed regional characteristics. There was an increase of realism, a new attitude toward nature, a new feeling for matter, volume and space. This development, beginning about 1430, also changed the idiom of the International style practiced by its last representatives.

Both indigenous forces and an influx of the *ars nova* of the Netherlands helped this development reach a climax in the decade 1440-1450. This new realistic style shows increased interest in material weight, surface values, tangible form, and space displacement. This *schwerer Stil*, so called to distinguish it from the preceding *weicher Stil*, displays a heroic realism in sculpture and painting as well as in drawing and the graphic arts. Whereas the woodcut technique was more appropriate to the formal grammar of the International style, engraving corresponded to the new "hard style." Important personalities appeared, some already known by name, such as the painters Konrad Witz (No. 316) and Stephan Lochner (No. 319); others are known only by their initials (such as the monogrammist-engraver E S [No. 318]), or are named from characteristic works (such as the Master of the Worcester "Carrying of the Cross" [No. 315]).

Netherlandish influence exerted by Rogier van der Weyden, Dirck Bouts, Hugo van der Goes, Joos van Gent, and the Dutch painters dominated German art in the second half of the fifteenth century—a period prolific in production—surpassing all other Northern nations. Painting, with numerous local schools spread over the German-speaking countries, manifests a certain decline in quality, but the contrary is true of the graphic arts and sculpture. Great carvers such as Michael Pacher and Veit Stoss (No. 329), great engravers such as Schongauer (No. 321) and the Master of the House-Book (No. 324), outstanding designers of woodcut and illustration such as Michael Wolgemut (No. 328) now appear. The arts that make use of line were ideally suited to the artistic expression of the late Gothic period. The inventions of the late Gothic artists are of confusing richness, with dynamic swing in space and an overwhelming display of decorative qualities. Such leading masters as Schongauer, however, developed monumental accents that pointed the direction for the following centuries.

The first half of the sixteenth century is the most important era of German art; with great creative personalities promoting new artistic and ethical values, its only equal was the High Renaissance of Italy. More than ever, artistic production is narrowed down to a geographically small region: Southern Germany and the adjacent mountain countries. Prosperous cities, Nuremberg, Augsburg, Regensberg, Ulm, Strasbourg, and Basel provided a social and economic basis for this art; princes and bishops searched the city guilds for artistic promoters of their fame. Emperor Maximilian I was discriminating enough to choose the best of them, so that his reign (1495-1519) became representative of this most splendid period in the history of German art.

More than ever before, the fate of art depended on great artistic personalities, apparent in the examples that illustrate less trends and movements than artists with distinct identity and characteristics. This great era can in fact be called the age of Dürer, for he represents the nation and its spirit at their best. Dürer has become the symbol of the creative German genius. Emerging from the late-Gothic guild system, he became the first example of the Renaissance artist and his intellectual freedom in the North. He strove for truth in art, science, and religion. Although Dürer was a great painter, painting was occasionally laborious to him. He was more at ease cutting in wood or engraving in copper. Drawing, the most immediate expression of his personality, best represents him and his achievement, and many of his drawings have been preserved. Although some were merely designs for later development, many are complete works in their own right, already attracting collectors in his own time. We can trace his progress from the late-Gothic tradition of Nuremberg (No. 330) through his journey to the Upper Rhine, to Basel, Colmar, and Strasbourg. His horizon widened in Schongauer's influence (No. 333). He was the first to open the eyes of the German artists to the accomplishments of the Southern Renaissance; twice he traveled to Italy to study and work. En route, he discovered the mountains of the Austrian and Italian Alps and portrayed them in watercolor landscapes that offer an entirely new concept of scenery (No. 335), one quite independent of Leonardo.

Italian contacts stimulated Dürer's creative imagination and strengthened it to develop a new manner of representing the dramas of religious history, the mysteries of faith, and divine revelation (No. 341), articulating the religious experience of a profound believer. Dürer's eyes eagerly probed and absorbed the beauties of nature, sought the reality in man and beast (No. 339), in town and country. To balance this penetration into the diverse manifestations of reality, Dürer strove for the lofty style and monumental design apparent in his great altar compositions (No. 347). He endeavored to resolve into law the beauties of nature. What is most striking to the modern spectator about his drawings, however, is the grand human likenesses in which the representation of man reaches the sublimity of religious knowledge (No. 352).

Dürer's drawing art encompassed the widest range of artistic communication, from the most fugitive sketch to the most consummate work of art. In this regard, all German artists have learned from the draughtsman Dürer. But his influence went far beyond Germany—it was truly European. First of all, he conveyed the mode and style of his artistic expression in his studio to the circle of his immediate pupils, who came from all *lands* of Germany, among them the Franconians Kulmback (No. 366) and Springinklee (No. 372), the Suabians Schaeufelein (No. 369) and Baldung (No. 373).

Baldung was an ingenious artist who settled in Strasbourg and established the transition from Franconian art to that of the Upper Rhine. His late works are in the style known as Mannerism, as are those of the last generation of Dürer's pupils, the so-called Little Masters.

From Franconia also came Lucas Cranach, whose precise origin is still unknown; he is first historically traceable about 1500 in Vienna, where, with Joerg Breu (No. 397), he created the Danube style, one that combined achievements of the young Dürer and Austrian components. From 1505 he was active as court painter to the Elector of Saxony and established in Wittenberg, distant from the great centers of German art.

One of these flourishing centers was Augsburg, which supplanted Ulm as the heart of Suabian art. Suabian bridgers between the old century and the new were Bernhard Strigel (No. 391) and Hans Holbein the Elder (No. 393), a distinguished draughtsman and painter, the father of a still more distinguished son. The splendor of the Augsburg Renaissance, so different from the late-Gothic idiom of the elder Holbein, begins with Hans Burgkmair, whose portraits reveal affinity to Dürer (No. 395), as do those of Joerg Breu (No. 397).

In enigmatic grandeur the figure of Mathis Gothart Nithart, commonly called Grünewald, now rises in German art. He is, next to Dürer, the greatest of the Germans, his equal in depth of expression, surpassing him in mysterious, visionary, and religious exaltation. Less universal than Dürer, Grünewald is exclusively a religious painter. His large altarpieces continued the tradition of the past, yet he was not merely a belated medieval artist, older than Dürer. He seems actually to have been five or even ten years younger. His draughtsmanship indicates that he knew Dürer and had learned from him. Extremely modern for his time, he was so appraised by his contemporaries. What was hallowed convention for the late-Gothic painters, even for Dürer, became for Grünewald personal vision and arousing inner sight; the retention of medieval features in his art was deliberate. His mastery of color, his manifestation of light are incomparable. What few drawings remain seem to have served only as preparation for his paintings. Some are studies from nature (No. 401), some free inventions; but for the most part they are both (No. 406), as if experience of reality and imaginary vision had merged. His draughtsmanship is as outstanding as his painting; even in black and white he evoked the subtlest gradations of light and semblance of color. His drawings are done with black chalk, the favorite medium of the period. While Dürer never penetrated the epidermis except spiritually or theoretically, Grünewald developed an almost magical empathy. He laid bare nerves and fibers of the living tissue; he caught the flavor and breath of his subjects, animate and inanimate, giving a tremendous degree of reality to his overwhelming visions. That such a man, an episcopal court painter, should partake of the revolutionary religious and social movements of his time seems indeed a strange conclusion to his mysterious life. After dismissal from office, he earned his living as a technical worker and hydraulic engineer in the service of a Protestant community.

Grünewald appeared and disappeared like a comet, but something of his flaming spirit illuminates the German art of the upper Rhine; of Augsburg, from which he had acquired stimulation; and along the Danube.

The Danube School is an enchanting part of German art, in both painting and drawing. Originating in the Danube region of Austria, strongly promoted by Cranach and Breu, it produced outstanding Austrian and Bavarian masters, the most important of whom were Albrecht Altdorfer in Regensburg and Wolf Huber in Passau. Here we encounter a new pantheistic approach toward nature, as if everything were the outgrowth of a cosmic unity. This brings a strong humanization of the old religious themes and a predominance of landscape, with its connection to the infinity of space and its luministic phenomena. Altdorfer became a great painter and, next to Grünewald, the greatest master of color among the Germans. But he also acquired particular importance in the history of drawing.

German drawings of the fifteenth century, if not executed with silver- or metalpoint, were mostly pen drawings in bistre, iron-gall ink, or carbon ink. About the year 1500 drawings appeared with the pen dipped in India ink and white bodycolor, on paper grounded in different shades (blue, green, brown, brick-red), permitting a rich gradation. Altdorfer brought this technique of chiaroscuro drawing to extraordinary perfection. His numerous drawings were frequently copied by his pupils and followers and much appreciated by amateurs (No. 417).

The poetic element prevails in Altdorfer's drawings, the factual portraiture of scenic motifs in those of his younger contemporary Wolf Huber. Some of Huber's landscape drawings foreshadow modern landscape art in an amazing way (No. 427). Altdorfer's poetic approach has a counterpart in the works of Swiss artists, with their love for adventure: Hans Leu (No. 430), Niklaus Manuel Deutsch (No. 428), and Urs Graf (No. 432).

Hans Holbein the Younger brought this great era of German art to a dignified conclusion. Son and pupil of a father who was outstanding as a draughtsman and painter, heir to the rich tradition of Augsburg, he achieved classical balance of form, so rare in German art, and developed it to crystalline clearness. No other artist of the North so closely approached the ideal of the Italian classical High Renaissance. He retained, in addition, the Northern penetrating spirit, the deep scrutiny of human character, becoming the most objective depicter of man of all time. His portrait drawings are unsurpassed in simplicity of presentation, surety of line, and revelation of character. With him, at the middle of the century, ends the succession of great originators in the history of German art.

The selection of drawings that follows may be called representative. A few examples have been chosen to illustrate the later centuries, if only as evidence that the art of drawing never slackened in Central Europe and that the great German draughtsmen of the past have found worthy followers up to the present.

—OTTO BENESCH

PLATES

SCHOOL OF SALZBURG
Ca. 1230

304 **The Glory of the Almighty with Scenes
from the Book of Daniel and
from the Revelation of St. John**

Pen and brown and colored inks (violet in trees, red in fire)
on vellum, 400 x 585 mm.

Salzburg, Treasury of the Monastery of St. Peter (Inv. 975)

Used as binding for an account book of the
years 1439-1470

THE PRESENT drawing, previously unpublished, was discovered years ago by the author in the treasury of the monastery of St. Peter in Salzburg. It is a document of unique importance in the history of drawing. It is the only known design for a cycle of frescoes of the thirteenth century. It has always been clear that the large cycles of medieval wall paintings were executed on the basis of designs discussed by the ecclesiastical patrons with the painters. Yet such a design could never be produced. This is the first example that has come to light.

The design was destined for a small chapel in the shape of a quadrangle. There exist in Austria several chapels of this kind in late Romanesque and early Gothic churches. The most famous are the Episcopal chapels of the Abbey churches of Gurk in Carinthia and of Goess in Styria. The chapel of Gurk combines a scheme of two cupolas; the present design is limited to one. The iconographical program is composed of prophecies from the Old Testament and scenes from the Revelation.

In the center of the circle of the cupola, the raised right hand of the Lord appears, surrounded by four angels representing the Evangelists holding scrolls with quotations from their writings. In the following outer circle the four world empires appear: The Assyrian, the Persian and Median, the Greek and the Roman, riding over the waves of the sea between the winds of heaven on their symbolical beasts, according to the description in Daniel 7. Rome is riding on the beast with ten horns.

This central circle is flanked by four semicircles containing the design for the upright walls beneath the cupola. In the spandrels the four riders of Revelation 6 are riding. The inscriptions identify them: Christ as horseman on the white horse, the Devil as horseman on the red horse, Hypocrisy as horseman on the black horse, and Death as horseman on the pale horse.

The semicircle below the Roman Empire to the left of the raised hand of the Almighty represents the Almighty crowning Jesus Christ, both seated on the heavenly throne. To the left of it the Saints of the New Testament appear, to the right the Prophets and Patriarchs. Below the throne, the Holy Martyrs appear crying for revenge, according to the opening of the fifth seal in Revelation 6.

The lowest zone from left to right is filled with representations of (1) the altar of the Old Testament with the Ark of the Covenant, the Archangel Michael lighting the incense; (2) the woman clothed with the sun and the red dragon (Revelation 12), her son removed to heaven; (3) the dragon and Ecclesia flying to heaven from the face of the dragon; (4) St. John the Evangelist, between trees, on the island of Patmos, exhorted by Solomon and the Apostle Paul; (5) the convivium in which the bridegroom Jesus crowns the bride Ecclesia, seated between the Holy Confessors, the Apostles, and the Virgin Mary.

On the opposite wall, below the Persian and Median Empire, Chapter 4 of the Revelation is illustrated: The Lord enthroned upon the rainbow with the twenty-four elders and the beasts of the Apocalypse.

In the zone below, the different heresies appear beginning at the left with the Jews seduced by Gog and Magog (Revelation 20, vv. 7, 8), Antichrist and the false Prophets, the Devil cast into the lake (Revelation 20, vv. 7-10). The semicircle below the raised hand of the Lord and the Assyrian Empire contains in roundels the angels blowing the seven trumpets. In the center, the angel appears chaining the dragon (Revelation 20, v. 2). In the spandrels to the left and right, the fire falling from heaven and the volcano cast into the sea are represented according to Revelation 8, vv. 7, 8. The drawing is cut along all sides; the opposite semicircle is cut off.

The linear style of the drawing corresponds with Austrian frescoes of the thirteenth century. Those most closely related in style are to be found in the little Romanesque church of St. George in the town of Bischofshofen, Province of Salzburg (O. Demus, "Die Wandmalereien der Georgskapelle im Bischofshofen," *Oesterreichische Zeitschrift fuer Kunst und Denkmalpflege*, VII, Vienna 1953, pp. 89 ff.). They decorate the apse with representations of the Glorified Christ between the Evangelists, the Crucified Christ between the Evangelists, the Crucified Christ between the twelve Apostles, and with single figures of the saints. These frescoes are much more modest in program and composition, but the stylistic character of the figures corresponds best with the Salzburg drawing. The frescoes have been dated at about 1230, which seems to be also the best suitable dating for the drawing. It may be mentioned that Bischofshofen belonged to the ecclesiastical administration of the monastery of St. Peter, therefore this stylistic relation seems to have also a concrete historical background.

AUSTRIAN MASTER, Ca. 1320

305 **The Flight into Egypt
and the Baptism of Christ**

Pen in red and India ink, pen and brush in water colors
and gouache, white body-color on vellum, 225 x 375 and
393 mm. (irregularly cut)

Vienna, Albertina (Inv. 25109)

PROVENANCE

Abbey of Rein, near Graz, Styria

LITERATURE

Garzarolli-Thurnlackh, *Belvedere*, XI, pp. 23 ff.

Albertina Catalogue, IV, No. 3

LIKE THE preceding No. 304, the present drawing also has been used
as binding for a manuscript. Its fragmentary character does not per-
mit a conclusive judgment on its original purpose. It could have served
as a design for a mural or stained glass. The latter is suggested by
the way Joseph's hands overlap the frame separating the scene of the
"Flight" from the "Baptism."

On the other hand, the careful execution in different colors and
the unusually high level of artistic quality make it possible that it was
a work of art in its own right. Its linear character is a continuation of
that style of drawing which we saw in No. 304, now marked by a
strong wave of influence that Western (French and English) art had
upon the art of Austria in the first half of the fourteenth century. We
recognize the same style of drawing in Austrian and Bohemian manuscripts of the period, for instance in the *Biblio pauperum* of St. Flor-
ian, and the Codex 370 in the National Library, Vienna.

The same style enhanced to full round plasticity occurs in the
"Passionale Cunigundae" of the University Library in Prague. We
meet with related creations also in panel painting: the most important of them the backs of the wings of the Verdun Altar in Klosterneuberg.

AUSTRIAN MASTER, Ca. 1400

306 St. Margaret and the Dragon

Red chalk, brush and India ink, 214 x 140 mm.

Budapest, Museum of Fine Arts

LITERATURE

Schoenbrunner-Meder, No. 665

Parker, *Drawings of the Early German Schools*, No. 1

Benesch, *Die Meisterzeichnung V*, No. 3

THE DRAWING was formerly attributed to the School of Cologne by Meder and Parker. The exact knowledge of Austrian art of the International style brought about by research since 1920 made it possible to locate the present drawing in the circle of Austrian court art, which was strongly dependent on Bohemia. Numerous examples of painting and sculpture illustrate this.

Particularly related are the drawing in a model-book of a journeyman, Kunsthistorisches Museum, Vienna, published by J. von Schlosser, *Jahrbuch der Kunsthistorischen Sammlungen des Allerhoechsten Kaiserhauses*, 1902, and also two little heads for an "Annunciation," Fogg Museum of Art, Cambridge, Massachusetts (*The Bulletin of the Fogg Museum of Art*, Harvard University, XI, I, January 1949, p. 27).

MASTER OF THE UTRECHT LIFE
OF THE VIRGIN, Ca. 1410-1415

307 A Courtly Company

Silverpoint, retouched with ink, on prepared paper,
175 x 202 mm.

Uppsala, Royal University Library (Inv. No. H.N. 74)

LITERATURE

Benesch, *Die Graphischen Kuenste*, II, 1936, p. 14, Fig. 1

Dodgson, *Vasari Society*, 2d Series, XVI, 1935, No. 8

CAMPBELL DODGSON, who first published the present drawing, attributed it to the circle, perhaps even to the hand of Pol de Limbourg.

The present writer first gave it to an exquisite master of the German School of the International style, venturing the identity of the hand with the anonymous painter of the "Life of the Virgin" in the Museum of Utrecht. This artist was active in the Lower or Middle Rhine.

A. Strange, *Deutsche Malerei der Gotik*, III, pp. 116-117, suggests an attribution to another artist of the same circle: The illuminator of the prayer book of Mary of Geldern in the Staatsbibliothek, Berlin, which, however, neither in style nor in quality reaches the level of our drawing.

AUSTRIAN MASTER, Ca. 1415

308 The Mocking of Christ

Pen and brush in India ink, 139 x 208 mm.
Copenhagen, Royal Museum of Fine Arts (No. tu.103.4)

LITERATURE
Benesch, *Die Meisterzeichnung V*, No. 14

THE DRAWING is one of the most precious specimens of the International style. France, the Netherlands, Germany, Bohemia, and Austria formed an artistic unit at that time, and the artists frequently traveled, so that it is often difficult to give an exact place of origin. The situation was almost similar to that of the late Renaissance.

A drawing comparable in style is the "Betrayal of Christ" in the Louvre (*Inventaire Général des Dessins des Ecoles Allemande et Suisse*, II, No. 386), located by K. T. Parker, *Drawings of the Early German Schools*, No. 2, as from the Lake of Constance.

The group of men issuing from a doorway to the right is a feature to be found in several paintings of the School of Vienna. Therefore, the drawing can be tentatively given to an artist active at the artistically highly refined Court of Vienna.

AUSTRIAN MASTER OF 1424

309 Emperor Sigismund with the Kings of Bohemia and Poland

Pen and wash on white paper, 203 x 265 mm.

Date in bistre: 1424

Inscribed: *Sigismundus* rex *Romanorum*

Paris, Louvre, Collection Rothschild

LITERATURE

Blum, *Chefs-d'oeuvre de la collection Rothschild*, No. 17

EMPEROR SIGISMUND is shown between his step-brother Wenceslaus, King of Bohemia, and King Wladislaw of Poland.

The subject matter of the present drawing was erroneously described in the catalogue of the Rothschild Collection as the Emperor between the Kings of Bohemia and Hungary. Sigismund himself became King of Hungary in 1386, and German Emperor in 1410. In 1419 he followed his deceased step-brother on the throne of Bohemia. In our drawing, three different persons are shown. Thus the situation represented was, in 1424, already a historical one; in fact it corresponds to the division of power at the time of the Council of Constance, 1414-1418.

Stylistically the drawing belongs to the derivatives of No. 306 and the model-book of a journeyman, mentioned above. Although the figures are still flush with the picture surface, a strong feeling for cubic values comes to the fore. Thus it represents a trend of Austrian, particularly of Viennese, art developing independently from that shown in our Nos. 310 and 311.

This trend prepared for the first era of realism (the so-called "heavy style" in sculpture and painting between 1430 and 1460 to which Konrad Witz belonged). See the note to the following No. 310.

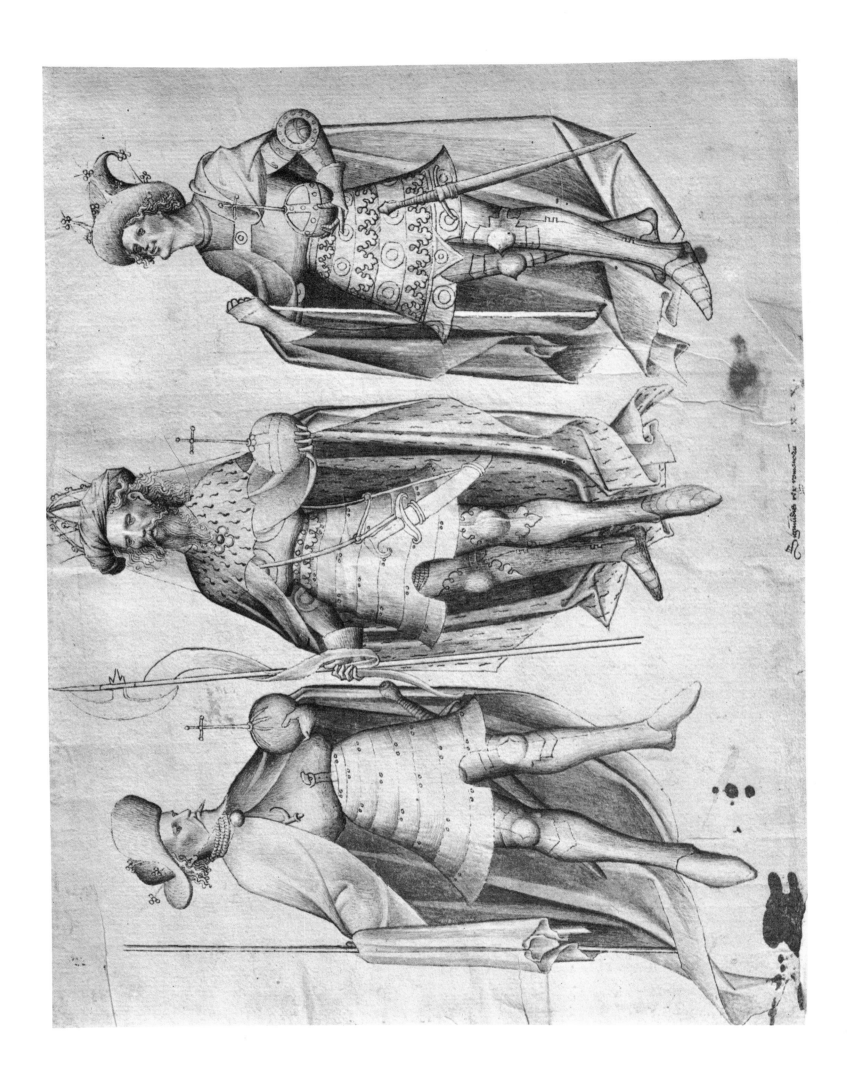

VIENNESE MASTER, 1425-1430

310 The Annunciation

Pen and brush in India ink, touches of water color,
   402 x 276 mm.

Vienna, Albertina (Inv. 25447)

PROVENANCE

Rumohr

LITERATURE

Benesch, *Die Meisterzeichnung V*, No. 21

Benesch, *Jahrbuch der Kunsthistorischen Sammlungen*, II,
   1928, p. 70

Albertina Catalogue, IV, No. 7

THIS IS a work by an artist of the circle of the Master of the Votive Panel of St. Lambrecht, with distinct features recalling the previous stage of development, mainly the Master of the Vienna Adoration, and the artistic circle of Burgundy and southwestern Germany (Melchior Broederlam). The Western features come to the fore, particularly in the rich architectonic stage and the landscape background. The types of the figures remind us of the works of the so-called Master of the Presentation, whose *oeuvre* was established by W. Suida among the Viennese followers of the Master of the Votive Panel.

THE MASTER OF THE VOTIVE PANEL OF ST. LAMBRECHT
Ca. 1430

311 **The Lamentation for Christ (Recto)**

312 **The Entombment of Christ (Verso)**

Pen and wash in India ink, 140 x 208 mm.

London, British Museum

LITERATURE

Parker, in *Old Master Drawings*, I, 1926,
  Pl. XXXIII, XXXIV

Benesch, *Die Meisterzeichnung V*, Nos. 18 and 19

FIRST RECOGNIZED as belonging to the Austrian School by K. T. Parker. The artist was one of the leading masters of the Austrian School of the late International style. His activity is ascertained for the Abbey of St. Lambrecht in Styria and the city of Wiener Neustadt, then the capital of Styria. He is also called the Master of the Linz Crucifixion and tentatively, but not conclusively, identified with Hans von Tuebingen (by K. Oettinger). His main works are the Votive Panel of St. Lambrecht representing the "Victory of Louis the Great over the Turks" and the large "Crucifixion" in the Museum in Linz on the Danube. His style grew out of the School of Vienna where he had also most of his followers. His influence can be traced in almost all Austrian provinces.

THE MASTER OF KING ALBERT
Ca. 1440

313 **The Virgin of the Annunciation**

Black chalk, pen and bistre, 128 x 145 mm.
Cambridge, Fitzwilliam Museum (No. 3170)

PROVENANCE
Kerrich

LITERATURE
Exhibition of 15th and 16th Century Drawings, 1960, No. 4

AT THE time Konrad Witz was active in Basel and Hans Multscher in Ulm, their style of weighty plasticity was represented in Viennese art by an anonymous master who began in 1438 to paint a large double-winged altar now in the Abbey of Klosterneuberg near Vienna (*Catalogue of the Gallery* by O. Benesch, pp. 52-68). This altar, commissioned by King Albert II after his election, was completed only after his death in 1439. It represents the same restful monumentality that we admire in the works of Witz. The present drawing, hitherto unpublished, can be attributed to him. Like the paintings, it is enlivened by the inclusion of enchanting still lifes.

VIENNESE MASTER OF 1441-1442

314 St. Catherine

Pen and bistre, water color over preparatory traces in black chalk, 219 x 140 mm.

Vienna, Albertina (Inv. 26857)

PROVENANCE

Abbey of Kremsmuenster

LITERATURE

Benesch, *Monatsschrift fuer Kultur und Politik*, I, March, 1936, opposite p. 246

THE DRAWING formed the frontispiece to the Codex of Georgius Gwiner de Stira, written in Vienna in the years 1441-1442. The draughtsman belonged to the circle of the Master of King Albert (see No. 313).

MASTER OF THE WORCESTER CARRYING OF THE CROSS
Ca. 1440-1450

315 Group at Calvary

Pen and wash in India ink, 153 x 231 mm.

Frankfort-on-Main, Staedel Art Institute (No. 6976)

PROVENANCE

Endris

LITERATURE

Benesch, *Die Meisterzeichnung V*, No. 30

Benesch, *Monatsschrift fuer Kultur und Politik*, I,
    March, 1936, opposite p. 247

THIS MOST impressive drawing was done by an anonymous Viennese artist working in the 1440's. His activity can be followed in a group of drawings and also in a little panel painting of the "Carrying of the Cross" in the Worcester Collection, Chicago. His works are characterized by dramatically moved figures with heavy heads and trunks, and slender expressive limbs. They are of a strong plastic eloquence in space, which makes them akin to a group of sculptures (the so-called Znaimer Altar in the Oesterreichische Galerie, Vienna, and a gilt bronze relief of the "Crucifixion" in the Walters Art Gallery, Baltimore). An engraver, the Master of the Kalvarienberg, also belongs to the Viennese artists of this group (Lehrs, Vol. I). This realistic current reached its climax shortly before the middle of the century. It eclipsed the last representatives of the International style.

KONRAD WITZ

(1400/10-1445)

KONRAD WITZ *Born at Rottweil (Wuerttemberg). In 1434 became a member of the Basel guild. Was active for the Bishop of Geneva in 1444. Died at Basel in 1445.*

316 The Virgin and Child in a Chamber

Pen and wash in India ink, water color, 291 x 200 mm.

Berlin, Ehem. Staatliche Museen, Kupferstichkabinett
 (K.d.Z. 1971)

PROVENANCE

von Nagler

LITERATURE

Ganz, *Handzeichnungen Schweizerischer Meister*, II, No. 1

Friedlaender-Bock, *Handzeichnungen Deutscher Meister des XV und XVI Jahrhunderts*, p. 43, Pl. V

Berlin Catalogue, p. 88, No. 1971, Pl. CXVIII

THE PRESENT drawing and another drawing of "The Virgin in a Chamber," Erlangen (Parker, *Drawings of the Early German Schools*, No. 5) are the two most outstanding examples of the realistic style of the great master working in Basel. A clear decision as to whether they are copies after his paintings or originals by his own hand has not yet been made. In any case, the preciseness of plastic articulation and refinement of pictorial values raise the drawing to a level that may justify its claim to be an original. The importance given to the interior reveals a dependency on the Master of Flémalle.

MASTER OF THE CIRCLE OF KONRAD WITZ, Ca. 1440-1450

317 **The Virgin and Child with St. Paul, Seated in a Landscape**

Pen and India ink, 180 x 272 mm.
Budapest, Museum of Fine Arts

LITERATURE
Schoenbrunner-Meder, No. 580
Hugelshofer, *Die Meisterzeichnung I*, No. 4

THE PLASTIC quality of the figures within the scenery is most strongly emphasized. The latter is indicated with delicate strokes of the drawing pen only. The shading, which is still in the technique of the early fifteenth century, reminds us of the texture of fur. Nevertheless, the figures acquire an almost metallic luster, which recalls such early German engravers as the Master of the Playing-Cards and the Master of St. John the Baptist.

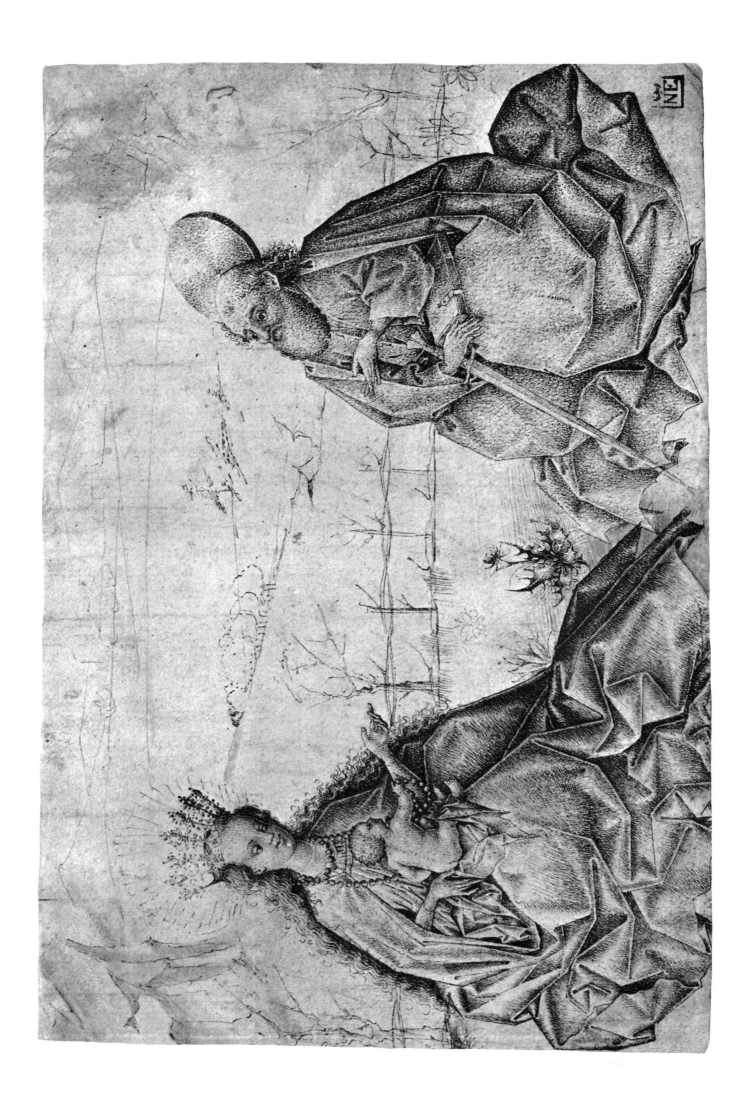

THE MASTER E. S.

(Active 1440-1470)

THE MASTER E. S. *The chief German engraver before Martin Schongauer. Active between 1440 and 1470 in the region of the Lake of Constance and the Upper Rhine.*

318 The Baptism of Christ

Pen and bistre, 290 x 211 mm.

Paris, Louvre, Cabinet des Dessins (No. 18.838)

PROVENANCE

Emigrés

LITERATURE

Demonts, No. 265, Pl. XLIII

Lehrs, *Jahrbuch der Preussischen Kunstsammlungen,* XI, p. 82

Parker, *Drawings of the Early German Schools,* No. 7

THE DRAWING was used by the artist for two of his engravings (Lehrs, Nos. 28 and 29). It is, however, much earlier in style than the engravings and seems to have originated at the latest about 1450. The dates 1466 and 1467 to be found on several engravings of the artist rather mark the end of the career of this most productive and important engraver before Schongauer.

STEPHAN LOCHNER

(Ca. 1400-1451)

STEPHAN LOCHNER *Born at Meersburg on the Lake of Constance. Settled in Cologne, where he is mentioned in documents from 1442. Died at Cologne in 1451.*

319 **The Virgin Seated,**
Presenting an Apple to the Child

Pen and wash in India ink, 125 x 95 mm.,
    the upper corners cut off

Paris, Louvre, Cabinet des Dessins (No. 20698)

LITERATURE

Demonts, No. 258

Winkler, *Die Meisterzeichnung IV*, No. 5

THE PRESENT drawing of very high quality and personal touch is, among those showing the style of Stephan Lochner, the only one that can claim to be by his own hand.

SOUTH GERMAN (SUABIAN?) ARTIST, Ca. 1470

320 **Mary with the Body of Christ at the Foot of the Cross**

Pen and India ink, heightened with pinkish-white and gold, on bluish-green prepared paper.
Fragment, 180 x 180 mm.

Vienna, Albertina (Inv. 2998)

LITERATURE

Schoenbrunner-Meder, No. 511
Albertina Catalogue, IV, No. 20

IN THE Albertina Catalogue the drawing is attributed by Tietze to the School of Nuremberg, but its stylistic character points rather to a Suabian follower of Hans Multscher. The technique in colors would be unusual for the School of Nuremberg. It is more in accordance with the Schools of Ulm and Augsburg. Tietze mentions a drawing related in style and technique in the Museo Civico in Pavia (R. Soriga, *I disegni del Museo Civico*, Pavia, 1912, Pl. LXVII), which is definitely Augsburgian in style.

MARTIN SCHONGAUER
(Ca. 1430-1491)

MARTIN SCHONGAUER *Born at Colmar, Alsatia. Active there as the son of the goldsmith Caspar Schongauer. Died at Breisach in 1491, where he had painted frescoes in the cathedral.*

321 **The Angel Gabriel for an Annunciation (half-length)**

Pen and India ink, 140 x 99 mm.

Monogram, perhaps by the artist

Berlin, Ehem. Staatliche Museen, Kupferstichkabinett (K.d.Z. 1019)

PROVENANCE

Lagoy

LITERATURE

Berlin Catalogue, p. 77, No. 1019, Pl. CX

Rosenberg, *Martin Schongauer*, Pl. XII

Parker, *Die Meisterzeichnung II*, Pl. VIII

ACCORDING TO Rosenberg, this is a work of the early maturity of the master. It is an excellent example of the new technique of hatching developed by the artist in his engravings and drawings. This technique gave rise not only to a more intense three-dimensional modeling in space, but also to a more eloquent gradation of light and shade. The Angel raises his left hand in an attitude of blessing, which seems to indicate that the drawing was meant to be a preparation for an **engraving**.

SCHONGAUER

322 The Virgin and Child on a Grassy Seat, with a Carnation Plant

Pen and bistre, 227 x 159 mm.

Berlin, Ehem. Staatliche Museen, Kupferstichkabinett
(K.d.Z. 1377)

PROVENANCE

von Nagler

LITERATURE

Berlin Catalogue, p. 77, No. 1377, Pl. CIX

Rosenberg, Pl. XXIV

Parker, *Drawings of the Early German Schools*, No. 8

Buchner, *Martin Schongauer als Maler*, p. 98 ff.

THE PRESENT drawing was considered by E. Buchner to be a careful preparation for an unknown panel painting, which seems to have originated about 1473-1475, thus close in time to the artist's best-known painting, "The Madonna in the Rose Arbor," in the Church of St. Martin in Colmar. We find an echo of this composition in a little painting in the National Gallery, London.

FOLLOWER OF
MARTIN SCHONGAUER,
Ca. 1490

323 **St. Dorothy Holding out a Basket
to the Christ Child**

Pen, bistre and India ink, 206 x 133 mm.

London, British Museum (No. 1949-4-11-98)

PROVENANCE

Desperet; Posony; von Lanna

LITERATURE

Schoenbrunner-Meder, No. 1416

Buchner, *Das Schwaebische Museum,* pp. 180-183

Benesch, *Monatsschrift fur Kultur und Politik,* I,
  March, 1936, opposite p. 249

FIRST PUBLISHED as a work of the School of Schongauer, to whose wider circle it certainly belongs, E. Buchner ventured an attribution of this drawing to the painter Ulruch Mair of Kempten in the Allgaeu. If a comparison with panel painting were drawn, the connection with the Austrian followers of Schongauer in the School of Vienna is still closer, mainly with the anonymous painter of the Holy Virgin in St. Stephan's Cathedral in Vienna.

THE MASTER
OF THE HOUSEBOOK

(Active 1 4 7 5 - 1 5 0 0)

THE MASTER OF THE HOUSEBOOK *So called after the illustrated manuscript of the* Hausbuch *in the Castle of Wolfegg in the Allgaeu. After Schongauer, the most important painter-engraver and draughtsman. Active in the last quarter of the fifteenth century on the Middle Rhine, probably at Mainz.*

324 **Maximilian I at the Peace Banquet at Brúges in 1488**

Pen and bistre, 277 x 192 mm.

Berlin, Ehem. Staatliche Museen, Kupferstichkabinett
   (K.d.Z. 4442)

PROVENANCE

von Lanna

LITERATURE

Berlin Catalogue, p. 71, No. 4442

Warburg-Friedlaender, *Jahrbuch der Preussischen Kunstsammlungen*, XXXII, pp. 180 ff.

Winkler, *Die Meisterzeichnung IV*, No. 13

THE PRESENT drawing and the one on the reverse illustrate one of the most dramatic events in the life of the young King Maximilian when, after the death of his wife Mary of Burgundy, he tried to save his rule over the Netherlands. In the revolution of Bruges he barely escaped the death penalty, to which his companions fell victim.

The great master of the earliest "dry-points" has created here a sublime example of his late style, full of vibrancy and nearness to life, which makes it akin to the drawings of Jerôme Bosch.

SUABIAN ARTIST OF THE CIRCLE OF BARTHOLOMAEUS ZEITBLOM, Ca. 1490-1500

325 The Genealogical Tree of Jesse

Pen and bistre, 280 x 323 mm.

Inscribed by a later hand: *Martin Schon (Schongauer)*
   Maistre d'Albert Durer

Stuttgart, Staatsgalerie, Graphische Sammlung (Inv. 5)

THIS DRAWING, rich in eloquent figures and types, is a fine example of the art of the circle of the great Ulm painter, Bartholomaeus Zeitblom. It is the work of a younger artist, who perhaps was contemporary with Bernhard Strigel. The figures recall the panels of the so-called Master of the Pfullendorfer Altar, preserved in the Staatsgalerie, Stuttgart. A comparison has also been made with the Altar of the Holy Kindred of Kirchheim and the drawings preparatory for it in the Germanisches Nationalmuseum, Nuremberg.

THE MASTER OF THE ALTARPIECE OF AIX-LA-CHAPELLE, Ca. 1500

326 The Resurrection of Lazarus

Pen in bistre and India ink, 287 x 200 mm.

Berlin, Ehem. Staatliche Museen, Kupferstichkabinett
(K.d.Z. 12045)

LITERATURE

Winkler, *Die Meisterzeichnung IV*, No. 46

AT THE beginning of the sixteenth century the artists of Cologne were strongly inspired by the art of their Dutch contemporaries: the masters of Delft, the followers of Geertgen tot Sint Jans, Cornelis Engelbrechtsen, Jacob Cornelisz van Amsterdam, and Jan Mostaert. Not very personal or original in their mode of expression, they are yet distinguished by the richness and inventiveness of their compositions.

The Master of the winged altarpiece with the "Passion of Christ" in the Cathedral of Aix-la-Chapelle was one of the foremost, remarkable for his crowded compositions, which give the impression of tapestries. The technique of the present drawing seems also to reveal familiarity with engraved work.

NUREMBERG ARTIST, Ca. 1480

327 Calvary

Pen and bistre, 370 x 282 mm.
Budapest, Museum of Fine Arts

PROVENANCE
Esterházy

LITERATURE
Schoenbrunner-Meder, No. 341
Woelfflin, *Die Kunst Albrecht Dürers*, p. 27
Schilling, *Die Meisterzeichnung III*, No. 2

THIS DRAWING is a characteristic example of the art of the generation of Dürer's masters. It has been variously attributed to Wolgemut and Pleydenwurff. E. Abraham and E. Schilling correctly noted its closeness to the anonymous Master of the "Landauer Altar" in the Germanisches Nationalmuseum, Nuremberg.

MICHAEL WOLGEMUT

(1434-1519)

MICHAEL WOLGEMUT *Born at Nuremberg. Traveled to the Netherlands in 1471. Active in Munich. Took over the studio of Hans Pleydenwurff in Nuremberg. Master of Albrecht Dürer. Died 1519 at Nuremberg.*

328 God the Father Enthroned

Pen in bistre and red ink, water color, 382 x 248 mm.

Dated 1490

London, British Museum

LITERATURE

Schilling, *Die Meisterzeichnung III*, No. 6

Colvin, *Jahrbuch der Preussischen Kunstsammlungen*, VII, pp. 98 ff.

THIS IS A design for the title page of the *Schedel'sche Weltchronik*, published in 1491. The *Weltchronik* is one of the most monumental works of book illustration in woodcut. The title page is full of imagination and fantastic life and gives an idea of the high tension of creative activity that must have filled Wolgemut's studio when the young Dürer was working there.

VEIT STOSS
(1447-1533)

VEIT STOSS *Sculptor, engraver, painter. Born at Dinkels-buehl or Nuremberg. Active in Cracow from 1477. Settled in Nuremberg in 1496. Died there in 1533.*

329 The Presentation in the Temple

Pen and bistre, 114 x 178 mm.

On reverse: the master's sign and signature:
feyt stwos 1505 inv.

Watermark: small circle

Berlin, Ehem. Staatliche Museen, Kupferstichkabinett
(K.d.Z. 17653)

PROVENANCE

Ehlers; Goettingen

LITERATURE

Schilling, *Die Meisterzeichnung III*, No. 8

Baumeister, *Muenchner Jahrbuch der Bildenden Kunst*,
IV, p. 386

IN ADDITION to his sculptures, the great Nuremberg carver was formerly known only for a group of signed engravings. The present signed drawing indicates that several other known drawings are his work. A group of panel paintings now also has to be added to their number (E. Buchner, "Veit Stoss als Maler," *Wallraf-Richartz-Jahrbuch*, XIV, 1952, pp. 111 ff.).

ALBRECHT DÜRER

(1471-1528)

ALBRECHT DÜRER *Born May 21, 1471 at Nuremberg. Pupil of his father and of Michael Wolgemut. 1490-94 in Basel, Colmar, and Strassburg. Journeys to Venice 1495-96, 1505-07; 1520-21 journey to the Netherlands. Died April 26, 1528 at Nuremberg.*

330 Self-Portrait at the Age of Thirteen

Silverpoint on prepared paper, 275 x 196 mm.

Inscribed in the artist's hand at a later time: *Dz hab Ich aws eim spigell nach mir selbs kunterfet Im 1484 Jar do ich noch ein kint was Albrecht Dürer (This I have portrayed after myself from a mirror in the year 1484 when I was still a child Albrecht Dürer)*

Vienna, Albertina (Inv. 4839)

PROVENANCE

Imhof

LITERATURE

Winkler, *Die Zeichnung Albrecht Dürers*, No. 1

Lippmann, *Zeichnungen von Albrecht Dürer*, No. 448

Tietze and Tietze-Conrat, *Kritisches Verzeichnis der Werks Albrecht Dürers*, No. 1

Albertina Catalogue, IV, No. 30

THE EARLIEST preserved drawing by the artist. Dürer did this drawing during the time of his apprenticeship in the goldsmith studio of his father (see No. 331). It is a most extraordinary document of a great artist, still as a child, bound in its general arrangement to the conventional idiom of the Late Gothic style in Nuremberg, but revealing the future genius in the piercing and questioning eyes. Some *pentimenti* are visible in the outlines of the forefinger. A painted self-portrait by Dürer at the same age is in the collection of the Pommer'sche Geschichtsverein in Stettin (E. Buchner, "Das deutsche Bildnis der Spaetgotik und der fruehen Dürerzeit," Berlin, *Deutscher Verein fuer Kunstwissenschaft*, 1953, No. 164). It shows the same features, turned slightly to the front. A tassel is hanging down from the cap at the left in both portraits. The draughtsman may have used two mirrors.

Dz hab Ich aws eim spigell nach
mir selbst kunterfet Im 1484 Jor
Do Ich noch ein kint was

Albrecht Dürer

DÜRER

331 Albrecht Dürer the Elder

Silverpoint on prepared paper, 284 x 212 mm.

Vienna, Albertina (Inv. 4846)

PROVENANCE

Stromer

LITERATURE

Winkler, No. 3

Lippmann, No. 589

Tietze, No. A168

Albertina Catalogue, IV, No. 23

THIS DRAWING was recognized as a portrait of Dürer's father, drawn by his son, by M. J. Friedlaender (*Repertorium fuer Kunstwissenschaft*, 1896, p. 15 ff.). A copy of the drawing, formerly in the Castle of Rheinstein, bears Dürer's monogram and the date 1486, the very year Dürer left his father's studio and entered that of Michael Wolgemut, who became his master in painting and woodcut.

The personality represented is doubtless the same as in the painted portrait of Dürer's father of 1490, Uffizi, Florence. The hands, massive and monumental in modeling, are holding here a small sculptured figure, an example of the goldsmith's art; in the Uffizi portrait, they hold a rosary. The upper body was first outlined in its entirety, but afterwards covered in its lower part by a parapet.

The elder Dürer had migrated from Hungary to Germany, where he settled down as a goldsmith in Nuremberg.

DÜRER

332 Soldiers beneath the Cross

Pen and bistre, 216 x 168 mm.

Monogram by a later hand.

Frankfort-on-Main, Staedel Art Institute (No. 14400)

PROVENANCE

Peltzer (?)

LITERATURE

Winkler, No. 12

Lippmann, No. 597

Tietze, No. A82

THE SOLDIERS in the foreground are casting dice for Christ's garment. Those behind them are discussing the event. At the left margin the outlines of the cross are visible. The attribution to Dürer was voiced by E. Schilling (*Beitraege zur Geschichte der Deutschen Kunst*, edited by Buchner and Feuchtmayr, Vol. I, 1924, p. 129). He emphasized its close affinity to other works of Dürer's early youth such as the "Group of Soldiers," dated 1489, in the Kupferstichkabinett, Berlin (Winkler, No. 18).

Because of its rough and sketchy character this drawing takes a unique position among Dürer's early works. It was first outlined with a sharply pointed pen, which was also used for the man kneeling, and later carried further with a broader pen in harsh and expressive strokes.

DÜRER

333 Young Couple

Pen and bistre, 258 x 191 mm.
Hamburg, Kunsthalle (No. 23918)

PROVENANCE

Harzen

LITERATURE

Winkler, No. 56
Lippmann, No. 620
Tietze, No. 34

THIS DRAWING was done during Dürer's stay on the Upper Rhine from 1490 to 1494 and is correctly considered as a self-representation of Dürer's escorting a Basel girl to a dance. It is one of the most charming and lively genre scenes in German art of the fifteenth century, deriving from the tradition of the great engravers such as the Master E. S., Schongauer, and the Master of the Housebook.

The character of the pen strokes reveals the progress Dürer made since his Nuremberg beginnings under the influence of Martin Schongauer. There are close relations to his Basel book illustrations, *The Knight of the Tower*, and Sebastian Brant's *Ship of Fools*.

DÜRER

334 Female Nude, Seen from the Back, Holding a Staff and a Drapery

Brush and India ink, 320 x 210 mm.

Monogram and date 1495 by another hand

Paris, Louvre, Cabinet des Dessins (No. 19.058)

PROVENANCE

From the sketchbook in the Louvre, which contained many
drawings of the studio of Peter Vischer

LITERATURE

Demonts, No. 142, Pl. LVI

Winkler, No. 85

Lippmann, No. 624, Pl. DCXXIV

Tietze, No. 87

THIS IS one of the most magnificent of Dürer's figure studies, showing the freedom and mastery in the handling of the nude human body that he had gained in Italy. The pen supplements the work of the brush in the modeling of the body along the right outlines.

The influence of this study is still evident in the nude in the engravings "The Four Naked Women" of 1497 (Bartsch, No. 75), and "The Little Fortune" (Bartsch, No. 78).

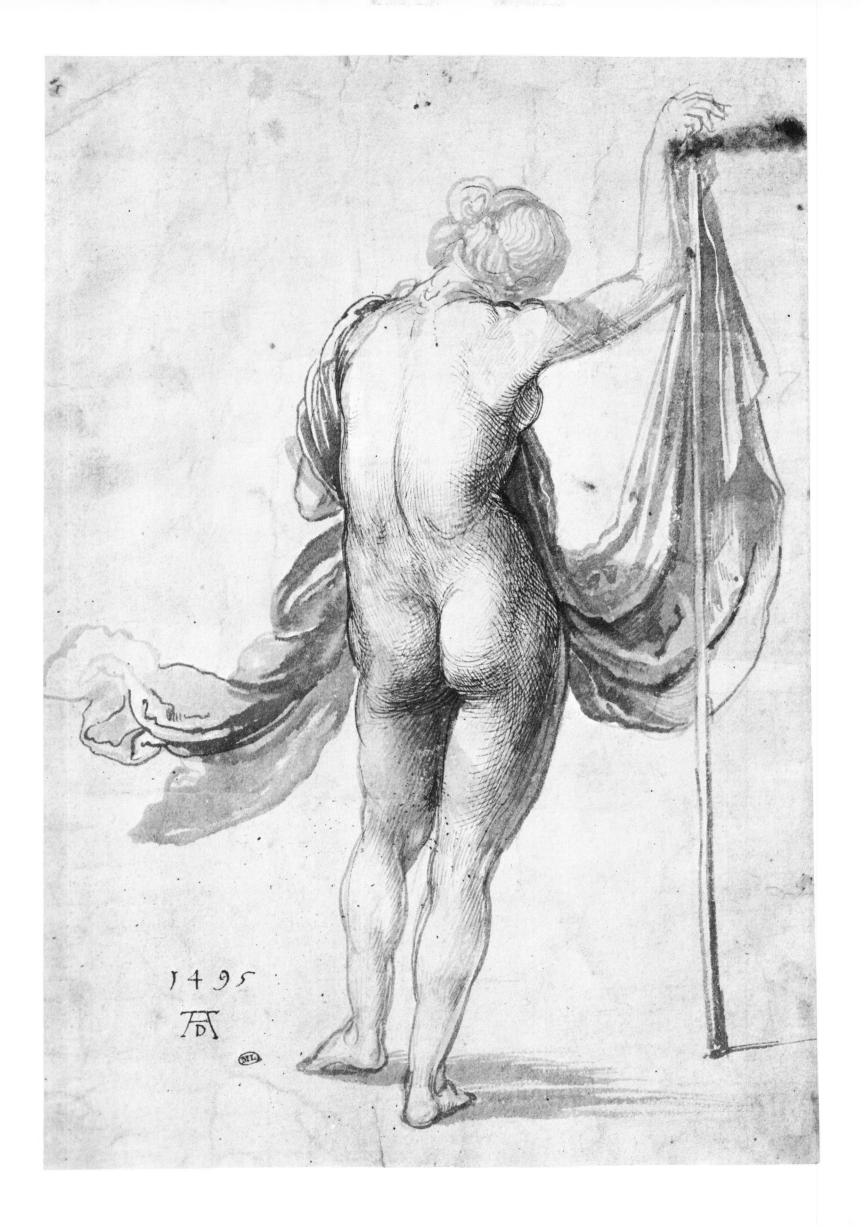

DÜRER

335 View of Arco

Water color and gouache, 223 x 223 mm.

Inscribed in ink by the artist: *fenedier klawsen*

Monogram by a later hand

Paris, Louvre, Cabinet des Dessins (No. 18.579)

PROVENANCE

Jabach; bought by Louis XIV in 1671

LITERATURE

Demonts, No. 144, Pl. LVII

Lippmann, No. 303, Pl. CCCIII

Winkler, No. 54, Pl. LIV

Tietze, No. 92, Pl. XCII

REPRESENTED IS the fortified castle of Arco near Lake Garda in Upper Italy. Shortly after his return from the Upper Rhine Dürer undertook his first journey to Venice in 1494, where he stayed until 1495. His stay was filled with eager study and learning. The immediate results of this journey, however, was the tremendous impression made by the majestic mountain scenery in the Tyrol and in Upper Italy.

During the journey there originated a number of water colors that reveal an entirely new conception of nature: freed from the old medieval schemes, filled with keen observation of cosmic structure, color, and atmosphere. They are indeed the very first products of modern landscape painting and herald a new era of artistic representation of the universe. They are works in their own right and therefore also surpass the works of the Late Gothic Netherlanders who dared a new approach to nature only within the framework of hallowed schemes of religious imagery.

The present water color, made on Dürer's way home, is extraordinary not only because of the observation of the geological character of the scenery, but also because of its typical North Italian color spell: the blackish purple shades of the rocky cliffs and the crumbling walls of old houses, the bluish hues of olive trees with their silvery highlights.

DÜRER

336 Studies of Two Horsemen

Brush and bistre, wash in bistre and India ink,
130 x 121 mm.

London, Count Antoine Seilern

PROVENANCE

Antonio Tempesta (?); Skippe; Rayner Wood

LITERATURE

Winkler, No. 949

Panofsky, No. 1234 (as by another hand)

Dodgson, in *Old Master Drawings*, XIV, p. 14

Christie's, *Sale Catalogue*, London, November 20-21, 1958,
lot 299, Pl. XXXIX

*Paintings and Drawings of Continental Schools other than
Flemish and Italian at 56 Princes Gate, London*, No. 252

THIS DRAWING was recognized by C. Dodgson as forming part of a large composition of "Calvary" to which the "Group of Holy Women," British Museum (Winkler, No. 192), also belongs. It is executed in the same technique with the same shades of ink. The spirit of that composition may have corresponded with the woodcuts (Bartsch, Nos. 11 and 59).

Dodgson dated the drawing as of about 1499. Winkler suggested a somewhat earlier date on the basis of stylistic affinities to the works of the years of Dürer's travels. The effect of the brushwork in both drawings is utterly pictorial and colorful. Dürer had acquired that mastery of the brush in Venice.

DÜRER

337 Christ Taken into Captivity

Pen and ink, 253 x 202 mm.

The so-called "geschleuderte" Monogram probably
    by another hand

Watermark: Gothic p with flower

Berlin, Ehem. Staatliche Museen, Kupferstichkabinett
    (K.d.Z. 74)

LITERATURE

Winkler, No. 318

Lippmann, No. 33

Tietze, pp. 109, 335, No. A47 (as Baldung)

Berlin Catalogue, p. 24, No. 74

THIS DRAWING, full of dynamic and expressive vigor, was correctly dated before 1500 by E. Bock in the Berlin Catalogue. It is full of the pathetic spirit of the "Apocalypse" and the "Large Woodcut Passion." After 1500, Dürer's penstroke becomes more organized and no longer has the rhapsodic passion of the present drawing. The motif of a warrior thrusting Christ in the back with the handle of a martel also occurs in the woodcut of the "Carrying of the Cross" (Bartsch, No. 10). The composition was later used by Dürer for the so-called "Green Passion," Albertina, Vienna (Winkler, No. 300).

DÜRER

338 A Lady of Nuremberg in Church Dress

Brush and water color, 317 x 172 mm.

Date, monogram, and inscription by the artist: *1500
A D Ein Normergerin als man zw kirchen gatt
(A Nuremberg lady as one goes to church)*

London, British Museum (No. 198)

PROVENANCE

Russell; Malcolm

LITERATURE

Winkler, No. 232

Lippmann, No. 703

Schilling, *Die Meisterzeichnung III*, No. 16

THE PRESENT water color, first mentioned by Waagen (*Galleries and Cabinets of Art in Great Britain*, London, 1857, p. 188), was originally considered a replica of the drawing of the same year (Albertina Catalogue, IV, No. 45 and Winkler, No. 224). Later opinion changed in favor of the present drawing, which evidently is the first version, done as a direct study from nature.

The present drawing was executed with the brush only and is particularly subtle in its scale of colors. The Albertina drawing, in its calligraphic character, lacks this immediateness (pen is used in addition to the brush and the color scale is more schematic).

The inscription of the Albertina drawing, beginning with the words "Gedenckt Mein In Ewerm Reych..." is also a hint of the artist's intention to use this study finally for a religious theme. It was used in the woodcut "The Betrothal of Mary" (Bartsch, No. 82) in the cycle of "The Life of the Virgin."

DÜRER

339 Head of a Roebuck

Water color, 228 x 166 mm.

Monogram and date 1514 added later (according to
Flechsig and Winkler) by Hans von Kulmbach

Bayonne, Musée Bonnat (No. 1271/655)

LITERATURE
Winkler, No. 365
Lippmann, No. 358
Tietze, No. 197a

IN THE years before his second Venetian journey, when working on
"The Life of the Virgin," Dürer devoted many of his most beautiful
drawings to the plant and animal kingdom. They prove his eagerness
for experience in all things existing in nature, a symptom of a new
intellectual era. The experience gained therein was used again by
Dürer for enlivening the old hallowed subjects. Another brush drawing of the head of a roebuck was formerly in the Lubomirski Museum
in Lwów (Winkler, No. 364).

DÜRER

340 Head of the Virgin

Charcoal, 265 x 178 mm.

Monogram and date 1503 by the artist; colors added by a later hand

Watermark: Bullock's head with snake

Berlin, Ehem. Staatliche Museen, Kupferstichkabinett (K.d.Z. 56)

LITERATURE

Winkler, No. 275

Lippmann, No. 6

Tietze, No. 227

Berlin Catalogue, p. 25, No. 56

THE DRAWING has been used by Dürer for the head of Mary in the woodcut of "The Adoration of the Magi" (Bartsch, No. 87), in the cycle of "The Life of the Virgin."

Dürer has based the design for the most charming of his narrative picture cycles not only on ingenious pen sketches as projects for entire compositions, but also on carefully detailed studies after a living model such as the present one, which is distinguished by its noble and amiable expression.

DÜRER

341 Head of the Dead Christ Crowned with Thorns

Charcoal on brownish paper, 360 x 210 mm.

Monogram and date 1503 by the artist, beside a hardly
    legible inscription by him referring to the fact that he
    made the drawing during illness

London, British Museum (No. S.5218-18-29)

PROVENANCE

Sloane

LITERATURE

Winkler, No. 272

Lippmann, No. 231

Tietze, No. 225

THE PRESENT drawing, together with the "Head of a Suffering Man"
(also in the British Museum, Winkler, No. 271), is a preparatory
study for a "Lamentation for Christ." Shortly before, in 1500, Dürer
had painted a large panel of this subject for the Nuremberg goldsmith
Glimm, which is now in the Munich Pinakothek. It is a deeply expressive work, which shows that for Dürer religious representation was
not a matter of convention but of personal experience. The artist's
anxiety of soul during hours of illness finds its expression in this
gripping image of the Saviour.

DÜRER

**342 Standing Female Nude,
A Staff in Her Right Hand**

Pen and ink, 236 x 96 mm.
Monogram and date 1508 by another hand
Ottawa, National Gallery of Canada (No. 6652)

PROVENANCE
Lubomirski Museum, Lwów

LITERATURE
Winkler, No. 265
Lippmann, No. 751
Tietze, No. 251a

DÜRER WAS convinced that the structure of the human body is based on lawful proportions and relations, which the artist has to discover in order to master its representation. At the end of his life he concluded a book on the subject. Dürer's studies in this direction had begun in the first years of the sixteenth century and reached their first climax in the famous engraving "Adam and Eve" of 1504 (Bartsch, No. 1).

Most scholars place the origin of the present drawing convincingly in the years preceding the above-mentioned engraving. The figure is obviously not drawn from a living model, but constructed out of a geometrical scheme visible in straight lines drawn with the help of a ruler.

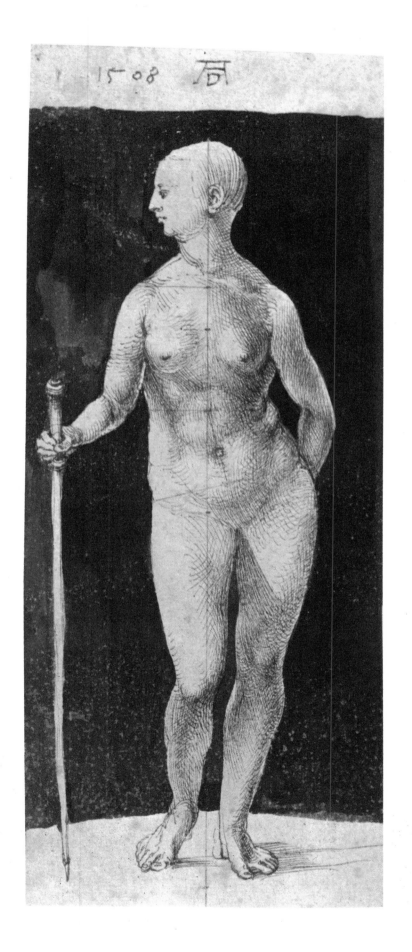

DÜRER

343 The Dead Christ, Lying on a Pall

Charcoal, 172 x 235 mm.

Signed with monogram and dated 1505 by the artist

Watermark: Briquet 2110

Cleveland, Ohio, The Cleveland Museum of Art
  (No. 52.531), Gift of Hanna Fund

PROVENANCE

Lubomirski Museum, Lwów

LITERATURE

Winkler, No. 378

Lippmann, No. 718

Tietze, No. A339

Panofsky, No. 619

Francis, *The Bulletin of The Cleveland Museum of Art*,
  XLII, January, 1955, pp. 3-5

THIS VIGOROUS and powerful drawing demonstrates how Dürer did not shun even repellent and sinister aspects in representations of holy subjects if they increased the dramatic intensity and the overwhelming impression on the beholder. The spirit of the "Small Woodcut Passion" is anticipated here. (The swollen hands with the stigmata prove the Lord's suffering.) The violent realism of the foreshortening, following the example of Mantegna, distorts the beauty of the human body and reveals its helplessness in death.

DÜRER

344 The Mantle of the Pope

Water color, 427 x 288 mm.

The profile and figure of the Pope partly redrawn in
    pencil in the nineteenth century

Monogram and date 1514 in pen and bistre, inscribed by
    Hans von Kulmbach

Watermark: Two crossed arrows

Vienna, Albertina (Inv. 3102)

LITERATURE

Winkler, No. 401

Lippmann, No. 494

Tietze, No. 314

Albertina Catalogue, IV, No. 77

A STUDY for the cope of Pope Julius II in the "Feast of the Rose Garlands." The figure was first sketched in thin outlines, the mantle
afterwards thoroughly executed in water color. This is perhaps
Dürer's most magnificent and representative drapery study, distinguished because of its high pictorial quality.

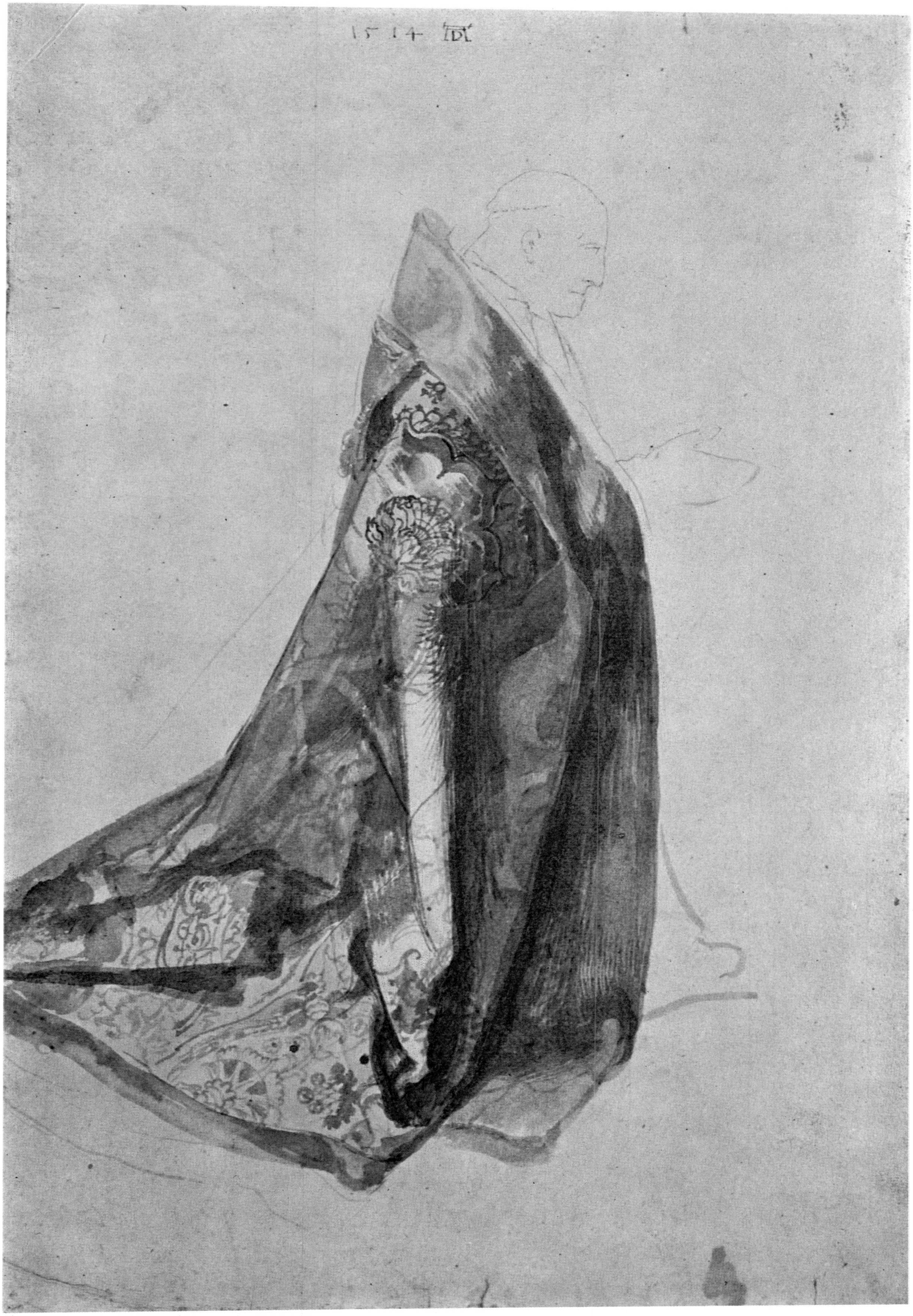
1514

DÜRER

345 Donor with Rosary Kneeling in Prayer

Brush and India ink and white body-color on blue
   Venetian paper, 323 x 200 mm.

Monogram and date 1506 by the artist

New York, The Pierpont Morgan Library

PROVENANCE

Andréossy; Lawrence; Holford; von Lanna

LITERATURE

Winkler, No. 384

Lippmann, No. 428

Tietze, No. 311

SEE NOTE to the previous drawing. The man represented here is kneeling in the painting to the right, behind the Emperor. He must have been one of the prominent members of the German colony, embodying the type of the wealthy German merchant in Venice who entrusted Dürer with the commission.

DÜRER

346 Portrait of an Architect

Brush and India ink and white body-color on blue
    Venetian paper, 386 x 263 mm.

Monogram and date 1506 by the artist

Watermark: Briquet 3391

Berlin, Ehem. Staatliche Museen, Kupferstichkabinett
    (K.d.Z. 2274)

PROVENANCE

Andréossy; Gigoux

LITERATURE

Winkler, No. 382

Lippmann, No. 10

Tietze, No. 313

Berlin Catalogue, p. 26, No. 2274

THIS DRAWING is supposed to represent Hieronymous of Augsburg, architect of the Fondaco dei Tedeschi (Community Center of the Germans) in Venice.

The so-called "Rosenkranzfest" ("Feast of the Rose Garlands") was the most important work painted by Dürer in 1506 (now in the National Gallery of Prague). It shows the Blessed Virgin and Child with St. Dominic placing wreathes of roses on the heads of the Emperor Maximilian, Pope Julius II, and the members of the German community in Venice. In it Dürer employed the solemn compositional device of the Italian High Renaissance: the triangular or pyramidal composition. In preparation for it Dürer made a number of wonderful brush drawings in the Venetian technique, which he had learned from Carpaccio and Bellini. The figure of the architect appears in the painting at the far right.

DÜRER

347 Head of an Apostle

Brush and India ink and white body-color on green
    prepared paper, 317 x 212 mm.

Monogram and date 1508 by the artist

Vienna, Albertina (Inv. 3111)

LITERATURE

Winkler, No. 450

Lippmann, No. 508

Tietze, No. 377

Albertina Catalogue, IV, No. 88

IN 1508 and 1509 Dürer painted a large altarpiece representing the "Assumption of the Virgin" for a wealthy Frankfort citizen Jacob Heller. It was placed in the Dominican church in Frankfort-on-Main and later entered the art collection of the Elector Maximilian of Bavaria in Munich, where it was destroyed by a fire in the residential castle.

This was the climax of Dürer's monumental painting. He prepared for it carefully, making a series of detailed studies for figures, heads, draperies, and hands. In this he followed the practice of the Italian masters of the High Renaissance, but he deepened it with the profundity of the searching German spirit, intent upon vivifying the religious characters. This is most evident in the heads of the Apostles, the finest of which entered the Albertina. The present drawing was used for an Apostle in the right portion of the painting.

DÜRER

348 The Virgin with the Child and Little St. John

Pen and bistre, 165 x 210 mm.

Monogram by another hand

Bayonne, Musée Bonnat (No. 1279/1508)

LITERATURE

Winkler, No. 515

Lippmann, No. 353

Tietze, No. 521

CLEARLY A representation of the Madonna by a Northern Italian Mantegnesque artist must have inspired Dürer when making this drawing. The cross section of a Bramantesque cloister in the right background also follows an Italian model. It was added by the artist afterward, yet it meant to form the background to the figures of the foreground. The drawing is commonly dated at the beginning of the second decade of the sixteenth century.

DÜRER

349 The Virgin Suckling the Child

Charcoal, 418 x 288 mm.
Monogram and date 1512 in pen and ink by the artist
Vienna, Albertina (Inv. 4848)

LITERATURE
Winkler, No. 512
Lippmann, No. 525
Tietze, No. 503
Albertina Catalogue, IV, No. 103

ONE OF Dürer's most beautiful drawings of the Virgin, full of motherly splendor and amiable serenity. Fugitive pen sketches of the Virgin by the master are as frequent as drawings in charcoal of such an imposing and monumental aspect are rare. In the following years of the decade, Dürer frequently made engravings of the same subject. One of them (Bartsch, No. 36), of 1519, may have been inspired by the present drawing.

A pupil of Dürer's used the figure of the Child for the "Madonna with the Iris," National Gallery, London.

DÜRER

350 Two Versions of the Virgin and Child

Pen and India ink, 159 x 132 mm.
Frankfort-on-Main, Staedel Art Institute (No. 13445)

PROVENANCE
Lawrence (?); von Lanna

LITERATURE
Winkler, No. 527
Lippmann, No. 726
Tietze, No. 601

DÜRER

351 The Virgin Seated on a Chair, Offering an Apple to the Child

Pen and bistre, 187 x 162 mm.
Dated 1514 by the artist. Monogram by another hand
Venice, Accademia (No. 471)

LITERATURE
Winkler, No. 532
Lippmann, No. 796
Tietze, No. A412

THE PRESENT drawing belongs to the group of spirited sketches of the theme that Dürer did in the first half of the second decade. The lower version is a further development of the idea of the engraving of 1503 (Bartsch, No. 34).

THE MOTIF of maternity, with a feeling of German domesticity, is combined with the strict triangular composition of the Italian Renaissance. Compare with the engraving "The Virgin at the Wall" (Bartsch, No. 40), done in the same year.

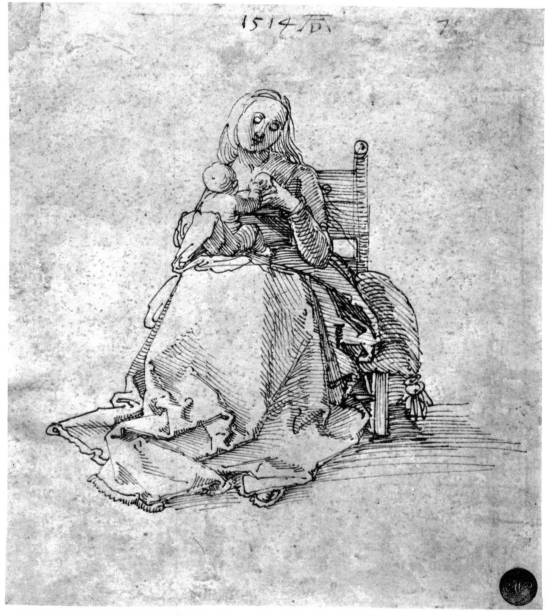

DÜRER

352 Portrait of the Artist's Mother

Charcoal, 421 x 303 mm.

Dated 1514 and inscribed by the artist in the same
charcoal: *Dz ist albrecht durers mutter dy was alt 63
Jor (This is Albrecht Dürer's mother at the age of 63)*

Later addition in ink also by the artist: *und ist verschiden
Im 1514 Jor am erchtag vor der crewtzwochn im zwey
genacht (and died in 1514, on May 16th at two
o'clock by night)*

Berlin, Ehem. Staatliche Museen, Kupferstichkabinett
(K.d.Z. 22)

PROVENANCE

Imhof; Andréossy; Firmin-Didot

LITERATURE

Winkler, No. 559

Lippmann, No. 40

Tietze, No. 591

Berlin Catalogue, p. 29, No. 22

THE ARTIST portrayed his mother here during the last year of her
life after she had been struck by an attack of severe illness. Inexorable
realism of representation is combined with an almost religious depth
of spirituality. The feeling of the son for his mother comes to the fore
in a sublime way, full of piety and reverence. Thus originated Dürer's
most monumental and also most famous portrait drawing. It initiates
the large portraits in charcoal that Dürer created in his mature years.

DÜRER

353 The Holy Trinity

Pen and bistre, 300 x 219 mm.

Monogram and date 1515 by the artist

Boston, Massachusetts, Museum of Fine Arts

PROVENANCE

Gutekunst

LITERATURE

Winkler, No. 583

Lippmann, No. 810

Tietze, No. 650

Dodgson, *Vasari Society*, VII, No. 24

THIS COMPOSITION, full of a sublime pathos, was created not for the purpose of preparing a certain engraving or woodcut, but out of Dürer's own inner urge, developing further the main group of the woodcut of 1511 (Bartsch, No. 122). The drawing was famous during the artist's lifetime and was copied frequently by his pupils, among them Hans von Kulmbach.

DÜRER

354 Sheet of Studies with Six Nude Figures, the Main Figure Tied to the Trunk of a Tree

Pen and bistre, 270 x 211 mm.

Date 1515 by the artist

Frankfort-on-Main, Staedel Art Institute (No. 698)

PROVENANCE

Lawrence

LITERATURE

Winkler, No. 666

Lippmann, No. 195

Tietze, No. 623

THE PRESENT drawing and a companion piece of 1516, also in Frankfort (Winkler, No. 667), have been investigated in vain for a literary source. The Prometheus myth was among those proposed, but no satisfactory solution has been found. Other scholars have assumed that it is just an assembly of studies after the nude. The drawing resembles Dürer's etching of the so-called "Man in Despair" (Bartsch, No. 70), which also combines different studies from the nude, but simultaneously introduces a figure resembling Michelangelo's features. This suggests that the scenes imply a literary content. Winkler is tempted to think of Michelangelo's fettered slaves.

DÜRER

355 Portrait of Hans Burgkmair the Elder

Charcoal, on discolored paper, touched with the brush in
  body-color, against a background of black (India) ink,
  374 x 265 mm.

Monogram and date: M⁰D⁰XVIII
  Below: 1515 and Monogram

Inscribed: ALBERTVS DVER PICTOR NORICVS GERMANICVS
  VACIEBAT

Oxford, Ashmolean Museum

PROVENANCE

Douce

LITERATURE

Winkler, No. 569

Lippmann, No. 396

Tietze, No. A397

Ashmolean Catalogue, I, No. 290

ACCORDING TO Parker the black background, the outlines, and inscription in white body-color are by Burgkmair, to whom Dürer gave
the drawing as a gift.

The monogram and date below seem to trace Dürer's signature in
charcoal.

The sitter was identified by F. Doernhoeffer (*Beitraege zur Kunst-
geschichte, Franz Wickhoff gewidmet*, Vienna, 1903, p. 129). A self-
portrait drawing of 1517 by Burgkmair in Hamburg made possible
the identification of the sitter.

DÜRER

356 Portrait of Emperor Maximilian I

Charcoal, 381 x 319 mm.

The reddish flesh-colors and the heightenings in white chalk added by the artist's hand afterwards

Inscribed in pen and ink by the artist: *Das ist keiser maximilian den hab ich albrecht durer zw awgspurg hoch obn awff der pfaltz In seine[m] kleinen stuble kunterfett do man zalt 1518 am mandag noch Johannis tawffer (This is Emperor Maximilian whom I Albrecht Durer have portrayed in his little chamber at Augsburg high up in the Palatinate on June 28, 1518)*

Monogram added by another hand

Vienna, Albertina (Inv. 4852)

PROVENANCE

Imhof

LITERATURE

Winkler, No. 567

Lippmann, No. 546

Tietze, No. 708

Albertina Catalogue, IV, No. 133

THIS MOST vivacious and human portrait of the great Renaissance ruler was done during the last year of Maximilian's life on the occasion of his sojourn at the Imperial Diet (Reichstag) in Augsburg. He returned from there to Austria. Growing illness, increased by a personal bitter experience in Innsbruck, prevented him from completing his homeward journey. He had to interrupt it in the little city of Wels in Upper Austria, where he died on January 12, 1519.

After the Emperor's death Dürer completed, in 1519, two portrait paintings of him on the basis of the present drawing: first, the painting in water colors on canvas in the Germanisches Nationalmuseum, Nuremberg; second, the stately panel in the Gallery of the Kunsthistorisches Museum in Vienna. The woodcut (Bartsch, No. 154) was also based on this drawing.

Das ist kaiser maximilian der hab ich albrecht dürer zu ogspurg hoch oben auff der pfaltz in seim kleinen stüblin kunterfet do man zalt 1518 am mantag noch Johannis zwischen [monogram: AD]

DÜRER

357 The Lamentation for Christ

Pen and bistre, 315 x 214 mm.
Date 1519 by the artist
Monogram by another hand
Vienna, Albertina (Inv. 3159)

LITERATURE
Winkler, No. 587
Lippmann, No. 559
Tietze, No. 544
Albertina Catalogue, IV, No. 106

IN HIS mature years Dürer returned to the representation of the Passion of the Lord with many figures, but now he welds his composition into a monumental group that exhales an almost architectural mood. The many bystanders, dressed in northern costumes of town and country people, are fused into a tight group that stands like a block in the void of the bare scenery. Thus, great emphasis is laid upon the drama of the content.

DÜRER

358 St. Anne (Portrait of Agnes Dürer)

Brush and India ink and white body-color on gray prepared
  paper, background laid out in black ink, 395 x 292 mm.

Monogram and date 1519 by the artist on a superimposed
  square paper

Vienna, Albertina (Inv. 3160)

LITERATURE

Winkler, No. 574

Lippmann, No. 560

Tietze, No. 734

Albertina Catalogue, IV, No. 136

THIS DRAWING breathes an almost sculptural grandeur. That Dürer's
wife, Agnes, is represented here becomes evident from a study of her
in the sketch-book of his journey to the Netherlands, which unde-
niably represents the same person. The drawing, however, was not
executed with the intention of creating a portrait, but of using Frau
Agnes as a model for the painting of "St. Ann, the Virgin and the
Child" in the Metropolitan Museum of Art, New York (see also note
to No. 359). A personal experience in Dürer's family life may be hid-
den behind the cool and smooth abstraction of the above-mentioned
painting, an example of how drama may brood behind the iron concentration and lawfulness of Dürer's late creations.

DÜRER

359 Head of a Young Woman with Her Eyes Closed

Brush and India ink and white body-color, 326 x 226 mm.
Monogram and date by the artist
London, British Museum (No. S.5218-43)

PROVENANCE
Sloane

LITERATURE
Winkler, No. 576
Lippmann, No. 270
Tietze, No. 748
British Museum Catalogue, No. 264

THIS MAGNIFICENT head of great sculptural quality is not the result of an abstract and theoretical construction as assumed by L. Justi, but a life study as has been brought forward by most other scholars. The drawing is related in technique to the preceding, further to the head of the same (?) "Young Woman" with the date 1519, formerly in Bremen (Winkler, No. 575), and the "Head of a Dead Baby" in Hamburg with the date 1520 (Winkler, No. 577). All these drawings are connected either as preparatory studies or models with the afore-mentioned painting in New York.

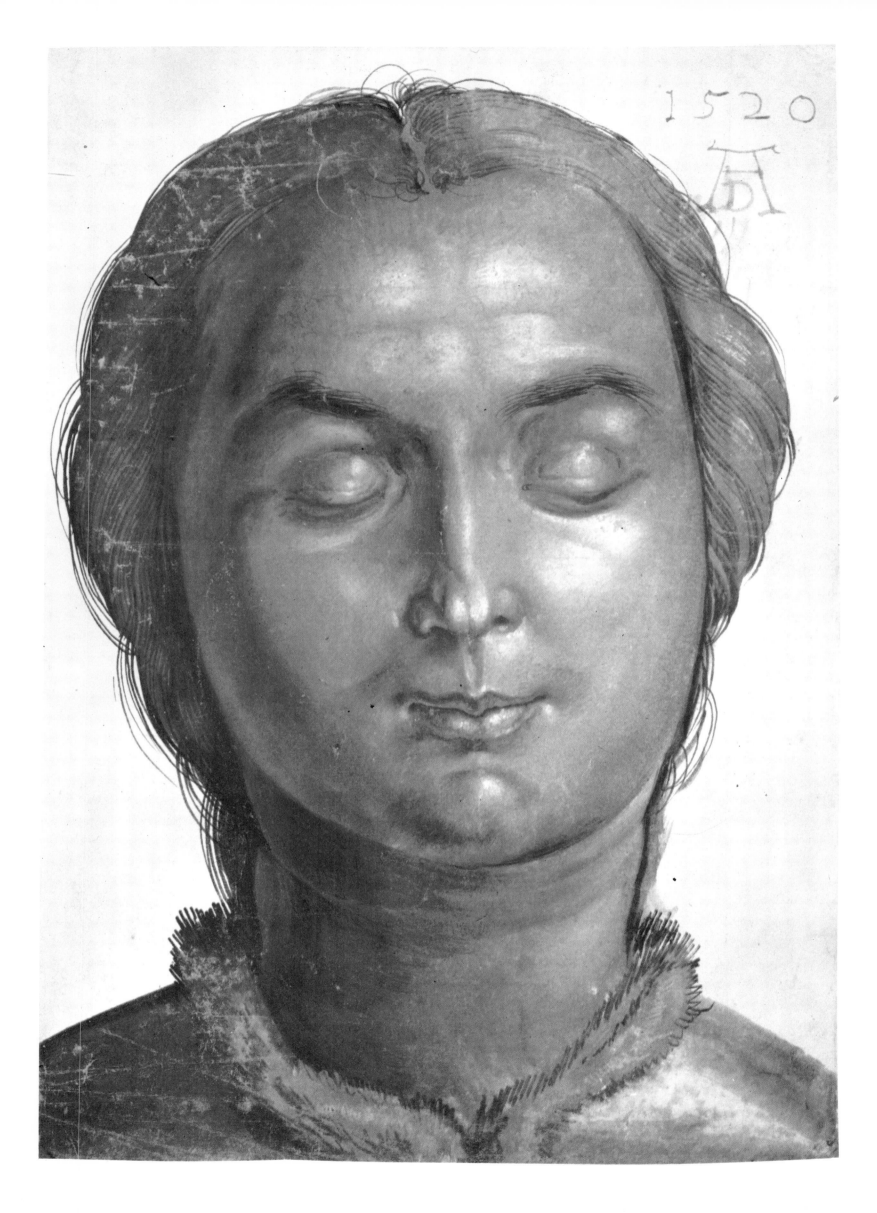

DÜRER

360 Heads of a Young Woman and of an Old Woman from Bergen

Silverpoint on prepared paper, 129 x 191 mm.

Inscribed by the artist: *zw pergen (at Bergen) feuertag (Holiday)*

Chantilly, Musée Condé

PROVENANCE

Vivant-Denon; Reiset

LITERATURE

Winkler, No. 771

Lippmann, No. 342

Tietze, No. 777

IN THE years 1520 and 1521 Dürer went to the Lower Rhine and the Netherlands in order to receive from the new Emperor Charles V confirmation of the pension that Emperor Maximilian had granted to him. This trip developed into a triumphal journey through the Netherlands, proving the great fame that the artist had acquired. It was a journey of importance for his artistic thinking as well.

A little silverpoint sketch-book accompanied him, which forms a kind of picture complement to his written diary. The leaves of this sketch-book are now scattered over many collections. At the beginning of December 1520, he visited Bergen op Zoom on a trip to Zeeland. In his diary he writes the following note about the present drawing: I have portrayed Jan de Has, his wife and his daughters with the charcoal, and the servant and the old lady with the silverpoint in my booklet."

On the reverse of this drawing is "Two Busts of Women from Bergen and Goes" (Winkler, No. 770).

DÜRER

361 Portrait of a Ninety-Three-Year-Old Man

Brush and India ink and white body-color on grayish-violet prepared paper, 418 x 282 mm.

Monogram, date 1521, and inscription by the artist: *Der man was alt 93 jor und noch gesunt und fermuglich zw antorff (The man was 93 years old and still healthy and vigorous at Antwerp)*

Watermark (?): Three lilies, coat of arms and a Gothic e

Vienna, Albertina (Inv. 3167)

LITERATURE

Winkler, No. 788

Lippmann, No. 568

Tietze, No. 804

Albertina Catalogue, IV, No. 144

WHEN DÜRER stayed in the Netherlands he painted for Rodrigo d'Almada, a noble art lover from Portugal, a half-length figure of St. Jerome (National Museum, Lisbon). Dürer prepared carefully for this painting, making large masterly drawings, five of which are preserved (two studies for the head, one in the Albertina and the other in Berlin; three further studies are also in the Albertina, one for the hand, one for the skull, and one for the lectern with the books). The present drawing is the most beautiful of them, the very climax of Dürer's sublime draughtsmanship.

DÜRER

362 Madonna and Child Enthroned with Saints and Angels

Pen and bistre, 317 x 446 mm.
Monogram by another hand
Bayonne, Musée Bonnat (No. 1276/1505)

PROVENANCE
Vivant-Denon

LITERATURE
Winkler, No. 839
Lippmann, No. 364
Tietze, No. 851

DÜRER HAD received the commission for a large altar painting of the Madonna surrounded by numerous saints and angels making music. It is, so to say, the rebirth of the idea of the "Feast of the Rose Garlands" in a new spirit. He began working on it during his stay in the Netherlands and devoted much care to it after his return home, but the work was never brought to a conclusion. Several pen sketches for the composition and also detail studies, carefully executed in black and white chalk on colored paper, give an idea of the grandiose project. Dürer certainly received some inspiration for it from the large altars by Quentin Massys, especially the altar of "The Holy Kindred," but he transformed the Netherlandish inspiration entirely into the German spirit, harking back to his experiences in Venice.

DÜRER

363 Study for St. Barbara (Bust)

Black chalk on green prepared paper, 415 x 286 mm.

Monogram and date 1521 by the artist

Paris, Louvre, Cabinet des Dessins (No. 18.590)

LITERATURE

Demonts, No. 129, Pl. LI

Reiset, No. 498

Winkler, No. 845

Lippmann, No. 326

Tietze, No. 852

AFTER DÜRER had fixed the poses of the figures in the total design for the "Madonna and Child Enthroned" (our No. 362), he used models posing in the attitudes needed for his figures. Winkler's opinion that this and the following drawing are "ideal studies" can hardly be maintained. The character of a realistic life study is too obvious in the present drawing of a girl of negroid type. The figure of St. Barbara appears in the left portion of the composition.

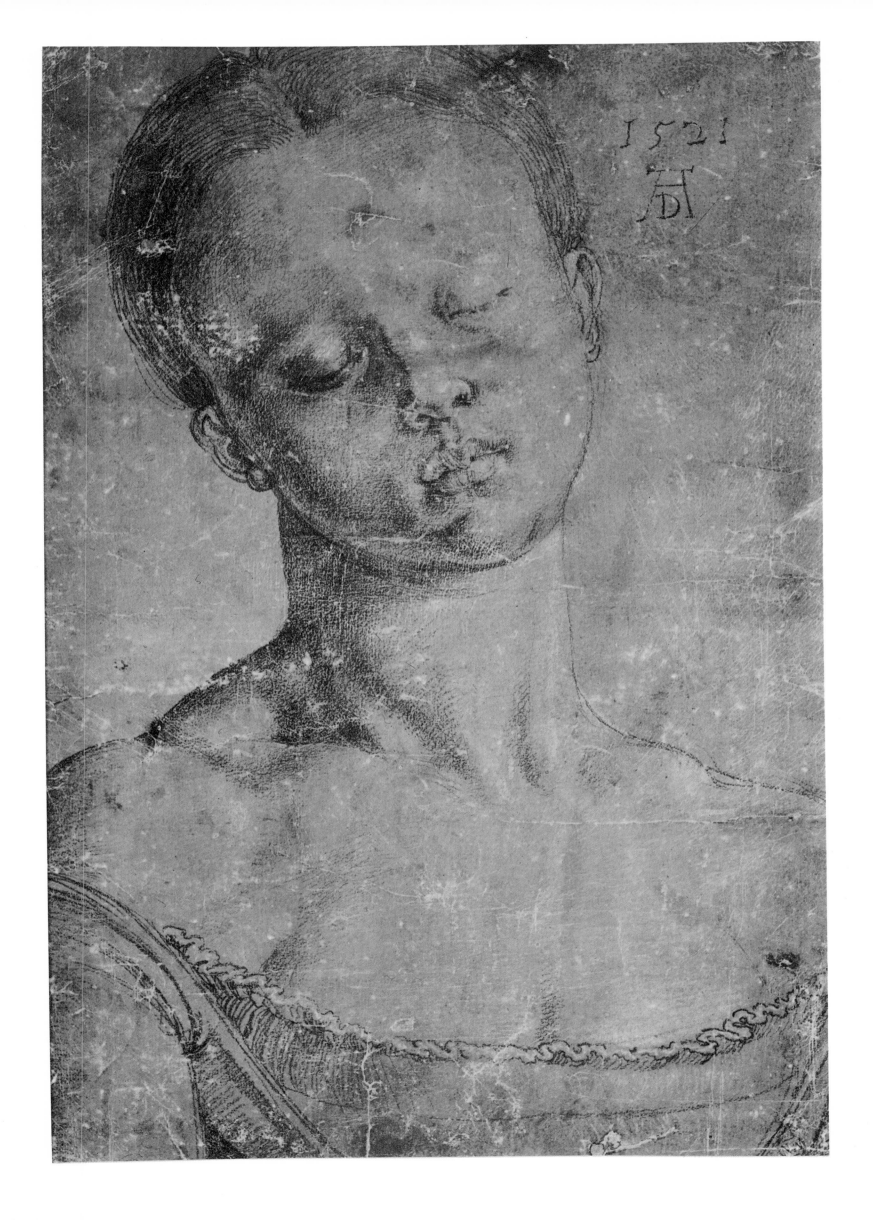

DÜRER

364 Study for St. Apollonia (Bust)

Black chalk on green prepared paper, 414 x 288 mm.

Monogram and date 1521 by the artist

Berlin, Ehem. Staatliche Museen, Kupferstichkabinett
(K.d.Z. 1527)

PROVENANCE

Robinson

LITERATURE

Winkler, No. 846

Lippmann, No. 65

Tietze, No. 853

Berlin Catalogue, p. 33, No. 1527

SEE NOTE to the preceding No. 363.
This beautiful woman appears in the same rigid attitude in the
right portion of the "Madonna and Child Enthroned" (our No. 362).

DÜRER

365 The Agony in the Garden

Pen and bistre, 208 x 294 mm.

Monogram and date 1521 below Christ's legs by the artist.
  Another monogram by a later hand

Frankfort-on-Main, Staedel Art Institute (No. 695)

PROVENANCE

Vivant-Denon (?); Reinhold; F. N. Fink

LITERATURE

Winkler, No. 798

Lippmann, No. 198

Tietze, No. 820

In the Netherlands Dürer drew a series of drawings of the "Passion of the Lord," which may hint that a plan existed to create a new cycle of prints. The compositions are no longer upright in the German tradition, but oblong under the influence of the early Netherlanders. This gave Dürer an opportunity to develop the breadth of scenic space and to give the single figures enhanced monumentality and importance. The present drawing is full of a deep seriousness of mood. The Saviour is extended flat on the rock and surrenders himself to the universe and the heavenly Father. Veils of fog, in their horizontal extension, increase the oppressive mood of the night in the forest. The angel with the chalice emerges from them. Perhaps this quiet monumentality answers better the meaning and spirit of the scene than the dramatic upright compositions of previous years.

HANS SUESS VON KULMBACH

(Ca. 1480-1522)

HANS SUESS VON KULMBACH *Studied in Nuremberg, first with Jacopo de Barbari, after with Dürer. In Cracow from 1514-16. Died 1522 at Nuremberg.*

366 Two Pairs of Lovers and an Old Woman

Pen and bistre over pencil traces, 184 x 253 mm.

Apocryphal Schongauer monogram

On reverse, the unexplainable inscription:
  Mathisz allerley schlecht

Munich, Staatliche Graphische Sammlung (No. 1928-101)

PROVENANCE

Roupell

LITERATURE

Weigmann, in *Muenchner Jahrbuch der Bildenden Kunst*, 1933, p. 325

Baumeister, in *Pantheon*, XXV, 1940, p. 101

Winkler, *Die Zeichnungen Hans Suess von Kulmbachs und H. L. Schaeufeleins*, No. 17

Munich Catalogue, p. 34

A CHARACTERISTIC specimen of Kulmbach's early drawing style, which is closely related to the works of the young Dürer. This and other drawings, first brought together by Winkler, seem to have been done around 1500 or in the first years of the new century, because they depend on Dürer's style of drawing after his return from Venice.

They emulate the expressive quality of Dürer's drawings without attaining Dürer's vigor and decisiveness. The pictorial and lyrical features of Kulmbach's work are already evident here.

KULMBACH

367 The Holy Virgin and Child with Angels Making Music, St. Jerome and St. Anthony. On the Wings: St. Sebastian, St. Roch

Pen in bistre and ink, 203 x 405 mm.

Design for a winged altarpiece; the center piece touched with water color

Date 1511 and Dürer monogram in pencil

Vienna, Albertina (Inv. 3131)

LITERATURE

Winkler, *Kulmbach*, No. 84

Schoenbrunner-Meder, No. 469

Meder, *Die Handzeichnung ihre Technik und Entwicklung*, p. 334

Albertina Catalogue, IV, No. 181

THE DRAWING was first outlined with the pen in bistre, as can still be seen in the figures of the Saints on the wings. The center piece was reworked afterwards in pen and black ink and touched with water color (only the Glory of God the Father and the angels remained unchanged).

Meder was the first to recognize Kulmbach's authorship of this drawing and of a similar one, also in the Albertina, which is dated 1508. It seems that these drawings were designs for an altarpiece commissioned by the Tucher family for the church of St. Sebald in Nuremberg. In the following years, Dürer and Kulmbach both made designs for the altar, which finally was executed by Kulmbach. Winkler assumed that Dürer, overburdened with work, left the commission to Kulmbach, but nonetheless influenced the work in its preparatory stages. Therefore, he gives documentary significance to the Dürer monogram on the present drawing and credit to the authenticity of the date, which has also been accepted by other scholars.

KULMBACH

368 The Nativity

Pen in bistre and wash in India ink, 299 x 191 mm.

Apocryphal Dürer monogram; date 1512 by another hand

Design for stained glass

Frankfort-on-Main, Staedel Art Institute (No. 15681)

LITERATURE

Winkler, *Kulmbach*, No. 138

Schilling, *Altdeutsche Handzeichnungen aus der
    Sammlung I. F. Lahmann*, No. 12

WINKLER assumes that the date, although in another than Dürer's hand, might still indicate the correct year of origin. The objects hanging from the ends of the garlands (left, a sword and a lute; right, a harp) may be symbolically connected with the donor who commissioned the design.

HANS LEONHARD SCHAEUFELEIN

(Ca. 1480-1538/40)

HANS LEONHARD SCHAEUFELEIN *Born at Nuremberg of a Noerdlingen family. Pupil of Dürer 1503-08. Traveled to the Tyrol. Active in Augsburg and elsewhere in Suabia from 1510. From 1515 active in Noerdlingen. Died there between 1538 and 1540.*

369 The Last Supper

Pen, 154 x 220 mm.

Date 1509, monogram, and inscription by the artist: *Da man die muschlan auf den huot band (when the shells were fixed to the hat)*

London, British Museum (No. 315)

LITERATURE

Winkler, *Die Zeichnungen Hans Suess von Kulmbachs und H. L. Schaeufeleins*, No. 42

Schilling, *Die Meisterzeichnung III*, No. 37

SCHAEUFELEIN IN his early work around 1510 was a most ardent follower of his master, Dürer, not only in paintings like the altar from Ober St. Veit, Vienna, but also in drawings. Dürer's influence is also evident here. Out of Dürer's idiom of pen drawing, the pupil developed a kind of baroque style with curls and flourishes. It is a style that fits well the types to represent the Apostles, chosen from artisans and the common people of Germany.

The inscription seems to refer to the festival of St. James, the patron of pilgrims, which is also the day when the Apostles separated and as pilgrims wandered in all directions on the globe. Curiously enough, one of the Apostles in the upper left-hand corner is dressed in the costume of an old mercenary. The Lord, holding out the sop to Judas, indicates the one who will betray Him.

1·5·0·9

Daran die mußstlan auf
den hüt dand
HS

SCHAEUFELEIN

370 Head of the Apostle St. James the Greater

Black chalk, 268 x 198 mm.

Monogram, date 1512, and inscription by the artist:
Hanns Scheyffl das gutt Scheif....

Stockholm, Nationalmuseum (No. 1787/1863)

PROVENANCE

Crozat; Tessin

LITERATURE

Winkler, *Schaeufelein*, No. 51

Schilling, *Die Meisterzeichnung III*, No. 39

Wallach, *Die Stilentwicklung Hans Leonhard
Schaeufeleins*, I, p. 66

SCHAEUFELEIN

371 Portrait of an Old Woman in Head Cloth

Black chalk, 377 x 230 mm.

Dated 1516 apparently by the artist; Apocryphal Dürer
monogram

Copenhagen, Royal Museum of Fine Arts (No. tu.98.5)

LITERATURE

Schilling, in *Kunstmuseets Aarsskrift*, XXXVIII,
p. 64, Pl. X

Schilling, in *Zeitschrift fuer Kunstwissenschaft*, IX, p. 165
No. 8, Pl. XV

Fischer and Sthyr, *Seks Aarhundreders europaeisk
Tegnekunst*, p. 110, Pl. XXIII

SCHAEUFELEIN SEEMS to follow in the footsteps of his master Dürer in this large and monumentally conceived head without hiding his more lyrical and sentimental temperament, so different from Dürer's powerful virility.

THE PRESENT drawing has tentatively been attributed to Dürer, and also to Grünewald, from whose expressive linework it is not too distant, although it lacks Grünewald's atmosphere. The attribution to Schaeufelein is due to E. Schilling.

HANS SPRINGINKLEE

(d. Ca. 1540)

HANS SPRINGINKLEE *Pupil of Dürer. Active as an illu-*
minator in Constance in 1511. Active in Nuremberg 1512-
22. One of Dürer's collaborators in his commissions for
Emperor Maximilian I. Died about 1540.

372 The Rest of the Holy Family
on the Flight into Egypt

Pen and India ink and white body-color on brown prepared
  paper, 224 x 162 mm.

Monogram and date 1514 by the artist

London, British Museum (No. 1876.12.9.618)

LITERATURE

Dodgson, in *Dürer Society*, VII, No. 12

Parker, in *Old Master Drawings*, I, 1926/27, Pl. XIX

British Museum Catalogue, No. 328

ALTHOUGH NO ass is visible, the traveler's dress of St. Joseph indicates that the subject is a "Flight into Egypt." The little angels seem
to urge the continuation of the journey; one of them puts a hat on
the head of St. Joseph, who is still asleep from exhaustion. The importance given to the idyllic scenic environment and the character of
the chiaroscuro show the influence of the Danube School, a school
with which the artist seems to have come into contact during his
travels. He was also a successful illuminator, active for the Bishop
of Constance.

HANS BALDUNG

(1484/85-1545)

HANS BALDUNG, called Grien   *Born at Weyersheim near
Strassburg. Member of a Suabian family from Gmund.
Pupil of Strassburg painter about 1500. From 1503, a pupil
of Dürer in Nuremberg. Citizen of Strassburg in 1509.
Active in Freiburg im Breisgau 1512-17. Court painter to
the Bishop and member of the city council of Strassburg.
Died there 1545.*

373 St. Jude Thaddeus

Black pencil and white body-color on dark brown
    prepared paper, 283 x 174 mm.

Lille, Palais des Beaux-Arts, Musée Wicar (No. 948)

PROVENANCE

Vallardi; Wicar

LITERATURE

Hans Baldung Grien, Staatliche Kunsthalle Karlsruhe,
    1959, No. 184

THE PRESENT drawing, hitherto not reproduced, was recognized as
Baldung's by the author in 1952. The catalogue of the Karlsruhe Exhibition dates it correctly in the early period of the master, com-
paring it to drawings of the first decade of the sixteenth century.

BALDUNG

374 **Portrait Study of an Old Woman
(half-length)**

Black chalk, 395 x 250 mm.

Background tinged in light grayish-green by another hand

Monogram by the artist

Jenkintown, Pennsylvania, Mrs. Lessing J. Rosenwald

LITERATURE

Sale Catalogue, Hollstein and Puppel, 1929, No. 11

Selections from the Rosenwald Collection, National
   Gallery of Art, 1943, pp. 50, 51

Tietze, *European Master Drawings in the United States*,
   p. 72, No. 36

THE DRAWING, still close in style to Dürer, seems to have originated
before 1510.

BALDUNG

375 The Lamentation over the Body of Christ

Pen and ink, 323 x 223 mm.

Date 1513 by the artist

Basel, Kupferstichkabinett (Inv. U.VIII.8)

PROVENANCE

Gaesch

LITERATURE

Koch, *Die Zeichnungen Hans Baldung Griens*, No. 34

Térey, *Verzeichnis der Gemaelde des Hans Baldung genannt Grien*, No. 3

THE DRAWING is of particular importance as a preparatory design for a painting preserved in the Museum Ferdinandeum, Innsbruck.

BALDUNG

376 Two Nude Men, Fighting

Pen and India ink and white body-color on reddish-brown
    prepared paper, 285 x 175 mm.

Date 1515 by the artist

Venice, Accademia (No. 477)

LITERATURE

Koch, No. 66

THE SUBJECT matter is without doubt inspired by Dürer's drawings
for his *Treatise on Fighting and Wrestling* (1512) in the Albertina,
which must have been known to Baldung. Related representations of
pairs of wrestlers are to be found in the roundel with the coats of
arms of Nikolaus Ziegler, Veste Coburg, Kunstsammlungen (Koch,
No. 82).

BALDUNG

377 Head of "Saturn"

Black chalk, 332 x 255 mm.
Monogram and date [1]516 by the artist
Inscribed by a later hand: *Saturno L.*
Vienna, Albertina (Inv. 17549)

PROVENANCE
Prince de Ligne (Cat. p. 141, No. 1)

LITERATURE
Koch, No. 48
Térey, No. 245
Albertina Catalogue, IV, No. 302

THE PRESENT work is perhaps the climax of Baldung's art of drawing. It was done toward the end of the Freiburg period and is full of an expressive grandeur, proving the influence of Grünewald's altar in neighboring Isenheim on Baldung. It is a token of the spiritual grandeur of that great era of German art, dominated not only by a new concept of religious thought, but also by the urge to penetrate the secrets of nature. Thus, old mythological figures gained a new significance as poetical embodiments of natural forces.

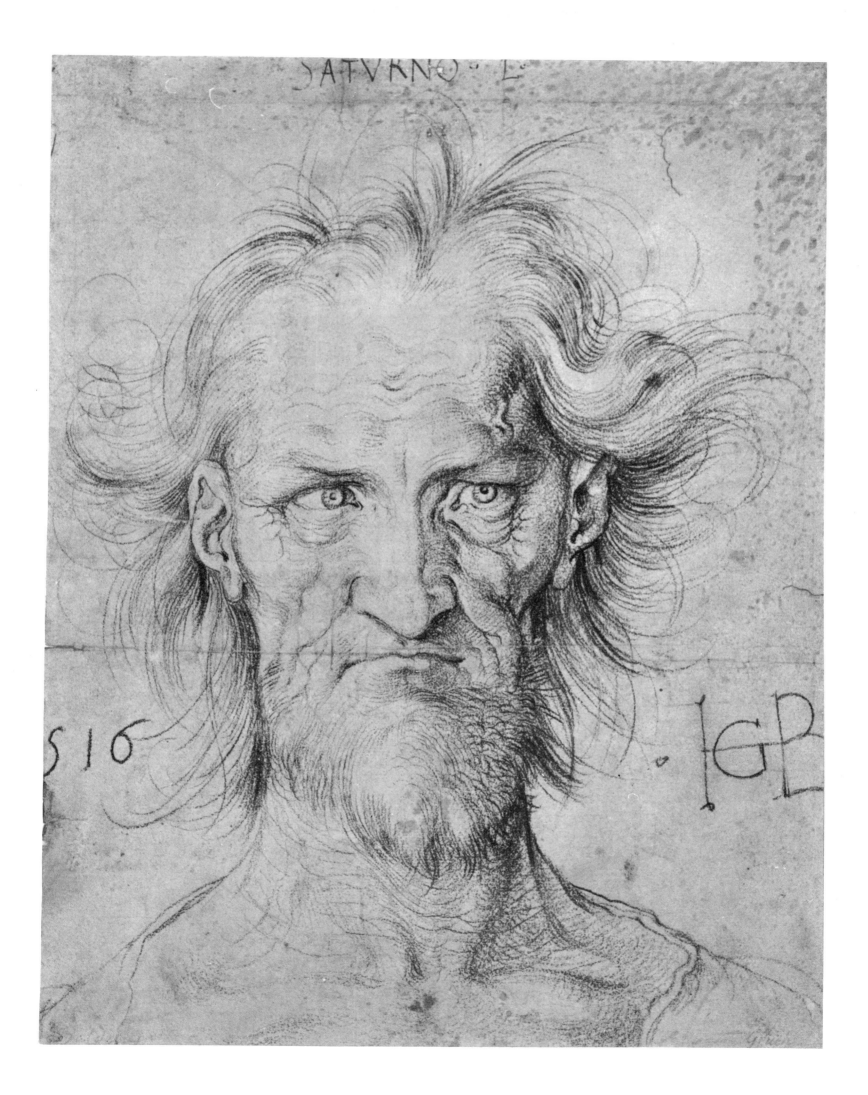

BALDUNG

378 **The Virgin and Child with Angels
and the Dove of the Holy Ghost**

Pen and bistre and white body-color on brown prepared
  paper, 277 x 194 mm.

London, British Museum (No. 5218)

LITERATURE

Koch, No. 38

Térey, No. 194

British Museum Catalogue, No. 179

THIS DRAWING is usually dated about 1516, during the period when
Baldung was working on the altar for the Cathedral in Freiburg im
Breisgau.

BALDUNG

379 Shooting at the Dead Father

Pen and wash in brown, 390 mm. diameter of roundel

Monogram and date 1517 by the artist

Berlin, Ehem. Staatliche Museen, Kupferstichkabinett
(K.d.Z. 571)

LITERATURE

Koch, No. 84

Térey, No. 45

Berlin Catalogue, p. 10, No. 571

THE LEGEND represented is contained in the *Gesta Romanorum*. Three princes had to shoot at their dead father for the purpose of determining by the best marksman, who should be his successor. The youngest son refused to shoot; thereupon he was regarded as the most pious and worthy one to succeed as king.

This is a design for a roundel of stained glass. The sinister scene of the *Gesta* was a topic well fitted to the imagination of the weird daemoniac. The half-decayed corpse of the king seems to accept life at the moment when the strange condition of his last will is being fulfilled. Ruthlessness, disgust, sadness, and silent obedience are wonderfully depicted in the protagonists and the bystanders.

BALDUNG

380 Venus with the Apple of Paris (?)

Pen in brown on yellowish paper, 298 x 166 mm.

Berlin, Ehem. Staatliche Museen, Kupferstichkabinett
(K.d.Z. 2171)

LITERATURE

Koch, No. 126

Térey, No. 29

Berlin Catalogue, p. 10, No. 2171

THIS IS a study of a model who posed for the mythological subject. No painting for which it served is known. A somewhat similar figure appears in the painting of 1523, "The Two Weather Witches," in Frankfort.

BALDUNG

381 **Portrait of a Young Woman
in Profile to Right**

Black chalk, heightened with the brush in white,
207 x 159 mm.

Dated 1519

Berlin, Ehem. Staatliche Museen, Kupferstichkabinett
(K.d.Z. 297)

LITERATURE

Koch, No. 28

Térey, No. 44

Berlin Catalogue, p. 10, No. 297

A VIVACIOUS portrait study from life, dated by Koch about 1510,
the beginning of the Strassburg period. Other scholars such as Bock
and Baldass do not doubt the authenticity of the date, which appears
plausible in view of the head-dress.

BALDUNG

382 Lucretia

Pen and India ink and white body-color, light washes on
brown prepared paper, 300 x 139 mm.

Monogram and date 1520 by the artist

Frankfort-on-Main, Staedel Art Institute (No. 649)

LITERATURE
Koch, No. 117
Térey, No. 95

HANS BALDUNG was a master in representing the female nude. Unlike Dürer, it was not the actual structure that interested him as much
as it was the pictorial splendor of the form. The same subject was
treated by Baldung in a drawing at Weimar in 1519 (Koch, No. 116).

BALDUNG

383 Portrait of a Man Praying with a Rosary

Black chalk with some additions in red chalk,
446 x 291 mm.
Monogram and date 1531 by the artist
Berlin, Ehem. Staatliche Museen, Kupferstichkabinett
(K.d.Z. 4234)

LITERATURE
Koch, No. 130
Berlin Catalogue, p. 10, No. 4234

BALDUNG'S PORTRAITS are outstanding in their power of characterization. The man represented here, who certainly belongs to the high patrician aristocracy, has himself portrayed ostentatiously in the attitude of prayer, with the rosary appropriate to the Catholic creed. The victorious advance of Protestantism in Germany was already marked in 1531.

LUCAS CRANACH THE ELDER

(1472-1553)

LUCAS CRANACH THE ELDER *Family name was Mueller. Born at Kronach in Franconia. Active in Vienna about 1500-04. From 1505 active in Wittenberg as court painter to the Elector Frederick the Wise of Saxony. Friend of Martin Luther. Died 1553 at Weimar.*

384 A Thief on the Cross, Turned to Right

Charcoal, heightened in white on reddish tinged paper, 226 x 121 mm.

Berlin, Ehem. Staatliche Museen, Kupferstichkabinett (K.d.Z. 4450)

PROVENANCE

Bamberger; von Lanna

LITERATURE

Rosenberg, *Die Zeichnungen Lucas Cranachs der Aeltere*, No.2

Berlin Catalogue, p. 19, No. 4450

LUCAS CRANACH THE ELDER

385 A Thief on the Cross, Turned to Left

Charcoal, heightened in white on reddish tinged paper, 215 x 128 mm.

Berlin, Ehem. Staatliche Museen, Kupferstichkabinett (K.d.Z. 4451)

PROVENANCE

Bamberger; von Lanna

LITERATURE

Rosenberg, No. 3

Berlin Catalogue, p. 19, No. 4451

THE PRESENT drawing and the one following originated during the Viennese period of the artist. They have to be compared with the two "Calvaries" in woodcut (Geisberg, Nos. 558 and 559) characterized by a blending of realism and an almost excessive expressiveness.

COMPANION PIECE to the preceding drawing.

LUCAS CRANACH THE ELDER

386 The Crucifixion

Pen and wash in bistre, on reddish tinged paper,
280 x 208 mm.

Later inscribed: *Lucas Van Leyden*

Cambridge, Fitzwilliam Museum (No. 2929)

PROVENANCE

Kerrich

LITERATURE

Rosenberg, No. 8

Dodgson, *Vasari Society*, III, 1907/08, No. 30

A COPY of this drawing is in Wuerzburg, University Collection. The early dating by Girshausen of 1505-1506, followed by Rosenberg, is not convincing. The opinion of Dodgson, who calls the present work "a drawing of Cranach's maturity," seems more probable. It could hardly have originated before 1510.

LUCAS CRANACH THE ELDER

387 **St. Eustace Kneeling in a Landscape**

Pen and wash, 255 x 194 mm.

Boston, Massachusetts, Museum of Fine Arts

PROVENANCE

Esdaile

LITERATURE

Rosenberg, No. 54

Rosenberg, *The Art Quarterly*, XVII, 1954, p. 281

THE DRAWING should be dated about 1520. The same subject was treated by Cranach in a painting (Friedlaender-Rosenberg, No. 95).

LUCAS CRANACH THE ELDER

388 The Death of the Virgin

Pen and bistre, 215 x 158 mm.

Apocryphal Dürer monogram

Berlin, Ehem. Staatliche Museen, Kupferstichkabinett
  (K.d.Z. 4182)

PROVENANCE

Liphart

LITERATURE

Rosenberg, No. A15

Berlin Catalogue, p. 19, No. 4182

DOUBTS ABOUT the authenticity of the drawing as voiced by Girshausen, followed by Rosenberg, are unjustified. It is a work of the artist's mature period between 1520 and 1530. Compare also the same representation in the woodcut (Geisberg, No. 563).

LUCAS CRANACH THE ELDER

389 Portrait of a Man in a Wide-Brimmed Hat

Brush, water color and body-color, 264 x 187 mm.
London, British Museum (No. 1896-5-11-1)
LITERATURE
Rosenberg, No. 72
Parker, *Drawings of the Early German Schools*, No. 33

CRANACH'S MAGNIFICENT studies in brush and colors, made from the living model, served him in preparing his finished portraits on wood. They give an idea of his ability to grasp the character of the sitter in all his straightforwardness and human immediacy. The study for the "Portrait of Luther's Father" in the Albertina (Albertina Catalogue, IV, No. 365), destined for a painting dated 1527, may serve as a clue to help date similar drawings such as the present one and the following one.

LUCAS CRANACH THE ELDER

390 Portrait of a Man in a Fur Hat

Brush in water color and body-color, 238 x 167 mm.

Apocryphal Dürer monogram

London, British Museum (No. S.5218.19)

PROVENANCE

Sloane

LITERATURE

Rosenberg, No. 71

Friedlaender-Bock, *Handzeichnungen deutscher Meister des XV und XVI Jahrhunderts*, p. 55, Pl. LXVIII

Parker, *Drawings of the Early German Schools*, p. 31

THE PRESENT drawing was previously ascribed to Dürer. It was first attributed to Cranach by Friedlaender-Bock. See the note to the preceding drawing.

BERNHARD STRIGEL

(Ca. 1460-1528)

BERNHARD STRIGEL *Born at Memmingen. Son and pupil of Ivo Strigel. Several journeys to Austria on commissions for Emperor Maximilian I. Active mainly in Memmingen, where he became councillor of the city. Died there in 1528.*

391 The Holy Family, 1491

Pen and bistre, heightened in white on reddish-brown tinged paper, 220 x 205 mm.

Date and inscription by the artist: *Nemt Zu Dank 91* (*accepts this with thanks 91*)

Watermark: high crown

London, British Museum (No. 1854-6-28-22)

LITERATURE

Parker, *Belvedere*, VIII, 1925, pp. 34, 35, Figs. 8 and 11

PARKER POINTED out that a related composition of a later time is preserved in a panel of the "Holy Family" in the Staatliche Museen, Berlin (No. 606D).

STRIGEL

392 A Pair of Unequal Lovers with the Devil and Cupid

Pen and India ink and white and reddish body-color on
   slate-gray prepared paper, 225 x 176 mm.

Inscribed by the artist:
DISCITE' A' ME QUIA' NEQUAM' SV'/'ET' PESSIMO' CORDE

Dated 1502

Berlin, Ehem. Staatliche Museen, Kupferstichkabinett
   (K.d.Z. 4256)

PROVENANCE

Rodrigues

LITERATURE

Friedlaender-Bock, *Handzeichnungen deutscher Meister
   des XV und XVI Jahrhunderts*, Pl. XCIII

Berlin Catalogue, p. 87, No. 4256, Pl. CXVIII

Parker, *Belvedere*, VIII, 1925, p. 30, Fig. 1

SATIRE AS it was cultivated mainly by Swiss artists. The young
woman has deprived the old wooer of his purse, which she hands
over to the little cupid.

HANS HOLBEIN THE ELDER

(1460/70-1524)

HANS HOLBEIN THE ELDER *Born at Augsburg. Studied at Ulm and in the Netherlands. Returned to his native city in 1494. Father of Ambrosius and Hans Holbein the Younger. Active for many churches and abbeys in Southern Germany and also for the Dominicans at Frankfort. Moved to Isenheim in 1516, where he died in 1524.*

393 Seated Woman with Long Loose Hair

Silverpoint on prepared paper with some heightenings in red and white chalk, reinforced in pen, 140 x 103 mm.

Inscribed in pen by another hand: *von mennigen (from Mennigen)*

Copenhagen, Royal Museum of Fine Arts (No. tu.95.1)

LITERATURE

Woltmann, *Holbein und seine Zeit*, No. 230

His, *Hans Holbein's des Aelteren Feder und Silberstift Zeichnungen*, Pl. XXXVI

Holbein Exhibition Catalogue, No. 55

Ussing, in *Kunstmuseets Aarsskrift*, XIII-XV, 1929/30, pp. 137 ff.

Fischer and Sthyr, *Seks Aarhundreders europaeisk Tegnekunst*, p. 105, Pl. XII

IT HAS been assumed that the same person was portrayed in a drawing in the Louvre (Catalogue, I, No. 215). It is one of the most beautiful portrait sketches by Holbein the Elder. It was made about the same time as the sketches for the Sebastian Altar (1515) in Munich.

HANS HOLBEIN THE ELDER

394 The Virgin Offering Her Breast to the Sleeping Child

Silverpoint on gray prepared paper, heightenings in white, reinforced with pen, 140 x 106 mm.

Basel, Kupferstichkabinett (Inv. 1662.204)

PROVENANCE

Amerbach

LITERATURE

Woltmann, No. 103

Ganz, *Die Handzeichnungen Hans Holbeins der Juengere*, No. 101 (wrongly attributed to Hans Holbein the Younger)

Holbein Exhibition Catalogue, No. 57

Baldass, *Beitraege zur Geschichte der deutschen Kunst*, II, p. 176, Fig. 131

THE DRAWING has always been correctly regarded as a work of Hans Holbein the Elder. Its connection with the "Madonna" in the Boehler Collection in Munich is so close that no doubt of the authorship of Holbein the Elder can be raised.

HANS BURGKMAIR THE ELDER

(1473-1531)

HANS BURGKMAIR THE ELDER *Born at Augsburg. Son and pupil of the painter Thomas Burgkmair. Pupil of Martin Schongauer in Colmar. Traveled to the Lower Rhine and Venice. Active in Augsburg, where he died in 1531.*

395 Portrait of Wolfgang von Maen

Black chalk, retouched with brush in bistre, 351 x 272 mm.
Dated in India ink by the artist: MDXVIII
Chatsworth, Devonshire Collections (No. 933)

LITERATURE
Dodgson, *Vasari Society*, IV, 1908/09, Pl. XXIX

WOLFGANG VON MAEN was the chaplain of Emperor Maximilian I. In 1518 he attended the Diet of Augsburg with the Emperor. On the same occasion when Dürer made the portrait of the Emperor (our No. 356), Burgkmair made this drawing of the chaplain to whose book *Das leiden Jesu Christi unnsers erloesers,* published in 1515, he had already contributed several woodcut illustrations. Among these is a portrait of the author, which gave the clue to the identification of the sitter in the present drawing.

M·D·XVIII·

HANS BURGKMAIR THE ELDER

396 The Virgin and Child

Brush and red chalk diluted in water, heightened in white
    body-color, the background laid out in India ink,
    295 x 249 mm.

Paris, Louvre, Cabinet des Dessins (No. 18. 683)

PROVENANCE

Abel Grimmer (?)

LITERATURE

Demonts, No. 74

Parker, *Beitraege zur Geschichte der deutschen Kunst,*
    II, pp. 208 and 218, Fig. 158

BURGKMAIR INTENDED to evoke something of the solemn effect of
a Byzantine icon, an effect frequently sought by the artists of Suabia
and Bavaria. Parker draws a comparison with the woodcut (Bartsch,
VII, p. 202, No. 8; Dodgson, II, p. 73, No. 13).

JOERG BREU THE ELDER

(1474/80-1537)

JOERG BREU THE ELDER *Born at Augsburg. Active in Austria 1500-02. Worked in Augsburg, where he died in 1537.*

397 The Crowning with Thorns

Pen and India ink, 217 x 143 mm.

Munich, Staatliche Graphische Sammlung
(No. 38009-8879)

LITERATURE

Buchner, *Beitraege zur Geschichte der deutschen Kunst,*
II, p. 304, Fig. 217

THE DRAWING shows the expressive qualities that the artist developed during his years in Austria, inspired by his surroundings there. It is close to the "Crowning with Thorns" for the altar of Wullersdorf in Lower Austria, painted in 1503, but now in the monastery of Melk. The character of the pen strokes is similar to that of the early drawings of Burgkmair.

JOERG BREU THE ELDER

398 **Portrait of a Young Woman**

Charcoal and red chalk, 307 x 221 mm.

Monogram and date 1519 by the artist

Berlin, Ehem. Staatliche Museen, Kupferstichkabinett
    (K.d.Z. 803)

PROVENANCE

von Nagler

LITERATURE

Friedlaender-Bock, *Die Handzeichnungen deutscher
    Meister des XV und XVI Jahrhunderts,* No.89

Berlin Catalogue, p. 15, No. 803

Buchner, *Beitraege zur Geschichte der deutschen Kunst,*
    II, p. 340

THIS IS a study from nature, used for the painting of 1521, "Madonna and Child with Angels," formerly in the Kaufmann Collection, Berlin.

MATTHIAS GRÜNEWALD

(1475/80-1527)

MATTHIAS GRÜNEWALD (Mathis Gothart Nithart) *Native of Lower Franconia. Lived in Seligenstadt. Active as court painter to the Archbishop of Mainz in Aschaffenburg, Frankfort, and Mainz. Main work for Isenheim in Alsace. Died at Halle in 1527, where he was a hydraulic engineer in the service of the city.*

399 Kneeling Man with Raised Hands

Black chalk, heightened in white body-color, gray wash on yellowish paper, 234 x 165 mm.

Red water color on sleeves and parts of garment applied by a later hand

The figure was cut to outlines and pasted on paper with inscription tablets of about 1560, now removed

Berlin, Ehem. Staatliche Museen, Kupferstichkabinett (K.d.Z. 4190)

LITERATURE

Friedlaender, *Die Zeichnungen von Matthias Grünewald,* No. 4

Behling, *Die Handzeichnungen des Mathis Gothart Nithart genannt Grünewald,* No. 8

Burkhard, *Matthias Grünewald,* Pl. LXXXIII

Berlin Catalogue, p. 44, No. 4190

THIS IS probably a study for one of the Apostles in the "Transfiguration of Christ" which Grünewald painted in 1511 for the Dominican church in Frankfort, where it was placed close to Dürer's "Heller Altar."

GRÜNEWALD

400 The Virgin Kneeling with Folded Hands

Black chalk on brownish paper, 160 x 146 mm.

Berlin, Ehem. Staatliche Museen, Kupferstichkabinett
   (K.d.Z. 12037)

PROVENANCE

Savigny

LITERATURE

Friedlaender, No. 14

Behling, No. 19

Burkhard, Pl. LXXIII

A STUDY for the figure of the Virgin in the "Annunciation" of the Isenheim Altar. The artist knew how to suggest vividly the almost frightening effect on Mary of the sudden appearance of the Angel while she prayed. A glare of supernatural light falls upon her in the drawing, which reduces her head and upper body to a mere indication of subtle lines. More emphasis is given to the rendering of the mantle through the rich modeling in different grades of light and shade. Grünewald's technique of mixing wash and chalk evokes a feeling of substance and colorful texture with an almost magical intensity.

GRÜNEWALD

401 An Elderly Woman with Clasped Hands

Charcoal (or black chalk?), 377 x 236 mm.

Inscribed in the same medium: *[M]athis*, and in ink
Matsis

Further inscribed: *Disses hatt Mathis von Ossenburg des Churfursten v[on] Mentz Moler gemacht und wo du Mathis geschriben findest das ha[tt] Er mit Eigener handt gemacht* (This has made Mathis of Aschaffenburg, the painter to the Elector of Mainz and where you find written Mathis, this he made with his own hand)

Oxford, Ashmolean Museum

PROVENANCE

Uffenbach; Grimmer; Douce

LITERATURE

Friedlaender, No. 21

Behling, No. 10

Burkhard, p. 70

Ashmolean Catalogue, I, No. 297

THE PRESENT drawing was apparently done during the artist's work on the Isenheim Altar (completed 1515). Grünewald, who in his paintings reached the climax of visionary expressiveness in German art, prepared for them by making drawings in which he faithfully studied the living model. These drawings were not only of full-length figures but also of such details as busts, heads, and hands. He had his models adopt the poses that his figures would have in the finished painting. In the present study he drew from a simple and pious woman of the people while he visualized the image of the Mother of Christ. Such drawings achieve an astonishing approach to nature and reality. They seem to encompass, as it were, both the breathing body and the very soul of the sitter. In this respect he even surpasses Dürer, in whose works the qualities of line and design prevail over those of color and keep to a lawful scheme of graphic expression that has been created by the artist himself.

GRÜNEWALD

402 **The Virgin and Child with Little St. John**

Black chalk and brownish water color in the dress,
   286 x 366 mm.

The oval form is due only to the mount

Berlin, Ehem. Staatliche Museen, Kupferstichkabinett
   (K.d.Z. 2040 verso)

PROVENANCE

von Radowitz

LITERATURE

Friedlaender, No. 25

Behling, No. 24

Burkhard, Pl. XCIII

Berlin Catalogue, p. 44, No. 2040 verso

IN THIS drawing the extreme sensitiveness of Grünewald's linework may be admired.

GRÜNEWALD

403 A Saint with a Staff Standing in the Forest

Black chalk, heightened with white body-color on
  yellowish paper, 368 x 296 mm.

Vienna, Albertina (Inv. 3047)

LITERATURE

Friedlaender, No. 26

Behling, No. 22

Burkhard, Pl. XCIV

Albertina Catalogue, IV, No. 296

IT HAS been assumed that the present drawing may be a study for a
St. Joseph in a "Flight into Egypt" or in a "Holy Family in the Forest."
The split old oak trees, whose roots twine about rocks and stones,
suggest a feeling for nature that Grünewald shares with the masters
of the Danube School. The same observation is valid for the drawing
of Nos. 404 and 405.

GRÜNEWALD

404 **Christ the King, Whose Train
Is Carried by Two Angels**

Black chalk, heightened in white body-color, gray wash,
    on brownish paper, 286 x 366 mm.

Berlin, Ehem. Staatliche Museen, Kupferstichkabinett
    (K.d.Z. 2040 recto)

PROVENANCE

von Radowitz

LITERATURE

Friedlaender, No. 24

Behling, No. 23

Burkhard, Pl. XCII

Berlin Catalogue, p. 44, No. 2040 recto

Parker, *Drawings of the Early German Schools,* No. 41

Zuelch, *Der historische Grünewald,* p. 335, Fig. 191

THIS IS perhaps a study for the altar of Oberissigheim. The composition seems to be the left half of a "Coronation of the Virgin." Scepter, crown, and astrolabe characterize the main figure as that of Christ. However, it is strange that the scene takes place between the trees of a young forest and not in the height of heaven. Again emphasis is laid on the drapery, whereas the figures dissolve in the atmosphere. Thus, the expression of a highly colorful and mysterious performance is achieved. A donation for the altar at Oberissigheim was made by Canon Reitzmann in 1514. This would correspond with the style of the drawing that points to the Altar of Isenheim, such as No. 403. The reverse of this drawing is our No. 402.

GRÜNEWALD

405 The Virgin and Child Seated by a Tree

Black chalk and brush in brown water color, 314 x 278 mm.

Berlin, Ehem. Staatliche Museen, Kupferstichkabinett
(K.d.Z. 12039)

PROVENANCE
Savigny

LITERATURE
Friedlaender, No. 23
Behling, No. 25
Burkhard, Pl. LXXVII

A STUDY for the central panel of the altar of St. Mary of the Snows in the Collegiate Church of Aschaffenburg (ordered in 1513, consecrated in 1516, and finally placed there in 1519), now in the Parish Church of Stuppach. The Virgin is represented on the altar seated in a landscape that seems to radiate from her person, surrounded by the symbols given to her by the visionary St. Bridget of Sweden. Only the triangular figure of St. Mary is shown in this drawing. In some features it differs from the finished painting in which the artist has eliminated Mary's crown and the holy veil with which she clasps the Child in the drawing, so that its corner protrudes as if it were the wings of a little angel. The drawing is of the utmost mastery. Although in a monochrome medium, it is full of pictorial suggestiveness. The upper parts become transparent in the light. The heavy drapery deploys an almost unbelievable richness of colors through the contrast of cool tones in the shades of the chalk and of warm tones in the pattern of the textile. Compare in style our Nos. 403 and 404.

GRÜNEWALD

406 The Virgin Kneeling and Turning a Leaf of the Bible

Black chalk, heightened in white body-color, gray wash, brush in India ink, 207 x 210 mm.

Berlin, Ehem. Staatliche Museen, Kupferstichkabinett (K.d.Z. 12040)

PROVENANCE

Savigny

LITERATURE

Friedlaender, No. 16

Behling, No. 20

Burkhard, Pl. LXXII

A STUDY for the "Madonna of an Annunciation." The gesture of Mary betrays her surprise at the appearance of the Angel. Like No. 400, this drawing has also been regarded as a preparatory study for the "Annunciation" in the Isenheim Altar. Whereas this assumption is correct in regard to No. 400, it is certainly wrong concerning the present drawing. Its style is much more advanced and points to a period later than the Isenheim Altar, e.g., the altar panels for the Cathedral of Mainz.

Here also the main emphasis has been laid upon the expressive eloquence of the garment. This kind of pleated garment occurs also in "St. Dorothy," No. 407; it was in fashion about 1400, in the time of the so-called "International style." It was an archaic requisite in the artist's studio, cherished by him, because it gave him the opportunity, even when studying nature, to have his figures approach the visionary and spiritual atmosphere of 1400. As in the case of Nos. 400, 404, and 405, the drapery was studied from nature whereas the figure itself was an addition of the artist's imagination.

N: 199

GRÜNEWALD

407 St. Dorothy and the Christ Child

Black chalk, heightened in white body-color, gray wash,
358 x 256 mm.

Berlin, Ehem. Staatliche Museen, Kupferstichkabinett
(K.d.Z. 12035)

PROVENANCE

Savigny

LITERATURE

Friedlaender, No. 18

Behling, No. 29

Burkhard, Pl. LXXXV

SEE THE note to the following drawing, No. 408. St. Dorothy wears the same garment as the "Madonna," No. 406. The Christ Child, who brought her the basket with flowers, balances on an astrolabe.

The present drawing is the very climax of the visionary and expressive art of the master. The gracile figure of the Saint bends like a flower under the weight of her garment.

GRÜNEWALD

408 St. Catherine

Black chalk, heightened in white body-color, gray wash,
316 x 215 mm.

Berlin, Ehem. Staatliche Museen, Kupferstichkabinett
(K.d.Z. 12038)

PROVENANCE
Savigny

LITERATURE
Friedlaender, No. 19
Behling, No. 27
Burkhard, Pl. LXXXVI

JOACHIM VON SANDRART saw in the Cathedral of Mainz three altars
by Grünewald, which are no longer in existence. In one of them the
Madonna appeared in clouds above female Saints standing on the
ground. The present drawing and the preceding one are preparatory
studies for some of those female Saints. Here once again the chief
emphasis was given to the expressive quality of the drapery. The
textile seems to become almost organic and living substance irides-
cent in light.

On reverse is an "Unfinished Study of a Female Saint," perhaps
St. Dorothy.

GRÜNEWALD

409 Portrait of an Ecclesiastic

Black chalk, 255 x 190 mm.
Apocryphal Dürer monogram
Stockholm, Nationalmuseum (No. 1853/1863)

PROVENANCE
Crozat; Tessin

LITERATURE
Friedlaender, No. 33
Behling, No. 35
Burkhard, Pl. XCIX
Reau, *M. Grünewald et le retable de Colmar*, p. 298
Feuerstein, *Grünewald*, p. 144
Graul, *Grünewaldzeichnungen*, No. 16
Schoenberger, *The Drawings of Mathis Gothart Nithart, called Grünewald*, No. 36

THE SITTER probably belonged to the circle of Cardinal Albrecht of Brandenburg, Archbishop of Mainz. Zuelch (Pl. CCII) suggested that the court astrologer, Johannes de Indagine, may be represented. The latter's head- and hairdress and costume, however, were different, as can be seen in his woodcut portrait by Hans Baldung (F. W. H. Hollstein, *German Engravings...* II, Amsterdam, 1959, No. 269).

albert Durer

1664

GRÜNEWALD

410 Head of a Screaming Angel

Black chalk, heightened with white, 244 x 199 mm.

Berlin, Ehem. Staatliche Museen, Kupferstichkabinett
  (K.d.Z. 12319)

LITERATURE

Friedlaender, No. 31

Behling, No. 30

Burkhard, Pl. LXXXIX

GRÜNEWALD

411 Head of a Weeping Angel

Black chalk, 276 x 196 mm.

Monogram by a later hand

Berlin, Ehem. Staatliche Museen, Kupferstichkabinett
  (K.d.Z. 1070 recto)

PROVENANCE

von Nagler

LITERATURE

Friedlaender, No. 30

Behling, No. 31

Burkhard, Pl. LXXXVIII

Berlin Catalogue, p. 44, No. 1070 recto

THE PATHETIC lament of this head reminds one of mourning angels in crucifixions by Giotto and his followers. With Grünewald it achieves an almost hysterical exaggeration of frenzy. Hence, Zuelch connects the drawing with an altarpiece by Grünewald in the Cathedral of Mainz; when crossing the frozen Rhone, a blind hermit is killed by two murderers. His body falls over the screaming boy who guided him.

See also note to following drawing.

THE EXPRESSION of the face has also been interpreted as that of a "Singing Angel." In analogy to No. 410 (see note there), it seems rather to be an angel for a "Lamentation." The intensity of the contraction of the facial muscles betrays pain.

On reverse of this drawing is our No. 415.

GRÜNEWALD

412 Trinity

Black chalk on brownish paper, 272 x 199 mm.

Monogram by the artist

Berlin, Ehem. Staatliche Museen, Kupferstichkabinett
(K.d.Z. 1071)

PROVENANCE

von Nagler

LITERATURE

Friedlaender, No. 5

Behling , No. 38

Burkhard, Pl. XCVII

Berlin Catalogue, p. 44, No. 1071

Benesch, *The Art of the Renaissance in Northern Europe*,
p. 36, Fig. 19

Schoenberger, No. 35

ALL SCHOLARS unite in considering the present drawing as one of the most powerful works of Grünewald's late period, an almost weird outburst of his visionary spirit. There prevails, however, wide divergence of opinion on its meaning. The interpretations range from seeing in it a blasphemous mockery (H. A. Schmid) to considering it a representation of the true Holy Trinity depicted in a strange shape inspired by the contemporary religious revolutionary movements (O. Benesch).

The interpretation first brought forward by G. Muenzel (*Zeitschrift fuer christliche Kunst,* XXV, 1912, p. 215 ff.) that these three heads represent a diabolic antithesis of the Holy Trinity, a Trinity of Satan, is now most commonly accepted.

Schoenberger voiced the opinion that the heads may be connected with the physiognomical theories of Johannes de Indagine, a scholar who belonged to the circle of Cardinal Albrecht of Brandenburg.

GRÜNEWALD

413 Man with Moustache and Clasped Hands (Bust)

Black chalk on yellowish paper, 434 x 320 mm.

Berlin, Ehem. Staatliche Museen, Kupferstichkabinett
    (K.d.Z. 12036)

PROVENANCE

Savigny

LITERATURE

Friedlaender, No. 22

Behling, No. 34

A STUDY of the model who posed for the figure of St. John the
Evangelist in the "Crucifixion" of Tauberbischofsheim, which is now
at Karlsruhe. The paintings preserved from this altar ("The Carrying of the Cross" and "The Crucifixion") are the last works of the
artist known up to now. Although a donation was made for the altar
as early as 1515, its execution certainly took place after 1520. It is
the last word of Grünewald in painting of which we know. The
shimmering and diaphanous quality of the drawing corresponds to
the utmost spirituality in the final phase of Grünewald's art.

GRÜNEWALD

414 Head of a Smiling Woman

Black chalk, 204 x 150 mm.

Apocryphal Dürer monogram

Paris, Louvre, Cabinet des Dessins (No. 18.588)

PROVENANCE

Jabach; R. de Cotte; A. Coypel

LITERATURE

Reiset, No. 501

Schmid, *Die Gemaelde und die Zeichnungen von M. Grünewald*, I, Pl. XLIX and II, p. 269

Demonts, No. 206, Pl. LXIX

Behling, No. 3, Pl. XXXIII

THIS DRAWING was recognized by Friedlaender as a very late work. It is of an extreme lightness and has a diaphanous quality that shows the master's ability to grasp the spiritual, using the most subtle means of drawing in their final perfection. The mysterious quality of her smile compares with the smiles of Leonardo's female heads.

GRÜNEWALD

415 Head of a Young Woman

Black chalk on yellowish paper, 276 x 196 mm.

Berlin, Ehem. Staatliche Museen, Kupferstichkabinett
(K.d.Z. 1070 verso)

PROVENANCE

von Nagler

LITERATURE

Friedlaender, No. 29

Behling, No. 32

Burkhard, Pl. XCI

Berlin Catalogue, p. 44, No. 1070 verso

THE STYLE of the drawing points clearly to the most mature period of the master's art. The recto of this drawing is our No. 411.

GRÜNEWALD

416 Margaret Prellwitz, Mother of Hans Schoenitz

Black chalk, slightly washed in bistre, heightened in red
and white chalk on yellowish paper, 228 x 289 mm.

Inscribed on reverse in a handwriting of about 1520 to
1530 (according to Zuelch):

HANS SCHENICZ MUOTTER, AETATIS SUE 71, and
below: *margret brellwitzin*

Paris, Louvre, Cabinet des Dessins (No. 18.936)

LITERATURE

Demonts, No. 208, Pl. LXVIII

Behling, No. 37, Pl. XXXIV

Baumeister, *Muenchner Jahrbuch der Bildenden Kunst,*
N. F. III, 1926, pp. 269-272

Tietze, in *Burlington Magazine,* XLIV, 1924, pp. 216 ff.

THE ATTRIBUTION of the present drawing to Grünewald by E.
Baumeister has not been unanimously accepted. There are strong re-
lations to the Danube School. However, the model represented was
the wife of a colleague of Grünewald in the service of the city of Halle:
Bornmeister (hydraulic engineer), Martin Schoenitz. Hans, the son of
Martin and Margarete, became Chamberlain to Cardinal Albrecht in
1528 and had himself portrayed by Konrad Faber, a painter of the
Danube School.

The present drawing has generally been reproduced upright. The
direction of the chalk lines, however, indicates that the model was
portrayed in a lying position. The features reveal the expression of a
dying or of a dead person. The light lines indicating the shoulders
seem to have been added later.

ALBRECHT ALTDORFER

(Ca. 1480-1538)

ALBRECHT ALTDORFER *Born shortly before 1480 at Ratisbon. Pupil of his father, Ulrich Altdorfer. Made several journeys to Austria in 1505, 1511 and after 1518, where he was commissioned by different abbeys to make prints and altar paintings. Active for Emperor Maximilian I and the Duke of Bavaria. Councillor and architect of the city of Ratisbon, where he died in 1538.*

417 St. Nicholas of Bari Rebuking the Tempest

Pen and India ink, heightened with the brush in body-color on brick-red prepared paper, 192 x 147 mm.

Monogram and date 1508 by the artist

Oxford, Ashmolean Museum

PROVENANCE

Douce

LITERATURE

Becker, *Die Handzeichnungen Albrecht Altdorfers*, No. 54

Winzinger, *Albrecht Altdorfer Zeichnungen*, No. 5

Friedlaender, *Albrecht Altdorfer, Ausgewaehlte Handzeichnungen*, No. 4

Ashmolean Catalogue, I, No. 268

THE DEVIL steps on the masthead in order to break the mast through the force of his weight while terror seizes the sailors.

The technique of chiaroscuro drawing was highly favored by the masters of the Danube School, particularly by Altdorfer. It corresponds to the strong pictorial tendencies developed by this school of German painting. The swings and curves of the pen fuse elemental phenomena, objects, and human beings into a single unit, assimilating them to each other. The present drawing is a characteristic example of Altdorfer's early style.

ALTDORFER

418 A Pair of Lovers Seated in a Corn Field

Pen and brown ink, 221 x 149 mm.
Monogram and date 1508 by the artist
Basel, Kupferstichkabinett (Inv. U.XVI.31)

LITERATURE
Becker, No. 1
Winzinger, No. 11

THIS DRAWING represents Altdorfer's early style of pure pen drawing, which corresponds closely to his early engravings. The figures are heavy and clumsy and lack the articulateness of those of the school of Dürer. In this respect they are characteristic of the so-called Danube style, distinguished by the affinity for anthropomorphic, zoomorphic, and vegetal forms. This furthered the development of landscape representation in the Danube School to which particular emphasis was given. The drawing achieves a surprising modernity when, above the stalks of the cornfield, a bell-tower, gables, and chimneys of a village and the slope of a wooded hill become partially visible, suggesting space and atmosphere.

ALTDORFER

419 The Agony in the Garden

Pen and India ink and white body-color on reddish-brown
   prepared paper, 210 x 157 mm.

Monogram and date 1509 by the artist

Lower right corner: apocryphal Dürer monogram and 1508

Berlin, Ehem. Staatliche Museen, Kupferstichkabinett
   (K.d.Z. 111)

LITERATURE

Becker, No. 7

Winzinger, No. 13

Friedlaender, No. 3

Berlin Catalogue, p. 4, No. 111

A FINE example of the importance of scenery in the works of the Danube School. The human figures are so embedded in the landscape that
they form a part of it. The figures of the Apostles, which derive from
a work of Mantegna, weigh down heavily like stone blocks, whereas
the rising of the slender pine tree emphasizes the Lord's readiness for
sacrifice. A mountain gorge in the aboriginal forest seen by night with
flickering lights on the branches of the trees forms the stage. The
drama of the event fuses with the lyrical mood of nature.

A copy on blue prepared paper was formerly in the Oppenheimer
Collection (Parker, *Sale Catalogue*, No. 191).

ALTDORFER

420 St. Andrew Enthroned

Pen and India ink and white body-color on green
   prepared paper, 161 x 116 mm.

Monogram and illegible date at the cut-off upper margin

Berlin, Ehem. Staatliche Museen, Kupferstichkabinett
   (K.d.Z. 88)

LITERATURE

Becker, No. 10

Winzinger, No. 20

Berlin Catalogue, p. 4, No. 88

EVEN IN a pure figure drawing, Altdorfer's predilection for vegetal forms comes to the fore. The canopy looks like an overgrown grotto.

ALTDORFER

421 Samson Rending the Lion

Pen and India ink and white body-color on yellowish prepared paper, 216 x 155 mm.

Berlin, Ehem. Staatliche Museen, Kupferstichkabinett (K.d.Z. 86)

PROVENANCE

von Nagler

LITERATURE

Becker, No. 11

Winzinger, No. 34

Berlin Catalogue, p. 4, No. 86 (a repetition, also in Berlin Catalogue, p. 4, No. 87)

THE UNSIGNED and undated drawing was made about 1512. The dramatic scene of the Old Testament takes place in a clearing of the Bavarian or Austrian high forest with a charming vista of distant mountains with castles, and valleys with villages. The rising sun beyond the mountains vaults the dome of the firmament with its rays.

ALTDORFER

422 Sheet of Studies with Five Heads and a Castle in the Background

Pen in light purple, 148 x 115 mm.

Vienna, Albertina (Inv. 26166)

PROVENANCE

Count Salm

LITERATURE

Becker, No. 180

Winzinger, No. 103

Albertina Catalogue, IV, No. 227

Benesch, *Mitteilungen der Gesellschaft fuer vervielfaeltigende Kunst*, 1932, p. 17

THIS DRAWING was first published by the present author. The attribution was refused by Becker and Tietze, but accepted by Winzinger, who correctly emphasized the close affinity to Altdorfer's drawings in the Prayer-Book of Emperor Maximilian I. Also, the technique of drawing in colored ink corresponds to the Prayer-Book. The ornamental curls in pen on the reverse are like those drawn by Altdorfer on the backs of his original wood-blocks for Emperor Maximilian's "Triumphal Procession" and the "Triumphal Arch," preserved in the Albertina.

On reverse of this drawing is a "Sheet of Studies with a Head and Ornaments."

ALTDORFER

423 Salome with the Head of St. John the Baptist

Pen in dark brown and Chinese white ink on brown tinted
  paper, 192 x 123 mm.

Lower left corner: "17" (perhaps remains of date 1517)

Cleveland, Ohio, The Cleveland Museum of Art
  (No. 48.440), John L. Severance Fund

PROVENANCE

Prince of Liechtenstein

LITERATURE

Winzinger, No. 64

Francis, *The Bulletin of The Cleveland Museum of Art*,
  XXXVII, June, 1950, p. 117

THE DRAWING is closely related to the series of the Apostles in the
monastery of Seitenstetten (Austria) dated 1517. Altdorfer's part
in the "Triumphal Procession of the Emperor Maximilian" also cor-
roborates the attribution of the drawing.

WOLF HUBER

(Ca. 1485-1553)

WOLF HUBER *Born in Feldkirch, Vorarlberg. Worked probably in the shop of Joerg Koelderer at Innsbruck about 1510. Settled at Passau as court painter to the Bishop. Journeyed to the Austrian Danube region and Vienna. Died at Passau in 1553.*

424 Portrait of a Man in a Cap (Bust)

Charcoal, heightened with white, on brick-red prepared
    paper, 275 x 201 mm.

Monogram and date 1522 by the artist

Berlin, Ehem. Staatliche Museen, Kupferstichkabinett
    (K.d.Z. 2060)

PROVENANCE

von Nagler

LITERATURE

Berlin Catalogue, p. 56, No. 2060

A NUMBER of heads exist in the same technique with monogram and date 1522 (R. Riggenbach, *Wolf Huber*, Basel, 1907, p. 68). See also our No. 425. Most of them represent mercenaries whose virile faces protrude in strong plasticity, modeled by glittering highlights. This handling is related to Huber's technique of painting curls and dots with the brush.

WOLF HUBER

425 Head of a Young Man

Black and white chalk on red prepared paper,
294 x 198 mm.

Monogram and date 1522 by the artist

New York, The Metropolitan Museum of Art
(No. 50.202)

PROVENANCE

Count Harrach, Vienna

LITERATURE

Schoenbrunner-Meder, No. 716

Voss, *Der Ursprung des Donaustiles*, p. 21, Fig. 3

THIS DRAMATIC head may be compared with the related one at the left margin in the "Raising of the Cross" in the Kunsthistorisches Museum, Vienna.

WOLF HUBER

426 View of Feldkirch

Pen and ink, 313 x 211 mm.

Dated 1523 by the artist

London, British Museum (No. 1883-7-14-101)

LITERATURE

Halm, *Muenchner Jahrbuch der Bildenden Kunst,*
  N. F. VII, 1930, No. 25, Fig. 24

Weinberger, *Wolfgang Huber,* frontispiece

FELDKIRCH IN the Vorarlberg was the native town of Wolf Huber. He painted the altar for the Parish Church there, commissioned by the Brotherhood of St. Anne: the main work in painting of his career. On that occasion he may have noted this scenic prospect of his native country, which exists in several versions. The rays of the setting sun form a magnificent unit with the rich growth of the pine trees in the foreground.

A replica of this drawing by the artist is in Munich (Halm, No. 29). Copies in Berlin (Catalogue, p. 57, No. 838), Erlangen, Schwerin.

WOLF HUBER

427 The Rapids of the Danube Near Grien

Pen and ink, 159 x 212 mm.

Dated by the artist: 1531

Monogram by a later hand

Washington, D. C., National Gallery of Art
(No. B-17.728), Rosenwald Collection

PROVENANCE

Prince of Liechtenstein

LITERATURE

*Rosenwald Collection. An Exhibition of Recent
Acquisitions,* 1950, No. 52

Halm, "Die Landschaftzeichnungen des Wolfgang Huber,"
in *Muenchner Jahrbuch der Bildenden Kunst,*
N. F. VII, 1930, pp. 1-104

HUBER'S FAITHFUL rendering of the Austrian landscape was of
pioneering importance in its time. The result of a new concept of
nature, it paved the way for Pieter Brueghel's landscape drawings
and for centuries of artistic topography to come.

NIKLAUS MANUEL DEUTSCH

(1484-1530)

NIKLAUS MANUEL DEUTSCH *Printer, draughtsman, and poet. Born at Berne. Member of the guild in 1512. Soldier in 1516 and 1522. Contact with Burgkmair. Died at Berne.*

428 The Unequal Couple

Pen and India ink and pen and brush in pink and white body-color, on red prepared paper, 203 x 188 mm.

Monogram and inscription NKAW by the artist

Basel, Kupferstichkabinett (Inv. U.XVI.42)

PROVENANCE

Amerbach·

LITERATURE

Koegler, *Beschreibendes Verzeichnis der Basler Handzeichnungen Niklaus Manuel Deutsch,* No. 16

Ganz, *Handzeichnungen Schweizer Meister,* No. 5, Pl. III

SATIRICAL REPRESENTATIONS like this one were common in late Gothic and Renaissance German art. The old man gains love only when paying for it dearly. The young man without means finds contempt instead of amorous reward.

The capitals NKAW were deciphered by Koegler as "Niemand kann alles wissen" (nobody is able to know everything).

NIKLAUS MANUEL DEUTSCH

429 Lucretia (Bust)

Colored chalks, 240 x 198 mm.
Monogram by the artist
Basel, Kupferstichkabinett (Inv. U.X.10a)
LITERATURE
Koegler, No. 74
Parker, *Drawings of the Early German Schools*, No. 56

THE STATELY young woman looks tragically upward after having inflicted the deadly wound upon herself. She is a magnificent example of the picturesque idea of classical antiquity formed by this poetic artist. The drawing should be compared with the canvas "The Judgment of Paris," also in the Kunstmuseum, Basel. Related in style to the portrait bust of a young woman in colored chalks (Koegler, No. 76).

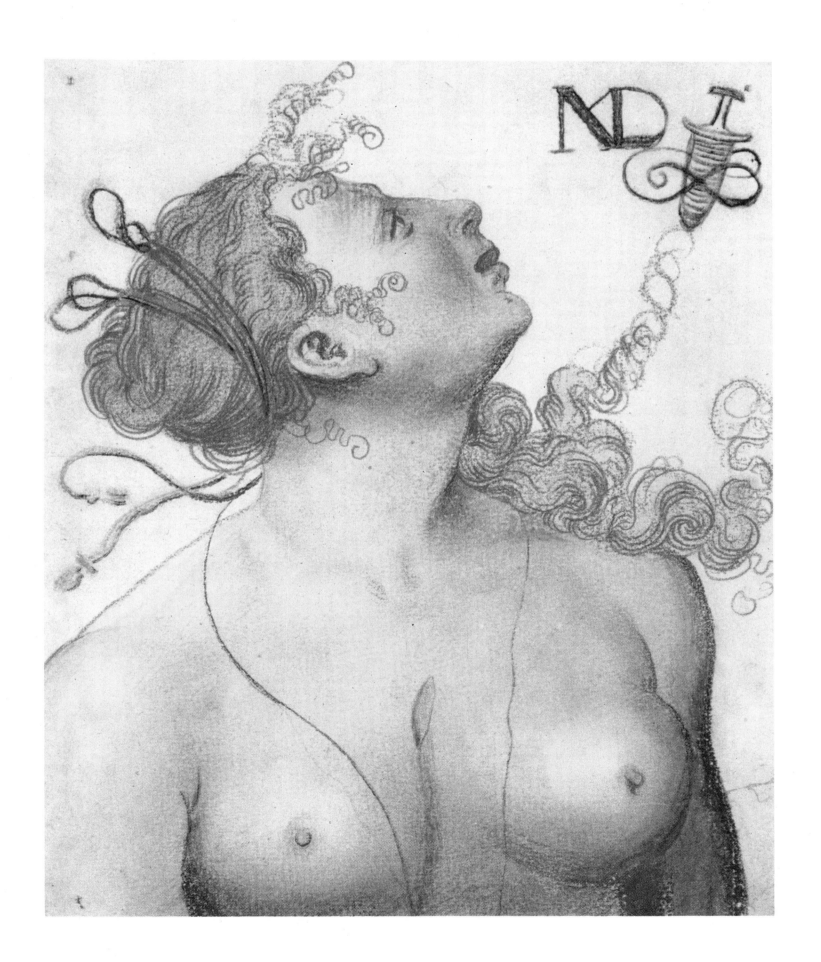

HANS LEU THE YOUNGER

(Ca. 1490-1531)

HANS LEU THE YOUNGER *Born at Zuerich. Pupil of Dürer in Nuremberg and of Baldung in Freiburg im Breisgau. Settled 1514 at Zuerich. Died in battle 1531.*

430 St. Jerome Repentant in a Mountainous Landscape

Pen and India ink and white body-color on grayish-purple prepared paper, 155 x 137 mm.

Frankfort-on-Main, Staedel Art Institute (No. 648)

LITERATURE

Handzeichnungen alter Meister im Staedelschen Kunstinstitut, XVIII, No. 3

AS IN the Danube School, there developed in Swiss art a feeling for nature and scenery. One of its main exponents was Hans Leu the Younger. The present drawing may be compared with the works of Altdorfer.

HANS LEU THE YOUNGER

431 Pietà

Pen and brush in carbon ink and gouache on green
   prepared paper, 275 x 207 mm.

Cambridge, Massachusetts, Harvard University, Fogg Art
   Museum (No. 1936.125), Gift of the Honorable Mr. and
   Mrs. Robert Woods Bliss

PROVENANCE

Weigel; von Lanna; Wauters; Oppenheimer

LITERATURE

Schoenbrunner-Meder, No. 1221

Mongan-Sachs, *Fogg Catalogue*, No. 390, Fig. 201

Parker, *Oppenheimer Sale Catalogue*, No. 392

LEU WAS strongly influenced by Hans Baldung. Parker correctly
emphasized the inspiration that he received for this group from the
woodcut of the "Lamentation for Christ" (Geisberg, No. 77).

URS GRAF

(Ca. 1485-1528)

URS GRAF *Goldsmith, painter, and engraver. Born at Solothurn. Traveled frequently, mainly to Strassburg. Settled at Basel in 1509. Participated in expeditions of the Swiss mercenaries to Italy and Burgundy.*

432 Place of Execution

Pen and India ink, 218 x 238 mm.

Monogram and date 1512 by the artist

Inscription on a broken post: LUG EBE / FVR DICH (watch out for yourself)

Vienna, Albertina (Inv. 3050)

LITERATURE

Koegler, *Beschreibendes Verzeichnis der Basler Handzeichnungen des Urs Graf*, No. 130

Albertina Catalogue, IV, No. 332

Schoenbrunner-Meder, Pl. CCCCLXVI

Parker, *Anzeiger fuer Schweizerische Alterumskunde*, N. F. XXIII, 1921, No. 34

THE LIFE of the mercenary, not only with its colorful adventures but also with all its misery, was the main content of Urs Graf's art of drawing. In a biblical allusion, the soul of the good thief is received in Heaven, whereas the soul of the bad thief is carried away by the devil.

URS GRAF

433 St. Sebastian Tied to a Tree

Pen and bistre, 318 x 213 mm.
Monogram and date 1519 by the artist
Basel, Kupferstichkabinett (Inv. U.X.85)

LITERATURE

Koegler, No. 86
Parker, *Zwanzig Federzeichnungen des Urs Graf*, Pl. XIV

THE RHAPSODIC and improvisatory character of the pen strokes is appropriate to the bold and modern interpretation of a theme of Christian iconography recorded as a sinister scene from the rough and warlike life of the Swiss mercenaries.

URS GRAF

434 The Beheading of St. Barbara

Pen and India ink, 204 x 118 mm.
Monogram by the artist, also date 1519? (cut below)
Basel, Kupferstichkabinett (Inv. U.X.36)

LITERATURE
Koegler, No. 82

THE PRESENCE of the tower is a clear indication that the woman suffering martyrdom is St. Barbara. The atrocity of the murder is further enhanced through the contrast it makes to the radiant Swiss lake scenery with high mountains in the background.

AUGSBURG DRAUGHTSMAN
Ca. 1515

435 **Reading of a Letter of Foundation
by a Bishop in the Presence of
Emperor Henry and Empress Kunigunde**

Pen and ink, 64 x 197 mm.

Munich, Staatliche Graphische Sammlung (No. 5634)

LITERATURE

Benesch, *Mitteilungen der Gesellschaft fuer
vervielfaeltigende Kunst*, I, 1931, p. 17

THE DRAWING has been attributed by Elfried Bock (oral communication) to Joerg Breu the Elder on the basis of comparison with the design for an *Epitaph* in the Nationalmuseum, Stockholm (E. Buchner, *Beitraege zur Geschichte der deutschen Kunst*, II, 1928, Fig. 270). It is, however, still closer to the drawings for the *Encomium Moriae* (No. 436). It is also drawn with the left hand, as are most of the drawings there. Whoever the creator of this delicate drawing was, it gives an excellent idea of the particular trend of Augsburg art from which the early works of the Holbein brothers derived.

HANS HOLBEIN THE YOUNGER

(1497-1543)

HANS HOLBEIN THE YOUNGER *Born at Augsburg. Son and pupil of Hans Holbein the Elder. Settled at Basel in 1515. 1517-18 in Lucerne and probably in Italy. 1519 member of the Basel guild. Journey to France in 1524. 1526 first journey to England, where he was introduced to Thomas More by Erasmus of Rotterdam. Returned to Basel 1528. From 1532 stayed in England. Died of the plague 1543 in London.*

AMBROSIUS HOLBEIN

(Ca. 1494 - Ca. 1519)

AMBROSIUS HOLBEIN *Born at Augsburg. Son of Hans Holbein the Elder. Active in Lake of Constance region and the Upper Rhine. Settled 1515 in Basel. 1517 member of the guild. Died about 1519 at Basel.*

436 The Astrologer and the Theologian

Pen and ink, 138 x 195 mm.

Marginal drawings in the *Encomium Moriae (Praise of Folly)* by Erasmus of Rotterdam, 1515

Basel, Kupferstichkabinett (Inv. 1662.166)

LITERATURE

Erasmi Roterodami Encomium Moriae. Edition in facsimile by H. A. Schmid, I, pp. 33, 89; II, p. 104

Holbein Exhibition Catalogue, No. 192

THE *Encomium Moriae* of Erasmus, printed by Johannes Froben in Basel in 1515, served the humanist Myconius as a textbook for teaching Latin to his pupils. Among them were the young Holbein brothers, newly arrived in Basel. They provided Myconius' copy with charming marginal drawings, which were done at the turn of the year 1515-1516, within ten days, according to Myconius' testimony.

The drawings are judged differently by the scholars. While Ganz attributes them to four different hands, H. A. Schmid is inclined to see in all of them the work of Hans the Younger and ascribes only a few of them to the hand of Ambrosius. The drawings are outstanding in liveliness and humorous comments on the scholarly text. They are drawn mostly with the left hand, a technique characteristic of all drawings by Hans Holbein up to his last English years.

Portentosa phȝ recē
nox uocabula, non ni
si a damonibz enarca
atq; abipis demu
colle ... ta.

litare. Vnde Circe ad
Vlyssem, de Tiresia lo
quens sic ait, ἦ τε φρεί
νες ἔμπεδοί εἰσι τῶ
ⲧⲉϑνεῶτι νόομ πόρε
ⲡⲉⲣσεφόνεια. οἷφ πεί
πνυϲϑαι πὲῖ ϳ σκίαι ἀϊϲ
σσοι.i. Huius mens
firma ē, Huicq; mor
tuo ,mentē dedit Per
sephone, ut solus sa/
pere possit, alij autem
umbræuolitant.

Mathe matici

Quia lippiunt) Ni
miū ob studiū. Ani
mus autem peregri/
natur, dum intēti co/
gitationibus, non su/
mus apud nos. Hora
tius, Dum peregre ē
animus sine corpore
uelox. Allusit ad du/
as fabellas, alterā de
philosopho, dum cō
templatur astra in fo
ueā lapso, quē anus
irrisit, quod conareē
uidere, quod esset in

Prognosta

On peregre ...

Theologi

Mouere Camarinā est
sibi ipsi malū accersere.

uideāt, uel quia lippiunt plæriq;, uel qa
pegrinantur animi, tamen ideas, uniuer
salia, formas sepatas, primas materias,
quidditates, ecceitates uidere se prædi
cāt, res adeo tenues, ut neq; lynceus(opi
nor)possit pspicere, Tum uero precipue
prophanum uulgus aspernant,quoties
ttriquetris,& tetragonis circulis,atq; hu
iusmodi picturis Mathematicis,alijs su
per alias inductis,& in labyrinthi specie
confusis,præterea literis uelut in acie di
spositis ac subinde alio, atq; alio repeti
tis ordine,tenebras offundūt imperitio
ribus. Neq; desunt ex hoc genere qui fu
tura quoq; prædicant consultis astris,ac
miracula plusq; magica polliceant,& in
ueniūt homines fortunati,qui hæc quo/
q; credāt. Porro Theologos silentio trā
sire fortasse præstiterit,κỳ ταύτlυ καμαρι

ναμ

coelis,cum quod ante pedes esset,non uideret. Alteram de Astrologo,qui re
uertens a coena,impegit in saxum,e pariete prominens,cuius meminit Ioā
nes Campanus. Quidditates ecceitates.) Hæc sunt portenta uerborum
a recentioribus Theologis excogitata. Alijs super alias) Hoc imitatus est
ex Icaromenippo Luciani,sicut alia nōnulla. In Labyrinthi) Dicunt & pi
cturæ quædam Labyrinthi,lineis ita circūductis,ut nō sit exitus.Notat aut
figuras Astrologorum. Tenebras offundunt.) Hinc palam est ,hoc loco
reprehendi eos,qui figuris his docendi causa utuntur,sed in hoc,ut res diffi
cilior cognitu uideaē,ut solent indocti ostētatores,aut certe molesti.Quor/
sum enim attinet rem per se facilem,huiusmodi difficultatibus inuoluere.
Ita ut fecit Rabanus suis literarijs figuris. ⲧ ταύτlυ καμαρίναμ οὐ κινῷ μ.)
.i. Et hanc camarinā non mouere. Camarina palus etat pestilenti exhalatiōe
noxia ciuitati proximæ.Consultus Apollo num eam deberent siccare,respō
dit,μὴ κινῷ τlυ καμαρίναμ.i.ne mouete Camarinā,post obliti miraculi,de
siccarunt,& cessauit quidem pestis,sed hostes per eam ingressi,populati sūt
ciuitatem

Camarinā mouere:

HANS HOLBEIN THE YOUNGER

437 Portrait of a Leper (so-called)

Black and colored chalks, water color, reinforced in
  pen on light tan paper, 205 x 152 mm.

Dated 1523 by the artist

Cambridge, Massachusetts, Harvard University, Fogg Art
  Museum (No. 1949.2), Meta and Paul J. Sachs Collection

PROVENANCE

Koller; von Lanna; Bonn

LITERATURE

Woltmann, *Holbein und seine Zeit*, No. 244

Schoenbrunner-Meder, No. 1125 (Hans Holbein the Elder)

Ganz, *Die Handzeichnungen Hans Holbeins der Juengere*,
  No. 8

Mongan-Sachs, *Fogg Catalogue*, No. 386

Holbein Exhibition Catalogue, No. 276

ON THE reverse of this drawing is inscribed: F. K(oller) 1856 Hans
Holbein Portrait U. von Hutten's in seinem Todesjahr (1523), "Portrait of U. von Hutten in the year of his death."

HANS HOLBEIN THE YOUNGER

438 Portrait of the Mayor Jakob Meyer (Bust)

Black and colored chalks on grayish-white paper,
   383 x 275 mm.

Study for Meyer's portrait in the "Darmstaedter Madonna"

Basel, Kupferstichkabinett (Inv. 1823.140)

PROVENANCE

Faesch

LITERATURE

Woltmann, No. 40

Ganz, No. 14

Holbein Exhibition Catalogue, No. 296

JAKOB MEYER zum Hasen, a shrewd man who played an important role in politics and financial history, belonged to the Catholic party of Basel. He was one of the first patrons of the artist, who portrayed him and his wife in 1516. In 1526 they ordered the famous "Madonna," now in Darmstadt, representing Jakob Meyer together with his family in adoration of the Virgin. The painting served as altarpiece in the Chapel of the Castle of Gundeldingen, the country seat of the former Mayor. Jakob Meyer's pose is almost the same as in the finished painting.

HANS HOLBEIN THE YOUNGER

439 Portrait of Anna, the Daughter of Jakob Meyer (in Profile to the Left)

Black and colored chalks on white paper tinged in a greenish tone, 391 x 275 mm.

Study for the kneeling maiden in the "Darmstaedter Madonna"

Basel, Kupferstichkabinett (Inv. 1823.142)

PROVENANCE

Faesch

LITERATURE

Woltmann, No. 42

Ganz, No. 16

Holbein Exhibition Catalogue, No. 298

ANNA MEYER is represented here seated and with unbound hair as a young girl. In the painting she is kneeling and dressed as a bride. See note to No. 438.

HANS HOLBEIN THE YOUNGER

440 Portrait of an English Lady in Hat and Coif

Black and red chalk, heightened with white, on paper tinted
in pink water color, cut to outlines, 280 x 190 mm.

London, British Museum (No. 1910-2-12-105)

PROVENANCE

Richardson, Sr.; Knapton; Gower; Sutherland; Salting

LITERATURE

Ganz, No. 93

Dodgson, *Vasari Society*, I, 1905/06, No. 31

Parker, *The Drawings of Hans Holbein...
at Windsor Castle*, Fig. 4

A DRAWING from the artist's second English period (1532-1543),
which represents a lady of the burgher class. The admirable certainty
of line in Holbein's portrait drawings suggests that he may have
used the technique of tracing the model's outline through a pane of
glass, not uncommon in his period. However, this perfection may
also be due to the artist's unsurpassable sureness of eye and hand,
combined with a classical calmness and scientific exactitude in
weighing the optical elements.

HANS HOLBEIN THE YOUNGER

441 Cardinal John Fisher, Bishop of Rochester

Black and red chalk, washed in brownish water color,
reinforced with brush and pen in India ink by a later
hand on primed paper, 383 x 234 mm.

Inscribed in italics with the pen by a contemporary hand:
Il Epyscop° de resester fo...ato Il Cap° lan° 1535

Windsor Castle, Royal Collection (No. 12205)

LITERATURE

Ganz, No. 35

Parker, *The Drawings of Hans Holbein...*
at Windsor Castle, No. 13

A copy is in the British Museum (Parker, p. 39, Fig. XIII);
another one formerly in the Heseltine Collection (reproduced in *Original Drawings...in the Collection of J. P.
Heseltine*, 1912, Pl. XXII)

JOHN FISHER, the Chancellor of Cambridge University and Bishop
of Rochester, was beheaded on June 22, 1535, for opposing King
Henry VIII's divorce. He was canonized in 1935.

R Epusco de rosester
fo facerdar Al cont carns 25

HANS HOLBEIN THE YOUNGER

442 Portrait of Sir Charles Wingfield

Black, red and colored chalks, reinforced with pen and India
  ink, light retouches by a later hand, on pink primed
  paper, 286 x 198 mm.

Inscribed in gold and scarlet: *Charles Winhfield Knight*

Windsor Castle, Royal Collection (No. 12249)

LITERATURE

Parker, *The Drawings of Hans Holbein...*
  at Windsor Castle, No. 36

THE UPPER body of the sitter is bare. He wears a medallion suspended
on his chest. A female wrist adorned with a bracelet is slightly indicated in the upper left corner.

Charles Winhfield Knight.

BARTHEL BEHAM

(1502-1540)

BARTHEL BEHAM *Born at Nuremberg. Pupil of Dürer. Prosecuted because of religious reasons and emigrated to Munich in 1525. Painter to the court of Bavaria. Died in Italy 1540.*

443 Portrait of a Bearded Man in a Flat Cap (J. Jost?)

Black and red chalk, wash, 352 x 281 mm.

Berlin, Ehem. Staatliche Museen, Kupferstichkabinett
   (K.d.Z. 1356)

PROVENANCE

Chennevières

LITERATURE

Schilling, *Die Meisterzeichnung III*, No. 46

Berlin Catalogue, p. 12, No. 1356

A STYLISTICALLY related portrait is also in Berlin, *Catalogue*, p. 12, No. 523. The attribution to Barthel Beham is not ascertained beyond any doubt. Nevertheless, the drawing is a characteristic example of the art portraiture in Nuremberg after Dürer.

On the reverse is a later inscription in pencil: J. Jost truchsess (High Steward) von Walthaus 1521.

HEINRICH ALDEGREVER

(1502-Ca.1558)

HEINRICH ALDEGREVER *Born at Paderborn. Active in Soest. Engraved the portraits of the Duke of Cleveland and the Anabaptists in Muenster. Died about 1558.*

444 Portrait of a Man in a Flat Hat

Black chalk, slightly touched in red chalk, 184 x 214 mm.

Watermark: coat of arms with monogram M P h

Paris, Louvre, Cabinet des Dessins (No. 18.273)

PROVENANCE

Emigrés

LITERATURE

Demonts, No. 1, Pl. I

Reiset, No. 258 (attributed to Cranach)

Winkler, *Die Meisterzeichnung IV*, No. 64, Pl. LXIV

THE ATTRIBUTION to Aldegrever was made by W. Hugelshofer, K. T. Parker, and F. Winkler on the basis of stylistic reasons. According to G. Habich, Sebald Stayber of Nuremberg is portrayed (*Jahrbuch der Preussischen Kunstsammlungen*, XLIX, 1928, p. 17).

TOBIAS STIMMER
(1539-1584)

TOBIAS STIMMER   *Born at Schaffhausen. Resident of his native city from 1560 after an apprenticeship in Zuerich and perhaps in Italy. In Strassburg from 1570. Member of the guild in 1582. Died at Strassburg in 1584.*

445   The Painter and His Muse

Brush and India ink and white body-color on
   red prepared paper, 403 x 314 mm.

Basel, Kupferstichkabinett (Inv. U.I.38)

PROVENANCE

Faesch

LITERATURE

Ganz, *Handzeichnungen Schweizer Meister*, No. 27, Pl. III

Thoene, *Tobias Stimmer, Handzeichnungen*, No. 18

STIMMER IN his powerful and ingenious drawings knew how to fuse the great tradition of the first half of the century with the new challenge of Mannerism.

HANS VON AACHEN

(1552-1615)

HANS VON AACHEN *Born at Cologne. From 1574 to 1588 alternately in Venice, Rome, and Florence. Active at Munich and Augsburg 1589-94. Called as court painter to Prague by Emperor Rudolph II in 1592. Died there in 1615.*

446 The Baptism of Christ

Black chalk, pen and bistre, wash heightened with white body-color.

Cambridge, Fitzwilliam Museum (No. 2856)

PROVENANCE

Peter Lely; Warwick; Clough

LITERATURE

Exhibition of 15th and 16th Century Drawings,
   No. 10 (as South German School)

THE DRAWING is a spirited example of that kind of Late Mannerism that was at home at the court of Prague during the reign of Rudolph II. It is distinguished by formal elements, which we may recognize also in the art of Jacques Bellange. A ray of light flames from the dove of the Holy Ghost, now turned black through oxidation of the medium.

The drawing has recently been catalogued in the Fitzwilliam Museum as "Attributed to Johann von Aachen," to whom it was given as early as 1947 by this author.

HANS VON AACHEN

447 Portrait of Giovanni da Bologna

Black and red chalk, 148 x 128 mm.
Monogram: *J O H F* (Johannes fecit ?)
Inscribed: *Joan de Boloniga*
New York, Dr. Julius S. Held

PROVENANCE
Ruth H. Heidsieck

THE PRESENT drawing, done from life, served as the basis for the painting in the Louvre, which A. Peltzer published, with good reasons, as a work of Hans von Aachen (*Jahrbuch des Allerhoechsten Kaiserhauses*, Vienna, 1911, XXX, p. 70). Van Mander reports that Hans von Aachen portrayed the great sculptor in Florence, and the drawing was made not later than 1587, when von Aachen left Florence. Emperor Rudolph II saw this portrait or a replica of it. He appreciated it so much that he called the painter to his court in Prague. The portrait was also engraved by Gijsbrecht van Veen in 1589.

ADAM ELSHEIMER

(1578-1610)

ADAM ELSHEIMER *Born at Frankfort-on-Main. Pupil of Philipp Uffenbach. Went to Munich to work in Rottenhammer's studio. Active in Rome from 1600. Friend of Rubens. Died 1610 at Rome.*

448 Classical Landscape

Brush and India ink, white body-color, 152 x 200 mm.

Basel, Dr. Robert von Hirsch

PROVENANCE

Esdaile; Count de Robiano

LITERATURE

Weizsaecker, *Adam Elsheimer*, p. 124, Fig. 66, Pl. LVII

Catalogue of The Hague Sale, 1926, No. 369

THE DRAWING repeats the setting of the painting "Tobias and the Angel" (the so-called "Large Tobias") known from copies in London and Copenhagen. It appears in the same direction as in the print by Hendrik Goudt. In its masterly handling of the medium with the brush it deploys an incredible richness of tones and gradations of light and shows Elsheimer as a true precursor of Rembrandt and Claude Lorrain.

COSMAS DAMIAN ASAM

(1686-1729)

COSMAS DAMIAN ASAM *Born at Benediktbeuren. Settled at Munich. Active with his brother Quirin Egidius in Bavaria, Bohemia, and the Tyrol. Died 1729 at the Abbey of Weltenburg.*

449 The Coronation of the Virgin

Pencil, pen and brush in bistre, heightened in white, indented for transfer, 411 x 259 mm.

Signed: *Cos: D: Asam Inven:*

Vienna, Albertina (Inv. 3825)

LITERATURE

Albertina Catalogue, IV, No. 957

Garzarolli, *Die barocke Handzeichnung in Oesterreich,* Fig. 41

THE BROTHERS Asam mastered alike architecture, sculpture, and painting, making of these three arts a Baroque unison of ravishing curving motion. The most outstanding of their works is the little church of St. John of Nepomuk in Munich.

The drawing is a design for an altarpiece.

FRANZ ANTON MAULBERTSCH
(1724-1796)

FRANZ ANTON MAULBERTSCH *Born at Langenargen on the Lake of Constance. Pupil at the Academy of Vienna, of which he became a member in 1759 and councillor in 1770. Active mainly in Austria, Hungary, Moravia, and Bohemia as painter of frescoes. Died 1796 at Vienna.*

450 Fides, Justitia, and Pictura

Pen and bistre, washes in gray and brown, 337 x 419 mm.

Vienna, Albertina (Inv. 25003)

LITERATURE

Albertina Catalogue, IV, No. 2193

Benesch, *Amicis*, I, 1926, pp. 4-8

DESIGN FOR a detail of the fresco (done in 1758) for the Palace of the Archbishop in Kremsier, Moravia. This splendid drawing shows the inventive genius of Maulbertsch. In all its strength it enhances the formal grammar of Late Baroque and Rococo to a fantastic and bizarre expressiveness.

FERDINAND OLIVIER

(1785-1841)

FERDINAND OLIVIER *Born at Dessau. Pupil of K. W. Kolbe. Contact with C. D. Friedrich at Dresden. Settled 1811 at Vienna. Journeys to Salzburg. Moved in 1830 to Munich, where he died in 1841.*

451 Landscape of Aigen near Salzburg

Pencil, light brown wash, heightenings in
 white body-color, 138 x 267 mm.

Monogram and inscription by the artist:
 Bey Aigen im Salzburgischen

Vienna, Albertina (Inv. 31441)

PROVENANCE

Prince of Liechtenstein

LITERATURE

Neuerwerbungen alter Meister 1950-58,
 Albertina, Cat. No. 160

OLIVIER, WHO traveled together with C. D. Friedrich in the Harz Mountains, is one of the most charming draughtsmen of the romantic period. He gave to his plain views of nature a religious contemplativeness that is reminiscent of the Old German masters. He used the present drawing for "Friday" in a series of lithographs of views of Salzburg, one for each day of the week, accompanied by a sentence of the Lord's Prayer.

HANS VON MARÉES
(1837–1887)

HANS VON MARÉES • *Born at Elberfeld. Studied at the Academy in Berlin. Settled at Munich in 1857. Extensive travels through Europe. 1873 frescoes in Naples. Settled 1874 at Rome, where he died in 1887.*

452 Ancient Chariot with a Pair of Horses and Several Female Figures

Red chalk, ca. 390 (irregular) x 405 mm.

Munich, Staatliche Graphische Sammlung (No. 1913-44)

LITERATURE

Meier-Graefe, *Hans von Marées*, II, No. 524

Degenhart, *Marées Zeichnungen*, No. 29

IN A period of commonplace naturalism in German painting, Marees upheld an ideal of grandeur of form, supported by a deep artistic ethos. His searching and powerful mastery of tectonic values comes to the fore in his drawings in a most convincing way. Filled with a solemn earnestness, they resuscitate an ideal world of antiquity.

Flemish and Dutch Drawings

Flemish and Dutch Drawings

WHEN ONE TURNS from the Italian drawings to those of the Netherlandish artists he enters another world, one in which nature and everyday life are much closer, where the human experience emerges more directly and human feelings communicate themselves with heightened immediacy.

Netherlandish is used here in its original meaning, including what we call today the Flemish and Dutch schools of art. During the fifteenth and most of the sixteenth century, when the seventeen provinces that now form Belgium and Holland were still united, one could speak with accuracy of a single school; regional distinctions did exist, but their importance was negligible. After 1575, however, when the northern and southern Netherlands began to go their own ways politically, the distinctions became marked.

The towering figures of each school in the seventeenth century illustrate the difference strikingly—the stanchly Catholic Rubens in Flanders, the liberal Protestant Rembrandt in Holland. The work of each is monumental, yet in what a different way! But as one begins to define the differences, he also discovers curiously striking similarities: each was deeply religious, each was blessed with greatness of conception; both were brilliant colorists, both attacked the widest range of subjects with the same masterful ease, both were superb draughtsmen.

Restricting ourselves simply to their drawings, we see that Rubens liked large scale and—especially in his chalk drawings—perfect outline. In preparatory drawings for paintings he gave attention to both composition and important details. From Rembrandt we find practically no preliminary studies for paintings, but countless indirect ones—he sketched one subject in various ways, then generally painted it differently. His early drawings have facility and consummate technique, but he soon developed a technique fully his own, especially with pen and wash, discarding all search for graphic perfection, hinting more than elaborating. In so doing he expressed more and probed deeper than his contemporaries. Little wonder his pupils (of whom Bol, Flinck, Backer, van den Beckhout, Maes, and Doomer are best known through their drawings) were captivated by their master's technique.

When Rubens' fame was well established, another genius, twenty-three years younger, appeared in Flanders: Anton van Dyck. His drawings were at first more or less dependent on those by Rubens, and often so nearly equal to them in quality and inspiration that even connoisseurs had difficulty distinguishing them. But after the age of twenty-five he showed a hand of his own: one of a loving precision, particularly in his portraits; one of weird hastiness in his compositional sketches. He stands out as the greatest among the crowd that surrounded Rubens, excelling by his aristocratic demeanor the clever but clumsier Jordaens. The landscape painters, headed by Jan Brueghel (the velvet Brueghel), produced their charming landscapes more independently. They had many excellent predecessors during the later part of the sixteenth century—the brothers Mathijs and Paul Bril, Valkenburgh, Verhaeght, as well as Coninxloo, Roeland Savery, and David Vinckboons, who moved to the North and had a stimulating effect on their Dutch colleagues. In citing Hendrick Avercamp (best known for his winter scenes, but equally captivating in his delicate summer landscapes) and such sympathetic interpreters of the area around Haarlem and Leyden as Cornelis Vroom, Esaias and Jan van de Velde, the prolific and always entertaining Jan van Goyen, the more refined, poetic Jacob van Ruisdael, we name only a few outstanding figures of the long line of landscapists who give luster to the Dutch seventeenth century. At the same time such other talents as the spirited Willem Buytewegh, wonderful but short-lived Adriaen Brouwer (who belongs both with Flanders and Holland), and the highly gifted brothers Adriaen and Isaac van Ostade were the leaders in figure painting.

Other masters did excellent portrait drawings (Lievens, Cornelis Visscher, Ter Borch); in architecture, especially church interiors, the name of Pieter Saenredam is pre-eminent.

It is hardly a surprise that among the seafaring Dutch, lovely marine subjects by Willem van de Velde (father and son), Simon de Vlieger, and Jan van de Capelle formed part of the enormous artistic output typical of the same period in Holland. And there were the marvelous animal painters, headed by the sharp observer Paul Potter.

Spirited pen drawings, mellow or strong sketches in chalk or pencil, soft tonalities of wash and water color fascinate in endless numbers. For those who wonder if the Netherlands produced any artists who, like Dürer in Germany, had a surpassing gift for the calligraphic line, Jacob de Gheyn and Hendrick Goltzius furnish the answer: their flowing, easy lines are often marvels for the eye. They form the bridge between the sixteenth and the seventeenth centuries, and many gifted hands had preceded them.

Drawing of course is as old as painting. The production of independent pictures started in the Netherlands around 1400; earlier expression in drawing can be found only in mural painting and in the illumination of manuscripts. Time has destroyed most of the sketches and finished drawings by such of the earliest great painters as van Eyck, Rogier van der Weyden, van der Goes, and Memling. Since their art derived from the great miniaturists, their handling was most precise and careful. An exception must be noted in the most original and fantastic mind embodied in Hieronymus Bosch, and with the advent of the Renaissance around 1500, more freedom characterized the work of Lucas van Leyden, Jan van Mabuse, Jan van Scorel, and Maerten van Heemskerck.

Around 1560 we meet another highly original figure of the type of Bosch, Pieter

Brueghel; like his son Jan, he was a most remarkable landscapist—as well as a sharp observer of man and a profound thinker.

This too-rapid bird's-eye view can only hint the riches in store. Many collectors and most beginners hunt for names, and there are names to be found here. But not all of the greatest names are represented. Some of the most extraordinary painters, such as Frans Hals or Vermeer of Delft, left no drawings.

From a period so rich, systematic representation in these pages of all the finest draughtsmen is physically impossible. Balancing some inevitable gaps and regrets, however, we do have a welcome compensation in reviving the memory of two remarkable Dutch artists whose talents blossomed most copiously in France—Jongkind and van Gogh. Each has a unique hand. Jongkind, with fluid pen, chalk, and brush, brings life and light in all his landscape sketches and water colors. Van Gogh, stubborn, fierce, angular, strikes forth vivid, radiant and timeless results in quite a different way.

—FRITS LUGT

PLATES

EARLY FLEMISH OR FRANCO-FLEMISH
Ca. 1420

453 The Betrayal of Christ

Silverpoint on grayish-green prepared paper, heightened with white, 117 x 132 mm.

London, British Museum (No. 1883-7-14-77)

LITERATURE

Popham, *Drawings of the Early Flemish School*, Pl. II

Beenken, *Old Master Drawings*, VII, 1932/33, pp. 18 ff.

Ring, *A Century of French Painting, 1400-1500*, No. 60, Pl. XXXV

Baldass, *Jan van Eyck*, No. 76, Pl. CLXIX

Panofsky, *Early Netherlandish Painting*, p. 452, Note 233b

THERE IS no doubt about the time of origin of this drawing, in which the "Betrayal of Christ" is dramatically depicted. The figures in their sweeping movements, the elongated and weightless bodies almost substituted by costumes that have a rather calligraphic more than an enveloping function, the particular use of the silverpoint, all point to the beginning of the fifteenth century.

Less certainty exists about the region where the drawing has been executed. Most likely a Flemish artist working in France close to the Limbourg Brothers, immigrants themselves, or a French artist influenced by them was the author of this rare document of the art of drawing, immediately preceding the revolutionary transformations caused in the Netherlands by van Eyck and Campin.

Attributed to ROBERT CAMPIN

(1375/80-1444)

ROBERT CAMPIN *Born probably at Valenciennes. Became citizen of Tournai in 1410, where he was the teacher of Rogier van der Weyden. Died 1444 at Tournai.*

454 Thief on the Cross

Silverpoint on gray prepared paper, 264 x 141 mm.

Cambridge, Massachusetts, Harvard University, Fogg Art
    Museum (No. 1950.60), Alpheus Hyatt Fund

LITERATURE

Rosenberg, *Art Quarterly*, XIII, 1950, p. 251

Panofsky, p. 423, Note 167[1]

ONLY FRAGMENTS and copies have been preserved of a large triptych by Robert Campin, famous in its time, representing a "Descent from the Cross" in the center, the Good Thief and the Donor on the left wing. The wing with the Good Thief is likewise lost, although the composition and details are known to us through a painted copy and the present drawing.

Such details as the shape of the deformed body, the treatment of the skin, and the fluttering bandage are entirely characteristic of the artist. The drawing, therefore, must be considered as a faithful recording of the lost figure, executed shortly after Campin finished his triptych.

JAN VAN EYCK
(Ca. 1390-1441)

JAN VAN EYCK *Born at Maaseyk (?). Worked under the patronage of the Dukes of Burgundy. Not later than 1425 was appointed Court painter and* valet de chambre *to Philip the Good. Diplomatic missions to Portugal. Worked also with his brother Hubert. From 1420-32 worked on the altarpiece of the "Adoration of the Lamb." Active at Bruges from 1430 until his death in 1441.*

455 Portrait of Cardinal Albergati

Silverpoint on grayish-white prepared ground,
212 x 180 mm.

Color notes by the artist: *geelachtich und witte blauwachtich* (yellowish and white-bluish), *rotte purpurachtig* (purplish-red), *die lippen zeer witachtig* (the lips very whitish), *die nase sanguynachtich* (the nose sanguinous)

Dresden, Staatliche Kunstsammlungen

LITERATURE

Weale and Brockwell, *The Van Eycks and their Art*, pp. 106 ff.

Friedlaender, *Die altniederlaendische Malerei*, I, p. 90

Baldass, *Jan van Eyck*, No. 28, Pl. CXXXIII

Panofsky, pp. 200 ff., Fig. 264

NICOLO ALBERGATI, Cardinal of Santa Croce in Gerusalemme, visited Bruges from December 8 to 11, 1431. On this occasion Jan van Eyck made this portrait of the Cardinal, who then was serving as a legate to the Kings of France and England and to the Duke of Burgundy. "This admirable prince of the church," as Panofsky writes, "was a man of proverbial wisdom and integrity, and the most successful diplomatist of the Curia."

Jan van Eyck made the drawing as the preparatory study for a portrait, which had to be painted without the benefit of the sitter's presence. For this reason the artist made extensive notes of the colors of parts of the face. The painted portrait, executed some time after the drawing, is now in the Kunsthistorisches Museum, Vienna.

This drawing, the only authentic drawing by the artist, is a monument to Jan van Eyck's sensitive eye, precision of hand, and insight into the human being. Without imposing himself on the image of the sitter, he gives us an interpretation of the man which is seemingly objective.

JAN VAN EYCK (?)

456 Portrait of a Man

Silverpoint on grayish-white prepared paper, 89 x 66 mm.

Inscribed by the artist: *R.egter*.

The man's left eye has been retouched

Rotterdam, Museum Boymans-van Beuningen (No. N. 73)

PROVENANCE

von Lanna; Wauters; Koenigs

LITERATURE

Schoenbrunner-Meder, No. 1407 (reproduced in reverse)

Panofsky, Note 200[3]

Haverkamp-Begemann, *Vijf eeuwen tekenkunst*, pp. 3-4

THE ATTITUDE, distribution of light and shade, and the turban-like headdress of this man remind us of portraits painted by Jan van Eyck, such as the "Portrait of a Man in a Turban" in the National Gallery, London. Because of the sketchiness and immediacy this must be considered as a portrait from life rather than as a copy after another drawing or after a painting. Furthermore, in such details as the way the shadows are drawn with dense silverpoint lines and in the more sketchy parts, the drawing is comparable to Jan van Eyck's "Portrait of Cardinal Albergati" (see No. 455). An attribution of this small but masterly drawing to Jan van Eyck seems therefore possible, although caution is required as long as the "Portrait of Cardinal Albergati" remains the only drawing undoubtedly executed by Jan van Eyck.

The inscription, meaning "judge," could be explained as an indication of the profession of the sitter. His identity, however, remains unknown.

DUTCH OR FLEMISH,
Ca. 1420-1450

457 Mary and St. John

Point of the brush or pen and brown ink, arched at top,
302 x 172 mm.

Annotated by a later hand: *Hieronimo Bosh f.*

Dresden, Staatliche Kunstsammlungen

LITERATURE

Woermann, *Handzeichnungen alter Meister...zu Dresden,*
IV, No. 2

Popham, *Drawings of the Early Flemish School,* No. 37

Friedlaender, *Die altniederlaendische Malerei,* V, 1927,
p. 127

de Tolnay, *Hieronymus Bosch,* p. 109

IN THE expression of grief Mary and St. John resemble, at least to a certain extent, figures painted by Hieronymus Bosch. Although this resemblance must account for the attribution to Bosch, it does not justify it. The shapes of the figures or rather of the costumes under which they disappear, the flowing lines of these costumes, the forms of the faces, and also the technique of the drawing are alien to Bosch. Friedlaender and de Tolnay, therefore, rightly rejected the attribution to this artist. However, the question as to who, instead of Hieronymus Bosch, was responsible for this remarkable drawing, cannot be answered without further study. De Tolnay, by stating the affinity to the work of Jan van Aken, undoubtedly came closest to an acceptable answer to this question.

The peculiar manner of depicting emotions, in such a way that a grimace results that could be understood as a caricature-like expression of joy as well as of grief, points to a considerably earlier period in the history of art in the Netherlands. Such an early date is confirmed by the gently curving folds of the costumes, which remind one of the "International style" of the beginning of the fifteenth century. The grinning faces expressing sorrow are close to similar ones in paintings by Hubert van Eyck or his younger brother Jan and in miniatures related to these paintings. In addition, the technique of this drawing resembles that of grisaille-miniatures in manuscripts executed in the Northern Netherlands in the first half of the fifteenth century. All this points to an origin in the Netherlands, probably between the years 1420 and 1450.

The numerous *pentimenti* in the drawing, such as in the shoulders of St. John, could be a point in favor of regarding it as a study for part of a composition. The completeness and high degree of finish, however, are generally found in copies rather than in studies from this early period. This question, therefore, has to remain unanswered.

The entire composition undoubtedly included either a representation of "Christ on the Cross" or a "Deposition," in either case placed to the right of the group of Mary and John. Whether the entire composition was a painting or a sculpture remains to be established. The unusually great difference in level between the two figures makes it likely that they belonged to a sculpture in relief. The angular ends of the folds of Mary's garment at the bottom at the left and the vague indication of the lower edges of the costumes of the figures agree with such a supposition; in both cases the transition from background to costume is indicated. Our scant knowledge of sculpture in the Netherlands in the first half of the fifteenth century would increase considerably if this beautiful and fascinating drawing definitely could be considered as a reflection of one of its numerous lost monuments.

ROGIER VAN DER WEYDEN

(1399/1400-1464)

ROGIER VAN DER WEYDEN *Born at Tournai. 1427 entered the school of Robert Campin. 1432 member of the guild. Worked at Brussels in 1436. 1450 traveled to Italy. Died at Brussels, 16 June 1464.*

458 Virgin and Child

Silverpoint on white prepared paper, 195 x 127 mm.

Cut out and pasted on larger sheet of paper, 216 x 127 mm.

Inscribed by a later hand: *Alberto Durer*

Rotterdam, Museum Boymans-van Beuningen (No. N. 9)

PROVENANCE

Cassirer; Koenigs

LITERATURE

Friedlaender, *Old Master Drawings*, I, 1926, pp. 29 ff.,
   Pl. XXXVIII

Friedlaender, *Die altniederlaendische Malerei*, VI,
   1928, p. 68

Degenhart, *Europaeische Handzeichnungen aus fuenf
   Jahrhunderten*, pp. 165-166, Fig. 12, Pl. XIV

Panofsky, p. 266, Note 266², Fig. 385

Haverkamp-Begemann, *Vijf eeuwen tekenkunst*,
   pp. 6-7, Fig. 3

THE VIRGIN and Child have been rendered with the greatest delicacy and sensitive precision. The drapery, the hands and faces have been represented with meticulous care and subtle gradations in light and shade. These qualities, combined with the fact that the composition is undoubtedly due to Rogier van der Weyden, are strongly in favor of the attribution of the drawing to Rogier van der Weyden himself. The gesture of blessing of the Christ Child, the fact that the background is indicated only slightly, and some other features prove that this "Virgin and Child" is only part of a larger composition. The original of this larger composition, a "Virgin Crowned with Stars," is lost but is known from a number of replicas.

Whether by Rogier van der Weyden or by a close follower, the drawing represents the high level of draughtsmanship as it was practiced by him and his circle.

ROGIER VAN DER WEYDEN

459 St. Mary Magdalen

Silverpoint on ivory prepared paper, 176 x 130 mm.

London, British Museum (No. 00.9.2)

LITERATURE

Popham, *Drawings of the Early Flemish School*, Pl. XII

Popham, *British Museum Catalogue*, V, p. 55

Panofsky, Note 275[4], Fig. 384

ST. MARY MAGDALEN, very elegantly dressed—whether the hat she wears is due to the fancy of the artist or really existed at the time remains uncertain—is depicted in front of a mountainous landscape, indicated with rapid and suggestive strokes of the silverpoint. She holds the ointment jar with her left hand, reverently covered with a cloth, and touches the lid of the jar with her right.

The figure corresponds closely with the same Saint on a triptych that Rogier van der Weyden painted for Jean de Braque and his wife, Catharine of Brabant, and which is now in the Louvre, Paris. The Magdalen on the right wing of the triptych has the same sad and tender expression as in the drawing.

Although the drawing is very accomplished and betrays a highly skilled and sensitive hand, it is not entirely beyond doubt whether Rogier van der Weyden executed it himself (see also No. 460).

After ROGIER VAN DER WEYDEN

460 Portrait of a Young Woman

Silverpoint on ivory prepared paper, 166 x 116 mm.

London, British Museum (No. 1874-8-8-2266)

LITERATURE

Winkler, *Der Meister von Flémalle und Roger van der Weyden*, p. 54, Fig. 25

Winkler, *Art Quarterly*, XIII, 1950, pp. 211 ff.

Popham, *British Museum Catalogue*, V, p. 54

IN POSE and dress this young lady resembles portraits by Rogier van der Weyden, especially one in the Museum in Berlin. This drawing undoubtedly reflects such a portrait, now lost.

As in Rogier van der Weyden's painted portraits of ladies, we find stressed here the roundness and volumes of forms and of cheeks, as well as of the carefully arranged headdress. The woman looks in the distance; her gaze is clearly directed, her countenance firm, her mouth expresses decision.

FLEMISH, Ca. 1450

461 Men Shoveling Chairs

Pen and brown ink over black chalk, 298 x 425 mm.

New York, Robert Lehman

LITERATURE

Mongan, *One Hundred Master Drawings,* No. 8, Pl. IX

Adhémar, *Bulletin de la Société des Antiquaires de France,*
     1952-53, p. 142

Lebeer, *Bruxelles au XVe siècle,* 1953, pp. 193-195

Exposition de la Collection Lehman de New York,
     Musée de l'Orangerie, 1957, No. 109, Pl. LIII

MEN SHOVELING stools is certainly a rare subject in art, and so is the shape of the drawing. Both shape and subject are explained by the fact that the drawing is the design for a sculptured capital crowning a round column. Column and capital are part of an arcade on the ground floor of the Town Hall in Brussels, and were executed between 1444 and 1450.

This scene may have been represented on the capital because previous to the building of the town hall a house called "Scupstoel" (Kick-Stool or Kick-Chair) stood on the same site. This word "scupstoel" or "schopstoel" is still in use today in Flemish. In Dutch the expression "op de schopstoel zitten" means "be likely to get kicked out." Since the word "schop" means a "kick" as well as a "shovel," the "schopstoelen" or "kick-chairs" could be represented by way of a pun as chairs being shoveled.

The fact that this pun was represented on a capital of the Town Hall certainly must have amused the citizens and may have reminded those who were in power that they too could be kicked out.

The style of the drawing is close to that of Rogier van der Weyden. This is not surprising because he was the official painter of the city of Brussels from 1435. It is not known which of his pupils executed the drawings. He was probably a painter rather than a sculptor.

After PETRUS CHRISTUS

(Ca. 1410-1472/73)

Petrus Christus   Born at Baerle. Became a citizen of Bruges in 1444. Worked there from 1444-72. Influenced by the van Eycks and Rogier van der Weyden. 1449 commissioned by the goldsmith's guild of Antwerp. Died at Bruges.

462 Portrait of a Man with a Falcon

Silverpoint on ivory prepared paper, 189 x 143 mm.
Frankfort-on-Main, Staedel Art Institute (No. 725)

LITERATURE

Friedlaender, *Die altniederlaendische Malerei*,
    I, 1924, Pl. XLVIII

Baldass, *Jan van Eyck*, Fig. 151

Panofsky, Notes 200[3] and 310[7]

THIS "PORTRAIT of a Man with a Falcon," executed with great precision as to his face, hat, and collar, and more freely handled in other parts, is very close in style to portraits painted by Petrus Christus, the artist who to a certain extent was Jan van Eyck's successor. The traditional attribution of the drawing to Jan van Eyck himself, therefore, is not surprising. Erwin Panofsky's opinion that it is an early copy after a painting by Petrus Christus is, however, more convincing. The way the light falls on the head, the modeling of face and hands, the interior and its perspective all point to Petrus Christus. The borderline at the bottom of the drawing, the fact that certain details such as hands and folds are not treated with the same certainty as other parts, point to a copy after a painting rather than a drawing done in preparation for it.

Only very few drawings of the latter type have been preserved from the fifteenth century in the Netherlands. Careful copying of paintings was a regular workshop practice and was frequently done also by highly gifted artists.

After PETRUS CHRISTUS

463 Portrait of a Man

Silverpoint on white prepared paper, 265 x 186 mm.

Vienna, Albertina (Inv. 4845)

LITERATURE

Albertina Catalogue, II, No. 15

IN THE pose of the man and the way his hands are arranged this drawing is close to late portraits by Petrus Christus.

It was probably executed after such a portrait.

School of ROGIER VAN DER WEYDEN

464 Portrait of a Man

Silverpoint on grayish-white prepared paper, 98 x 81 mm.

Berlin, Ehem. Staatliche Museen, Kupferstichkabinett
(K.d.Z. 1372)

PROVENANCE

Suermondt

LITERATURE

Berlin Catalogue, p. 5, No. 1372, Pl. VI

DIRK BOUTS

(1415/20-1475)

DIRK BOUTS   *Also known as Dierick Bouts and Dirk van
Haarlem. Born at Haarlem. From 1448 worked at Louvain,
where he became city painter in 1468. Died at Louvain, 6
May 1475.*

465 Portrait of a Young Man

Silverpoint on gray-white prepared paper, 139 x 106 mm.

Northampton, Massachusetts, Smith College,
Museum of Art

PROVENANCE

Dr. Henry Wellesley; F. Locker Lampson; Henry Oppenheimer; Rosenthal

LITERATURE

Popham, *Drawings of the Early Flemish School*, Pl. XVII

Schone, *Dieric Bouts und seine Schule*, p. 88, Pl. XIX

Panofsky, note 316, Fig. 423

Boon, *Dieric Bouts*, No. 32

THIS ELEGANTLY dressed man, holding a turban-like hat in his
hands, probably reflects a painting of the school of Rogier van der
Weyden.

THE MAN could be an artist, since he holds a metalpoint in his left
hand. The tall hat points to the drawing being executed about 1467,
as K. G. Boon established.

Compared with other Flemish silverpoint portraits of the fifteenth
century, the drawing is executed with a remarkable freedom and immediacy. It is therefore a portrait drawn from life, not after a painting. The angularity of costume and folds, unusual in Bouts's paintings, can likewise be explained by its being a study, in parts quickly
sketched.

HUGO VAN DER GOES

(1439/40-1482)

HUGO VAN DER GOES *Born at Ghent. History and portrait painter. It is not known to whom he was apprenticed. Died at Roode-Kloster, near Brussels, in 1482.*

466 The Meeting of Jacob and Rachel

Pen and brown ink, brown wash, heightened with white, on dark-gray prepared paper, 340 x 570 mm.

Oxford, Christ Church (Ref. No. Large Portfolio)

PROVENANCE

Guise

LITERATURE

Colvin, *Selected Drawings of the Old Masters in the University Galleries and in the Library of Christ Church, Oxford*, III, p. 15, Pl. XVII

Friedlaender, *Die altniederlaendische Malerei*, IV, 1926, p. 62, Pl. LXXVI

Oettinger, in *Jahrbuch der Oesterreichischen Kunstsammlungen*, N. F. XII, 1938, pp. 59-60

IN THE center of the composition Jacob embraces Rachel, who was shepherding her father's sheep. The sheep are drinking water from a well at the left, from which Jacob had removed a stone, visible in the drawing at the very left. Here the men from Haran are watching Jacob and Rachel. The woman at the right, shepherding cattle, is probably Rachel's sister Leah. A later moment of the story (Genesis 29) is represented in the background at the right, namely Jacob meeting Laban and telling him about his happy reunion with Rachel.

This drawing, related in subject and composition to a large painting by Hugo van der Goes representing "David and Abigael," is unusual in size and finish. Perhaps this unusual characteristic can be explained by assuming that the drawing was made as a design for a tapestry.

The figures, expressive in their restrained movements, are set in or rather before a landscape of peaceful tranquility, with thin-stemmed trees and bushes, which we often find in the paintings of Hugo van der Goes.

School of HUGO VAN DER GOES

467 Kneeling Woman

Pen and brown ink, 242 x 186 mm.

New York, The Pierpont Morgan Library

PROVENANCE

Sir Charles Greville; Earl of Warwick; Fairfax Murray

LITERATURE

Winkler, in *Kunstchronik*, N. F. XXXIII, 1921/22, p. 611

Popham, in *Apollo*, VII, 1928, p. 177

Boon, in *Nederlandsch Kunsthistorisch Jaarboek*,
    III, 1950/51, pp. 90-91, Fig. 11

EXECUTED ABOUT 1490-1500, this delicate study of a kneeling lady, probably a female Saint, has all the characteristics of draughtmanship as developed by Hugo van der Goes and in his school. A second study by the same anonymous artist, this time of two kneeling ladies, is in the British Museum, London.

School of HUGO VAN DER GOES

468 Virgin and Child

Pen and brown ink, 209 x 155 mm.

New York, Robert Lehman

PROVENANCE

Simon; Lasquin; Ten Kate; Leroy Backus

LITERATURE

Tietze, *European Master Drawings in the United States*,
No. 7, Pl. VII

IT IS generally the Infant Christ Child who is represented with the Virgin in fifteenth-century art of the Netherlands, and a six- or seven-year-old Christ Child in "Christ Disputing with the Doctors." When we find this older Child with His Mother it is generally in representatons of "The Virgin Teaching the Christ Child." This drawing is an exception.

The type of the Virgin and the modeling of her drapery are close to those of Hugo van der Goes; the handling of the pen and the way the shades are indicated with short cross-hatchings and occasional groups of dots were probably created by him, since we find this technique in a number of drawings from his school, although none by the master himself has come down to us. A "St. Luke" in the Boymans-van Beuningen Museum at Rotterdam, also very close to Hugo van der Goes, is probably by the same hand.

SCHOOL OF BRUGES, Ca. 1490

469 Lady Kneeling in a Landscape

Pen and brown ink over black chalk, 288 x 209 mm.
Rotterdam, Museum Boymans-van Beuningen (No. N.74)

PROVENANCE
Gelosi; Koenigs

LITERATURE
Catalogue Exhibition Dutch Art, 1927, No. 506

THIS LADY, a donor, is represented kneeling, surrounded by a low brick wall. Consequently she is represented in a "garden enclosed," a "hortus conclusus." Therefore the main scene of which she formed a part was probably a representation of the Virgin Mary and Saints.

The landscape background with tall trees and gently sloping hills points to an influence of Hugo van der Goes. It is not likely, however, that this drawing is a design for a painting, but rather a copy after one. The same composition is known from a drawing (pen, 275 x 190 mm.) sold with the Braz Collection, Paris, May-12, 1938. There a St. Michael was added behind the donor. See also No. 470.

SCHOOL OF BRUGES, Ca. 1490

470 Female Saint Standing in a Landscape

Pen and brown ink, 212 x 172 mm.

Copenhagen, Royal Museum of Fine Arts (No. tu.74.2)

PROVENANCE

Hudson; Donnadieu

LITERATURE

Fischer and Sthyr, *Seks Aarhundreders europaeisk
Tegnekunst*, p. 111, Pl. V

THE YOUNG lady holds a flower resembling a violet, symbol of
humility.

The drawing with its short, nervous lines, executed with the pen,
has some characteristics in common with the previous drawing. This
one has been executed, as the other one, by a late follower of Hugo
van der Goes.

FLEMISH, LATE XV CENTURY

471 **Scribe Writing,
the Author Presenting His Book**

Brush and blue water color on gray prepared paper,
heightened with white and gold, 164 x 185 mm.

Washington, D. C., National Gallery of Art (No. B-13.515),
Rosenwald Collection

LITERATURE

*Rosenwald Collection. An Exhibition of Recent
Acquisitions,* 1950, No. 26

Boon, in *Nederlandsch Kunsthistorisch Jaarboek,*
III, 1950/51, p. 95

THE SCENE in a Gothic interior is divided in two parts: at the left a scribe is writing a book that is being offered at the right by the author to the person for whom it was written, probably one of the high officials of the Burgundian Court.

This miniature formed part of an illuminated manuscript from which at least eight more are preserved (six in the Institut Néerlandais, Paris; two in the Van der Feer Lader Collection, Baarn). Other miniatures by the same hand are known and have been grouped together under the name of Alexander Bening, although he is not the author of them.

The technique of these and related drawings is reminiscent of drawings by van der Goes, such as the "Meeting of Jacob and Rachel" (see No. 466), and so is the style of the figures. Undoubtedly the artist was influenced by Hugo van der Goes, working in Bruges at the end of the fifteenth century.

Some of the miniatures of the book that contained the one here reproduced were copied in another book, now in the Museum Czartoryska, Cracow.

HIERONYMUS BOSCH

(Ca. 1450-1516)

HIERONYMUS BOSCH *Born at Bois le Duc. History and genre painter, brilliant colorist. Famed in Netherlands, Italy, and Spain during his lifetime. Little actually known of his life. Died at Hertozenboch 1516.*

472 Merry Company in a Giant Egg

Pen and brown ink, 176 x 257 mm.

Berlin, Ehem. Staatliche Museen, Kupferstichkabinett
(K.d.Z. 711 verso)

LITERATURE

Berlin Catalogue, p. 1, No. 711 verso
de Tolnay, *Hieronymus Bosch*, p. 110, No. 101

BOSCH

473 Two Pharisees

Pen and ink, 150 x 103 mm.

New York, Robert Lehman

PROVENANCE

Leroy Backus; Randall

LITERATURE

Rosenberg, in *Old Master Drawings*, XIII, 1939, Pl. LX
Baldass, *Jheronimus Bosch*, pp. 64, 69, 85, 246, Fig. 139

THIS SKETCH, on the reverse of the drawing of "St. Anthony," (see No. 477), served Bosch as a preparatory study for a painting which is lost but which is known through a number of replicas. Close study of the drawing makes it likely that two hands are responsible for it. The monster at the bottom right, the other one in the egg at the left, and the scribbles at the top right seem to have been drawn by Hieronymus Bosch; the egg, however, and all the figures probably have been added by another hand.

BOTH FIGURES are "types" that frequently recur in the paintings and in other drawings by Bosch with minor or greater variations. The physiognomy of the figure at the right is, for instance, very close to that of a beggar woman in the triptych of "The Last Judgment" in the Akademie der bildenden-Kuenste in Vienna: such highly expressive physiognomies, whether distorted as the one at the right or closer to nature as the other one, for Bosch generally represented either debased human beings or evil creatures, in this case perhaps Pharisees.

On the reverse of this sheet Bosch quickly jotted down the figures of Adam and Eve, one of the very few sketches for compositions that have come down to us.

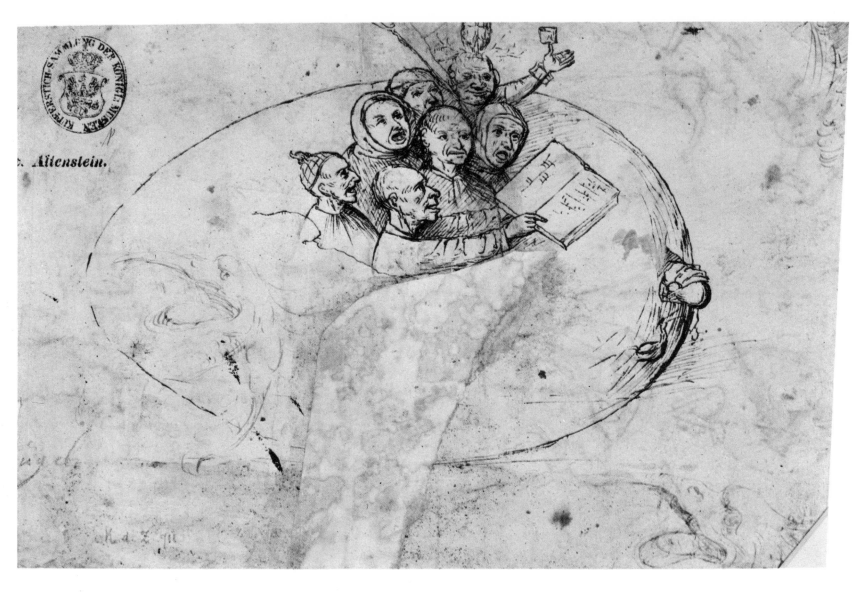

BOSCH

474 Two Witches

Pen and brown ink, 120 x 85 mm.
Inscribed by a later hand: *bosch*
Rotterdam, Museum Boymans-van Beuningen (No. N.190)
PROVENANCE
Vallardi; Rodrigues; Koenigs
LITERATURE
de Tolnay, p. 109, No. 2, Fig. 98
Baldass, pp. 67, 84, Fig. 135

BOSCH

475 The Owls' Nest

Pen and brown ink, 140 x 196 mm.
Rotterdam, Museum Boymans-van Beuningen
    (No. N. 175)
PROVENANCE
Koenigs
LITERATURE
de Tolnay, pp. 49, 111, Fig. 111
Baldass, pp. 77, 84, 88, 255, Fig. 154
Beets, in *Oud Holland*, III, 1935, p. 225, Fig. 48
Benesch, in *Konsthistorisk Tidskrift*, XXVI, 1957,
    pp. 125-126, Fig. 38

BOTH WOMEN are wearing dresses that at least partly resemble those of nuns. The figures are not represented, however, as devout members of one or another religious order. In this drawing, as in others, the activities of the women are a-religious, and their attitudes and expressions give them a witchlike character. This reversal of Christian values into their opposites is one of the main themes of the whole *oeuvre* of Jerome Bosch.

IN A seemingly simple scene, the charm of nature is connected inextricably with the mysteries and vagaries of human life and animal behavior. One owl is seated in a hole in an old tree; a second one approaches him, but the purpose of this remains unclear. Spiders, magpies, and another owl are the other inhabitants of the tree. In the landscape in the distance a cavalcade is passing by a wheel on a stick used as gallows; a cross occupies the foreground at the right. Perhaps the artist wanted to give a symbolic representation of man who hides from light, and of the punishment that follows sin.

The drawing is one of a group of late drawings by the artist in which an understanding of nature and atmosphere is expressed (see the note to No. 476).

BOSCH

476 Tree-Man in a Landscape

Pen and brown ink, 277 x 211 mm.

Inscribed by a later hand: *BRVEGEL*

Vienna, Albertina (Inv. 7876)

LITERATURE

de Tolnay, p. 111, No. 7

Baldass, pp. 64, 71 ff., 86, 247 ff., Fig. 152

Benesch, in *Konsthistorisk Tidskrift*, XXXVI, 1957, pp. 126-127, Fig. 39

THE FANTASTIC creature, half-man, half-tree, is imagined with great logic and represented in a seemingly naturalistic way. In these respects it is a part of the spacious landscape which, however, is truly naturalistic. Furthermore, the landscape is imbued with an idyllic sense of peace and restfulness in which it contrasts markedly with the tree-man.

Many explanations have been suggested for the meaning of this drawing. None, however, is completely satisfactory. Whatever the exact significance of all the details might be, it is most likely that the tree-man is a representation of one or another form of evil. The unity of landscape and tree-man, mentioned above, could perhaps be explained as an expression of the idea that evil is present everywhere.

A similar tree-man was included by Bosch in his representation of Hell, the right wing of the triptych "The Garden of Earthly Delights" in the Prado, Madrid.

In the way of rendering nature, space, and animals this drawing is close to "The Owls' Nest" (No. 475); both must be considered as late drawings by Bosch, executed about 1510-15.

BOSCH

477 St. Anthony

Pen and brown ink, 176 x 257 mm.

Berlin, Ehem. Staatliche Museen, Kupferstichkabinett
  (K.d.Z. 711 recto)

LITERATURE

Berlin Catalogue, p. 1, No. 711 recto

de Tolnay, p. 110, No. 101

THE DRAWING here reproduced is on the same sheet of paper as No. 472, but on the other side of it. The drawing could be considered as a study for a figure of St. Anthony as part of a larger composition representing the temptation of the saint by monstrous creatures. Most of the lines have been drawn twice, first by Hieronymus Bosch and subsequently, when these had faded considerably, by another hand. Extremely interesting and advanced is the landscape with a church and houses at the top of the sheet.

BOSCH

478 The Entombment

Brush and gray ink over black chalk, 250 x 350 mm.

Signed (?) in black chalk: *J HERONIMUS BOSSCHE*

London, British Museum (No. 1952-4-5-9)

PROVENANCE

Pepper Arden Hall

LITERATURE

Popham, in *British Museum Quarterly, XVII, 1952*,
  p. 45, Pl. XVIII

POPHAM WRITES of this drawing, "the theme is treated with a simple piety, and the oddity conspicuous in most of Bosch's religious compositions is absent, except perhaps in the costume of St. Joseph of Arimathea on the extreme right."

In contrast to most drawings by Bosch, which are either hasty sketches or finished drawings done with the pen, this large sheet has been executed with the brush. It is only comparable to such drawings as the "Death of the Miser" in the Louvre, and should be considered as a finished work primarily done for its own purpose.

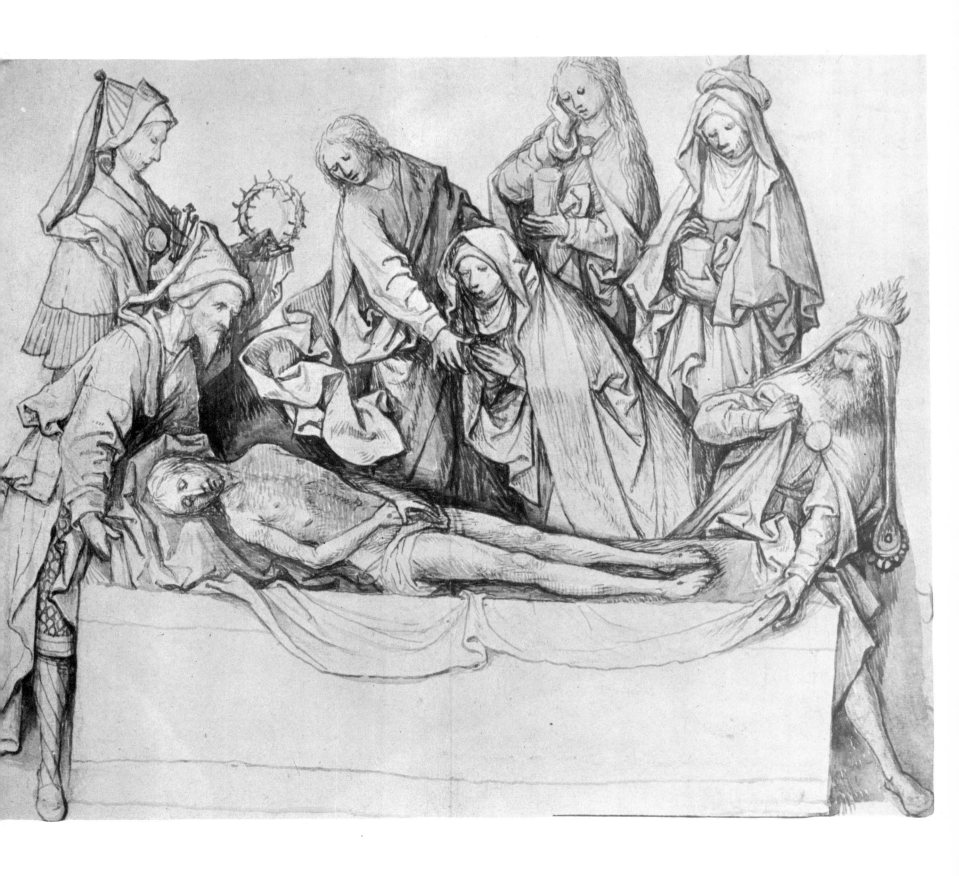

GERARD DAVID

(1450/60-1523)

GERARD DAVID *Born at Ouwater. Settled at Bruges in 1483, where he became member of the guild in 1484. 1515 in Antwerp. Returned to Bruges in 1521, where he died in 1523.*

479 Studies of Four Heads

Silverpoint on ivory prepared paper, 70 x 65 mm.

Ottawa, National Gallery of Canada (No. 6986)

PROVENANCE

Wauters

LITERATURE

Lees, *The Art of the Great Masters*, p. 63 (as Memlinc)

Exhibition of Old Master Drawings, 1956, No. 28

GERARD DAVID

480 Studies of a Young Woman's and of a Man's Head

Silverpoint, 128 x 93 mm.

Frankfort-on-Main, Staedel Art Institute (No. 6926)

PROVENANCE

Klinkosch

LITERATURE

Winkler, in *Pantheon*, IV, 1929, pp. 271 ff.

Friedlaender, in *Gentsche Bijdragen tot de Kunstgeschiedenis*, IV, 1937, pp. 5 ff.

THIS DRAWING originally belonged to a sketch-book from which other leaves are in the Louvre and elsewhere (see note to No. 480). The attribution to Gerard David, suggested by Conway and endorsed by Winkler, has been doubted by Friedlaender when he found that one of the drawings of this sketch-book had to be considered as a study for a portrait by an anonymous pupil of David.

All four heads derive from the group of the Holy Martyrs in van Eyck's Ghent altarpiece. Comparison shows that the artist carefully and exactly copied the heads of van Eyck's painting, which attracted the attention of artists through all ages.

THESE SILVERPOINT studies originally belonged to the same sketch-book as the previous drawing. The drawing shows the author as an accomplished and sensitive draughtsman, who knew how to render the tender formation of the face of the young girl as convincingly as the sterner features of the man sketched on the same sheet.

CORNELIS ENGELBRECHTSEN
(1468-1533)

CORNELIS ENGELBRECHTSEN (ENGELBRECHTSZ.) *Born at Leyden. Worked there, where he was the teacher of Lucas van Leyden. Died 1533.*

481 Heads of Men, Women, and Children

Brush with gray and white color on gray prepared paper
173 x 254 mm.

Amsterdam, Rijksmuseum, Rijksprentenkabinet
(No. 21.474)

PROVENANCE

Rodrigues

LITERATURE

Catalogue Exhibition Bosch, 1936, No. 36, Pl. XXXIV
De Jérôme Bosch à Rembrandt, 1937/8, No. 9, Pl. VI

THIS DRAWING has been presented as the work of Cornelis Engelbrechtsz in several exhibitions (Rotterdam, 1936, No. 36; Brussels, 1937/8, No. 9; Washington, 1958/9, No. 9). The style of draughtsmanship, however, does not correspond altogether with other works attributed to Engelbrechtsz (Vienna). Moreover, these typically early sixteenth-century figures show little relation to his paintings. The drawing can perhaps be explained as a collection of examples derived from older masters and intended for use in the atelier. For example, the man in the middle of the lowest row occurs in a painting by Memling (Friedlaender, No. 35). In the second row on the right, the man wearing a high bonnet might be taken from a fifteenth-century painting. Similarly, the delicate head of the woman in the lower right corner might come from a much earlier composition.

JAN DE BEER

(Ca. 1475 - Ca. 1536)

JAN DE BEER *Worked at Antwerp. Became Dean of the Antwerp guild in 1515. Contemporary of Mabuse.*

482 Aristotle and Phyllis

Pen and brown ink, 274 x 192 mm.

London, British Museum (No. 1929-4-16-1)

PROVENANCE

Lawrence; Donnadieu; Abbott

LITERATURE

Vasari Society, 2d Series, X, 1929, No. 8

Popham, *British Museum Catalogue*, V, p. 5, No. 3

THE LEGEND of the young and pretty woman riding on the back of the sage originated in the Middle Ages in Europe as a transformation of a much older but similar Indian legend. Especially in France and Germany it was often illustrated as one of those stories that proved the danger of the power of women over men, even the most learned and wisest ones.

Jan de Beer, the Antwerp mannerist, depicted the story vividly. Aristotle, bridled and bitted, looks up pathetically while Phyllis rides triumphantly on his back.

LUCAS VAN LEYDEN
(1489/94-1533)

LUCAS HUIGHENZ. VAN LEYDEN *Born at Leyden. Pupil of his father Hugo Jacobsz. van Leyden. Worked with Cornelis Engelbrechtsen, 1521 in Antwerp. Died at Leyden 1533.*

483 Study for David Victorious over Goliath

Black chalk on white paper, 240 x 154 mm.

The paper has been cut out and pasted on a second sheet and is signed ca. 1600: *L.*

On the reverse is written with pen in old script: *A° 1510 was Lucas 15 jaren out en maekte den Ecce Homo*

Amsterdam, Rijksmuseum, Rijksprentenkabinet (No. 24)

LITERATURE

Beets, *Lucas de Leyde*, p. 69

Catalogue Dutch Drawings, 1958/9, No. 13

THE STYLE of drawing corresponds to the one of a standing young man, which is now at Rugby School, Rugby (Warwickshire). A young lad, showing some resemblance to this boy, also occurs on the engraving "Ecco Homo" (1510), by Lucas. But the similarity is superficial and it is unlikely that the drawing was executed in 1510, as is indicated on the verso. This drawing must have been made later, around 1520, as is true of the one at Rugby. It is not impossible that both drawings served as studies for a representation of David as conqueror. The deeds of David occur repeatedly in Lucas' work. The style of draughtsmanship recalls German examples (for example, Dürer). The shadows are indicated with refinement. The expression on the boy's face is penetrating, keen, and full of determination. Arms, hands, and feet are rendered rather carelessly but for that reason our attention remains the more easily concentrated on the face of the youthful victorious David.

LUCAS VAN LEYDEN

484 An Old Man Drawing

Black chalk, 272 x 272 mm.

Signed (?) in ink at right bottom corner: *L*

London, British Museum

PROVENANCE

Barnard

LITERATURE

Colvin, *Jahrbuch der Preussischen Kunstsammlungen*, XIV, 1893, p. 171, No. 6

Popham, *British Museum Catalogue*, p. 30, No. 8

van Gelder, *Dutch Drawings and Prints*, No. 12

THIS IS one of the drawings by Lucas van Leyden originating in an album that was acquired by the British Museum in 1892. The album was bound in black leather with *Lucas Tekeningen 1637* in gold letters stamped on the side. The Dutch collector of 1637 has never been identified.

The old man, wearing spectacles, sits at a table and draws on a piece of paper which he holds with his left hand. He wears a cap and a coat with long sleeves. On the right, behind him, a woman is sketched very lightly. This drawing after life may have served as a study for an evangelist; the same type of man, representing St. Mark, occurs around 1518 in a print by Lucas. The mode of draughtsmanship does not yet show the tightness of the portrait drawings that Lucas made after his meeeting with Dürer in Antwerp (1521). The concentrated attention of the figure is caught vividly, however, and the drawing, for all its simplicity, is one of the earliest examples of what will later be called Dutch Realism.

LUCAS VAN LEYDEN

485 Girl Reading

Black chalk, 304 x 193 mm.
A narrow strip of paper, 12 mm. wide, is added at the top
Signed at upper right: *L*
Vienna, Albertina (Inv. 17550)

LITERATURE
Schoenbrunner-Meder, No. 56
Albertina Catalogue, II, No. 60

THE GIRL is portrayed in half length and is seen *en face*. She is reading a breviary, which is in a so-called bookbag that serves to protect the book when closed. This drawing, like No. 484, must likewise have been meant as a study for a Saint, perhaps St. Barbara. As yet, however, this figure has not been found in the painted *oeuvre* of Lucas van Leyden. It is also possible that the drawing might have served as a model for a glass-painting. As in the following drawing, the ornamental treatment of the pair points to a fairly early stage of Lucas' draughtsmanship. This is also confirmed by the sketchy execution of the hands and the folds of the garment, which are reminiscent of wood sculpture. In spite of some awkwardness, this drawing breathes a highly personal life, because of the tranquility that radiates from it. The sensitivity of this child prodigy, Lucas, not even eighteen years of age when he made this drawing, is here coupled with an unaffected personal vision, which has not yet quite reached the stage of virtuosity.

LUCAS VAN LEYDEN

486 Bust of a Young Man in a Fur Hat

Black chalk, washed with a tint of yellow,
205 x 164 mm.

Signed lower left: *L*

London, British Museum

PROVENANCE

Barnard

LITERATURE

Colvin, *Jahrbuch der Preussischen Kunstsammlungen*, XIV,
1893, p. 168

Popham, *British Museum Catalogue*, p. 28, No. 2

THIS DRAWING of a young man, turned in three-quarter view to the right, has a curiously uneven quality. The cap is indicated quite sketchily; the long locks, however, are curled like Gothic goldsmith's work and ornamentally treated. The eyes, too, are dissimilar, but show, like the rest of the body, the keen perceptiveness with which Lucas observed his models. The scarf and mantle are less true to nature. Various indications lead to an early dating, around 1508. Shortly after this year, Lucas painted scenes of chess players. In these works the spectators are conceived in the same fashion and moreover are chosen from a similar level of society. For the origin of the drawing see No. 484.

LUCAS VAN LEYDEN

487 A Mother Offering the Breast to a Child

Black chalk, 210 x 171 mm.

Signed lower right: *L*

London, British Museum (No. 1892-8-4-15)

PROVENANCE

Barnard

LITERATURE

Colvin, *Jahrbuch der Preussischen Kunstsammlungen*, XIV, 1893, p. 174, No. 9

Popham, *Drawings of the Early Flemish School*, No. 45

Popham, *British Museum Catalogue*, p. 30, No. 10

THIS DRAWING is undoubtedly the study for the "Virgin and Child" by Lucas, dated around 1525 and now in the Museum at Oslo. In the painting the mother stands behind the balustrade on which the child rests both feet. A preliminary sketch is still recognizable on the left and right sides of the drawing. The right arms of both mother and child were left in a more sketchy form than the rest of the drawing. The hands, face, and dress, especially, are provided with touches of shading and contours typical of Lucas' style. For origin see No. 484.

The mannered pose of the mother and the resisting action of the child are characteristic of Lucas and his sense of rhythm. But even at this early date the figures reveal an adaptation of the formal vocabulary of Raphael, which became especially well known in the Netherlands through the prints of Marcantonio Raimondi.

JAN GOSSAERT VAN MABUSE

(Ca. 1478-1533/36)

JAN GOSSAERT VAN MABUSE *Born at Maubeuge. Worked under the influence of Gerard David. Active in Italy 1508-09. Worked at Utrecht, Brussels, and Antwerp, where he died between 1533 and 1536.*

488 The Judgment of Paris

Brush and gray ink, heightened with white, on bluish-gray prepared paper, 235 mm. diameter.

Inscribed by a later hand: *Nicasius van Mabuse* (an architect, who was a brother of Jan Gossaert, and probably owned the drawing)

Edinburgh, National Gallery of Scotland (No. D.652)

LITERATURE

Bacou, in *Gazette des Beaux-Arts*, XCIII, 1951 (1960), p. 96, note 14

WITH JAN GOSSAERT and other artists of the beginning of the sixteenth century there is noticeable an increased interest in scenes from mythology and classical history. Although artists had traveled to Italy in the previous century, subjects of this nature had remained exceptions. "The Judgment of Paris" is one of the scenes depicted frequently about 1530-1550, the time this drawing was executed.

Although the drawing has an old attribution to a member of the Gossaert family, it is unlikely that Jan Gossaert made it. Other drawings by the same excellent hand are known, using the brush for small strokes that resemble pen lines, a technique developed by Albrecht Dürer. The name of the artist and the whereabouts of his activity remain to be established.

MABUSE

489 Portrait of Christian II, King of Denmark

Pen and brown ink of two shades, 267 x 215 mm.

Paris, Frits Lugt

PROVENANCE

Schneider

LITERATURE

Friedlaender, in *Annuaire des Musées royaux des Beaux-Arts de Belgique*, I, 1938, p. 95, Fig. 6

Folie, in *Gazette des Beaux-Arts*, XCIII, 1951 (1960), p. 92, No. 19, Fig. 9

CHRISTIAN II, King of Denmark, Sweden, and Norway (1481-1559), had to flee Denmark in 1523. By then the insurrection, first in Sweden and subsequently in Denmark itself, had become too powerful for him to resist. He went to the Netherlands, which he knew from a previous visit, and stayed with Adolph of Burgundy, patron of Gossaert, in the city of Middelburg.

It was here that Gossaert made this portrait, sketching the face first, probably from nature, and shortly afterward adding in a darker shade of brown the body, the arch with the coats of arms, and the balustrade. Like the true renaissance artist, Gossaert stressed the dignity and stature of man and caught the ambition for power in the face of the monarch.

Gossaert's mannerist ideas caused the arch to be almost obliterated by coats of arms, putti, and ornaments. The drawing was executed with care and precision as a design for an engraving.

MABUSE

490 Adam and Eve

Black chalk, 628 x 477 mm.

Providence, Rhode Island, Rhode Island School of Design,
Museum of Art

PROVENANCE

Albertina, Vienna; Friedrich August; Czeczowicka; Oskar
Bondy; Mrs. Elisabeth Bondy

LITERATURE

Meder, *Die Handzeichnung, Ihre Technik und Entwicklung,*
pp. 390, 533, Fig. 247

Schwarz, in *Gazette des Beaux-Arts,* 1953, pp. 157 ff., Fig. 5

Folie, ibid., p. 92, No. 18

THIS VERY large drawing, probably a "cartoon" for a painting, dates
from about 1523-26 and is characteristic of the mature style of the
artist: a mannerism based on Dürer, Jacopo de' Barbari, and the
antique. Gossaert visited Italy in 1509 and made sketches from the
classical sculptures and Roman ruins for his patron, Adolph of Burgundy, whom he accompanied to Rome.

After his return to the Netherlands the artist gradually developed
his own style, in which the knowledge of classical art was transformed
into a mannerist interpretation of the nude.

Attributed to PIETER BRUEGEL THE ELDER

(1525/30-1569)

PIETER BRUEGEL THE ELDER *Probably born at Breda. Pupil of Pieter Coeck van Aelst at Antwerp. 1551 member of the guild. 1553 in Rome. Worked at Brussels from 1563. Died there 1569.*

491 The Lamentation

Pen and brown ink over stylus preparation, 142 x 186 mm.

Vienna, Albertina (Inv. 7833)

LITERATURE

Albertina Catalogue, II, No. 18 (as copy after Hugo van der Goes)

Winkler, in *Nederlandsch Kunsthistorisch Jaarboek*, IX, 1958, pp. 107-108, Fig. 14

THIS DRAWING is a copy after a painting by Hugo van der Goes, now lost. The composition of this "Lamentation" is known from a large number of paintings. Nowhere, however, is it rendered in a more accomplished or more faithful way. The artist preserved the expression of sorrow and affliction peculiar to Hugo van der Goes in the grief-stricken faces of Joseph of Arimathea and of Nicodemus. He also caught in the face of St. John a bewildered curiosity as we know it in figures by van der Goes. Mainly these feelings must have urged the artist to copy the painting. It is in keeping with Brueghel's personality that he would have made this copy.

PIETER BRUEGEL THE ELDER

492 Studies of Crippled Men and Women

Pen and brown ink, 285 x 208 mm.

Vienna, Albertina (Inv. 7798)

LITERATURE

Albertina Catalogue, II, No. 24 (as Hieronymus Bosch)

Friedlaender, *Die altniederlaendische Malerei*, II, p. 127

ON A print of this drawing published in Antwerp by Hieronymus Cock, Hieronymus Bosch is mentioned as the artist who "invented" these dreadfully deformed people. Undoubtedly this is right. Bosch, however, did not draw this sheet himself.

It was Pieter Bruegel who copied the figures after Bosch, thus paying tribute to the artist he admired greatly.

Crippled and deformed people were not taken care of in hospitals or institutions. On the contrary, they were often regarded as the embodiment of God's punishment of sin and had to wander along the streets hoping they would receive a penny from those who had a feeling of mercy. Most of the crippled figures of this drawing are consequently depicted as beggars or street musicians.

Bruegel often represented beggars and crippled people such as those in this drawing, for example in his "Fight Between Carnival and Lent."

PIETER BRUEGEL THE ELDER

493 The Painter and the Connoisseur

Pen and bistre, 255 x 215 mm.

Vienna, Albertina (Inv. 7500)

LITERATURE

Romdahl, in *Jahrbuch der kunsthistorischen Sammlungen des Allerhoechsten Kaisarhauses*, XXV, 1905, p. 148, Pl. XXIV

Albertina Catalogue, II, No. 84

de Tolnay, *Die Zeichnungen Pieter Bruegels*, No. 118, Pl. LXXIII

Stridbeck, *Bruegel Studien*, pp. 15-42

ON THE basis of Stridbeck's recent investigations, it is likely that we have to interpret this fascinating drawing in the light of contemporary art theory as a didactic allegory, representing the art of painting in its relation to those who give commissions or buy paintings.

The unkempt hair of the artist points to his indifference to his appearance; the closed mouth indicates silent retirement as being favorable to intellectual activity and to his "speaking" with the brush instead of with his voice. The "connoisseur" holds his hand in his purse and looks over the artist's shoulder. In spite of his glasses—in the sixteenth century they expressed "short-sightedness" rather than wisdom—the "connoisseur" does not seem to see art, nor to understand it.

In the figure of the "connoisseur" Bruegel undoubtedly meant to express a certain amount of criticism of the contemporary art buyer. In other respects, however, the drawing is less of a personal confession of the artist's attitude toward the world and of the world's attitude toward the artist than has been supposed. The painter has also been considered as a self-portrait or as a portrait of Jerome Bosch. The reason for these assumptions is that Bruegel, even when thinking of the painter in general terms, gave him individual traits.

PIETER BRUEGEL THE ELDER

494 Ripa Grande, Rome

Pen and brown ink of two shades, 208 x 282 mm.
Inscribed *arypa,* and by a later hand, *bruegel*
Chatsworth, Devonshire Collections (No. 841)

LITERATURE
Egger, *Roemische Veduten,* I, Pl. LXX
Friedlaender, *Pieter Bruegel,* p. 41, Pl. XXIII
de Tolnay, No. 4, Pl. II
Michel, *Bruegel,* p. 91, Pl. LXIV
Ebbinge-Wubben, *de Van Dyck à Bruegel,* No. 9, Pl. VI

BRUEGEL MADE a journey to Italy in 1552 and the following year, and came as far south as the Strait of Messina. In Rome he sketched this view of the "Ripa Grande" in 1553. This was the harbor of the city, and was done from a point on the opposite bank of the Tiber. The building at the right with a long row of steps is the Dogana (custom house); the tower seen in the center behind the buildings is the Campanile of Leo IV.

This drawing is one of the earliest by Bruegel that have come down to us and is one of the very few landscape drawings that the artist did from nature. Here Bruegel rendered the main buildings faithfully, observing their location and size. The view at the right, however, differs from reality and is executed with ink of a darker brown color than the rest of the drawing. Apparently Bruegel sketched the buildings and the ships from nature and completed the drawing later.

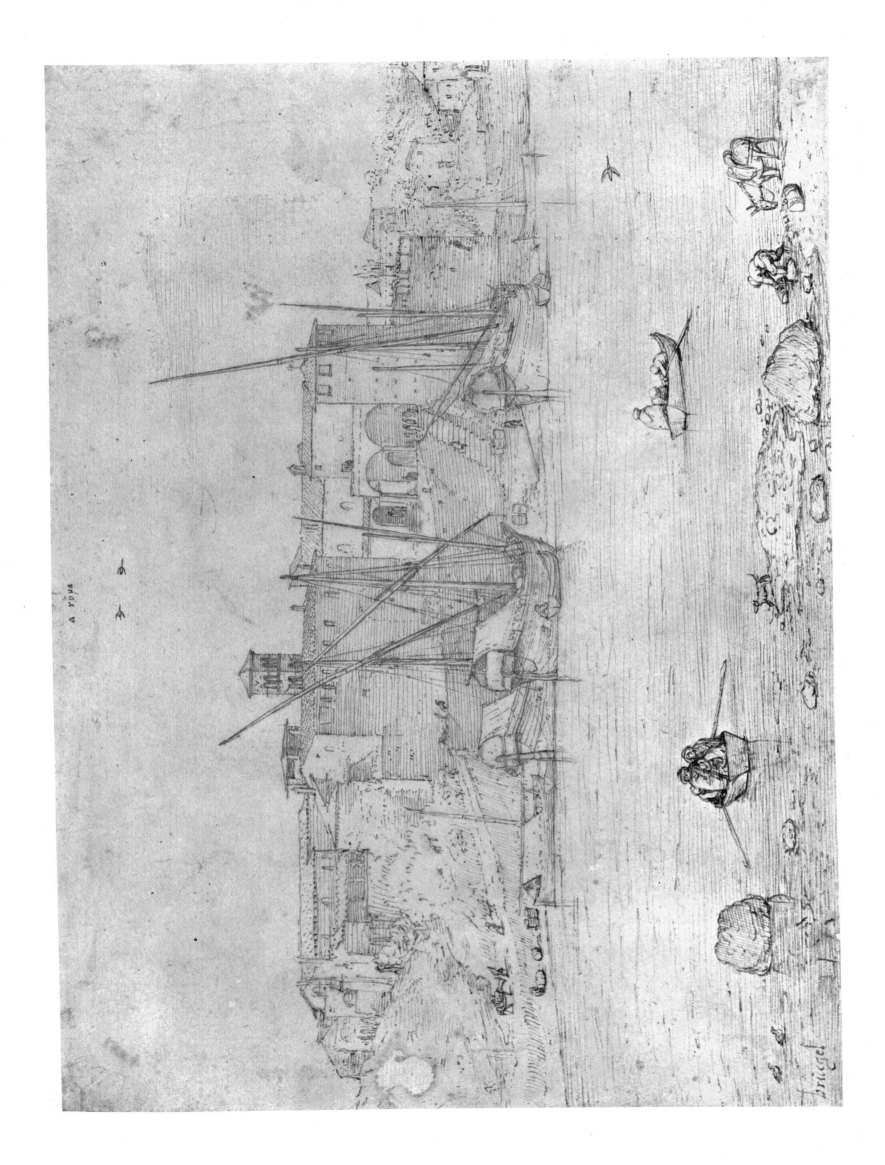

PIETER BRUEGEL THE ELDER

495 Landscape with Monastery at the Foot of a Mountain

Pen and brown ink, brush and water color, 186 x 328 mm.

Signed and dated: *brueghel 1552*

Berlin, Ehem. Staatliche Museen, Kupferstichkabinett (K.d.Z. 5537)

LITERATURE

van Bastelaer and Hulin de Loo, *Peter Bruegel l'Ancien, son oeuvre et son temps*, No. 2

Berlin Catalogue, No. 5537, Pl. XVIII

de Tolnay, No. 2, Pl. I

PIETER BRUEGEL executed this drawing on his trip through Italy. The Monastery itself and the mountain behind were probably drawn from nature, although it has not been possible to identify it. Subsequently, Bruegel added the foreground with ink of a slightly different color. The trees in the foreground are arranged in such a way that they form a slightly curved frame that closes the composition and stresses the distance of the background.

In this drawing, one of the early landscape drawings by Bruegel, the way of sketching the trees in the foreground with loose loops for foliage and quickly drawn parallel lines for the ground points to the influence of Matthijs Cock. In contrast to the heavier foreground, the mountains are indicated with light touches and dots for trees and foliage, a procedure enhancing the impression of distance.

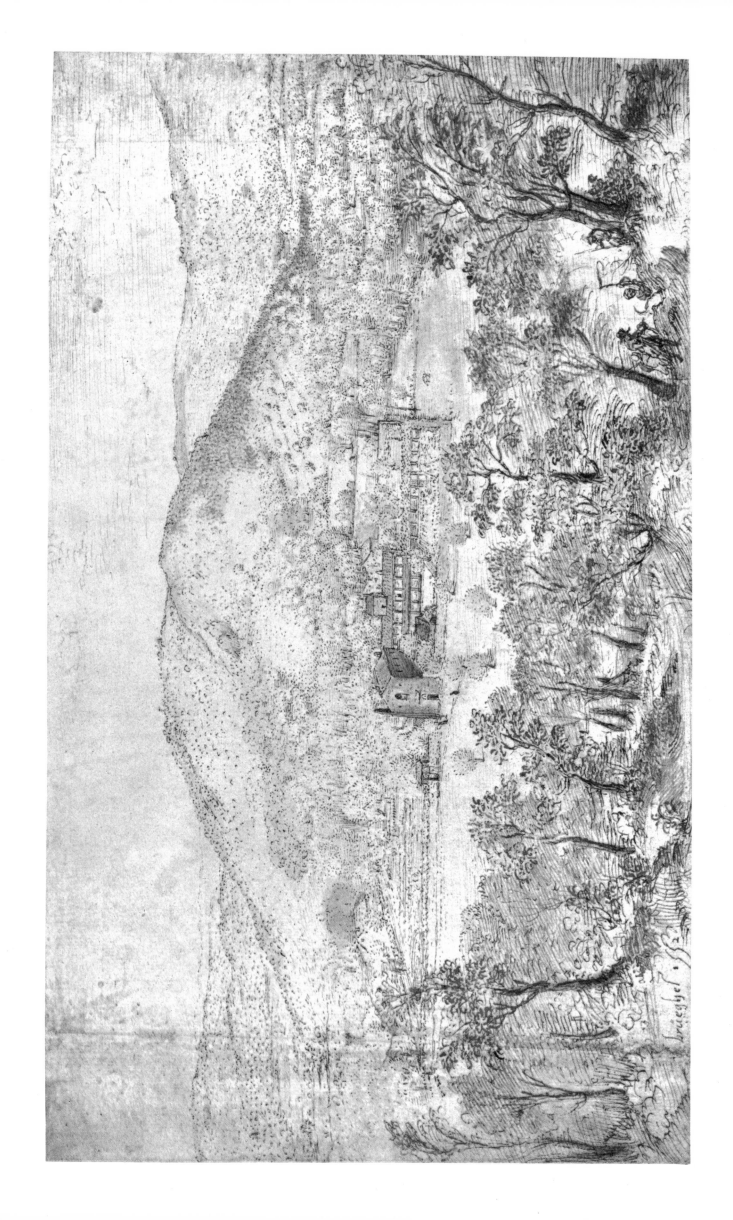

PIETER BRUEGEL THE ELDER

496 Landscape with Rest on the Flight into Egypt

Pen and brown ink of two shades, 203 x 282 mm.

Signed: *bruegel F.*

Berlin, Ehem. Staatliche Museen, Kupferstichkabinett
(K.d.Z. 5730)

LITERATURE

van Bastelaer and Hulin de Loo, No. 22

Berlin Catalogue, p. 18, No. 5730, Pl. XVI

de Tolnay, No. 6, Pl. III

As IN the view of the "Ripa Grande" in Rome, Bruegel probably first sketched the monastery in the middle distance, perhaps from nature, and subsequently added the surroundings and the foreground with the motif of the Virgin resting with her Child, while Joseph is enjoying the distant view.

The drawing probably originated about the same time as the "Ripa Grande" (see No. 494).

PIETER BRUEGEL THE ELDER

497 Alpine Landscape

Pen and brown ink, 322 x 267 mm.

Inscribed by a later hand: *156 Waltersspurg*

Brunswick, Maine, Bowdoin College, Walker Art Museum
(No. 1811.142)

LITERATURE

Mather, in *Art in America,* II, 1914, p. 108, Fig. I

de Tolnay, No. 16, Pl. IX

Benesch, in *Kunstchronik,* VI, 1953, pp. 76 ff.

Grossmann, in *Bulletin Museum Boymans Rotterdam,* V,
1954, p. 76

WHEN BRUEGEL returned from Italy to the Netherlands he went through the Alps. He was profoundly impressed by them and sketched views, some of which have come down to us. After his return he continued drawing Alpine motifs, partly from memory, partly using the sketches he had made *in situ.*

Bruegel created a new type of landscape by conveying the grandeur of nature, by representing the ponderous masses of mountains, the limpid air, and even by suggesting the silence reigning in the enclosed valleys.

The inscription *Waltersspurg* probably refers to Waltensburg on the Rhine in the Swiss canton of Graubuenden. Whether the drawing is a faithful rendering of the site or a variation of it remains to be established. The completeness and high degree of finish, however, are in favor of the latter supposition.

PIETER BRUEGEL THE ELDER

498 Alpine Landscape

Pen and brown ink, 305 x 456 mm.

Cambridge, Massachusetts, Harvard University, Fogg Art
    Museum (No. 1932.369), Bequest of Charles A. Loeser

PROVENANCE

Loeser

LITERATURE

de Tolnay, in *Jahrbuch der Preussischen Kunstsammlungen*,
    1929, p. 199 ff.

Mongan-Sachs, *Fogg Catalogue*, No. 459, Fig. 234

de Tolnay, No. 17, Pl. X

SEE THE note to No. 495. Probably this drawing, like the majority of
the Alpine landscapes, was executed some time after Bruegel's return from Italy (according to de Tolnay about 1554-55) and from
memory. It is completely in keeping with the art theories of the time
that the artist valued the freely imagined "recreations" of nature
higher than mere renderings of existing sites.

PIETER BRUEGEL THE ELDER

499 Alpine Landscape with a River, Village, and Castle

Pen and brown ink, and brown wash, 357 x 444 mm.

New York, The Pierpont Morgan Library

PROVENANCE

Rev. Thomas Carwardine (ca. 1734-1824) and descendents, including Colonel Oliver Probert

LITERATURE

Stampfle, *Landscape Drawings and Water Colors: Bruegel to Cézanne*, 1953, Pl. I

Benesch, in *Kunstchronik*, VI, 1953, pp. 76 ff.

Grossmann, in *Bulletin Museum Boymans Rotterdam*, V, 1954, pp. 76, 84, Fig. 8

IN THIS largest of all Bruegel's drawings, and certainly the most impressive of his Alpine landscapes, the artist combined all the motifs found in his other mountain views: huge rocky mountains, trees, a river with some boats, a castle, and houses. We look only in vain for human beings, except the tiny figures on the boats. This absence of human life, the smallness of the village and even of the castle, both seemingly deserted, add, however, to the feeling of grandeur conveyed by the towering masses of earth and rocks, sparsely covered with trees.

Professor Otto Benesch identified the castle with the castle of Joergensberg, situated on the river Rhine to the east of Waltensburg (see note to No. 497), and the village with the village of Ruis; the large mountain opposite would be the Piz Mundaun. The size and finish of the drawing are in favor of the assumption that Pieter Bruegel created a seemingly naturalistic landscape, basing it on impressions he received during his journey through the Alps (see note to No. 498).

PIETER BRUEGEL THE ELDER

500 Spes (Hope)

Pen and brown ink, 224 x 285 mm.

Signed and dated: *BRVEGEL 1559*

Berlin, Ehem. Staatliche Museen, Kupferstichkabinett
 (K.d.Z. 715)

LITERATURE

van Bastelaer and Hulin de Loo, No. 94

Berlin Catalogue, p. 18, No. 715

de Tolnay, No. 60, Pl. XXXVII

Stridbeck, pp. 143-148

THIS DRAWING is a design for an engraving, to be one of a series of seven "Virtues," published by Hieronymus Cock in 1559. The figure, crowned with a beehive and holding a shovel and sickle, traditional symbols of Hope, stands on an anchor floating on the water. The figure is surrounded by illustrations of various kinds of human hopes: those of people who are trying to extinguish a fire, to escape a whale, to be rescued from drowning, or of those who are tilling the soil (in the background). Some of these human hopes, however, are in vain; they illustrate the human folly in a foolish world, a theme constantly recurring in Bruegel's *oeuvre*.

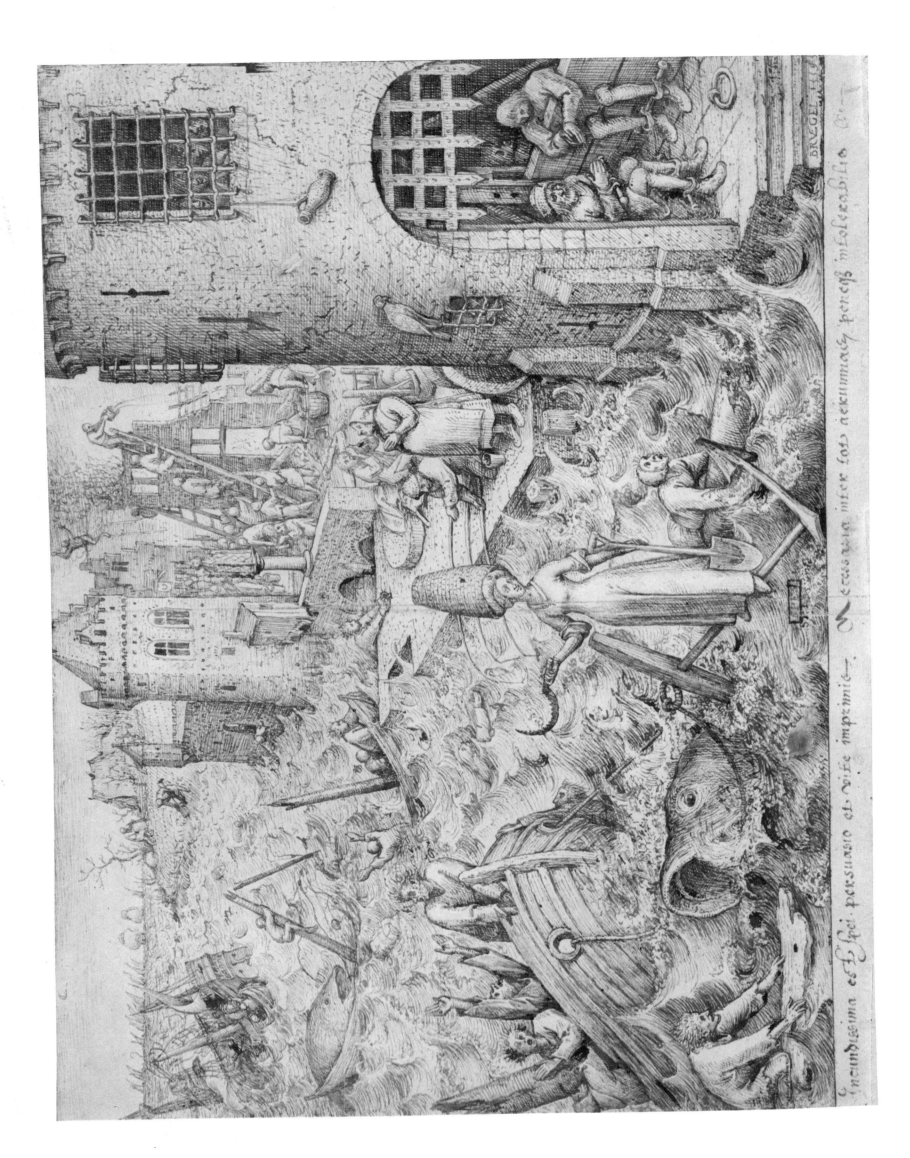

BRVEGEL

Incundissima est spei persuasio et vitae imprimis

Necessaria inter tot pene intolerabilis

PIETER BRUEGEL THE ELDER

501 The Temptation of St. Anthony

Pen and India ink on brownish (discolored) paper,
   216 x 326 mm.

Inscribed by a later hand: *brueghel 1556*

Oxford, Ashmolean Museum

PROVENANCE
Douce

LITERATURE
van Bastelaer and Hulin de Loo, p. 158
Ashmolean Catalogue, I, No. 30
de Tolnay, No. 46, Pl. XXV

ST. ANTHONY is kneeling at the right, seemingly unaware of the numerous devilish creatures in his immediate surroundings. These creatures, acting in a fantastic world, are in their activities as well as their shapes closer to similar figures that populate some paintings by Jerome Bosch than to any of Bruegel's other compositions. Therefore, this drawing perhaps reflects a composition of the earlier artist who often represented St. Anthony and his temptations.

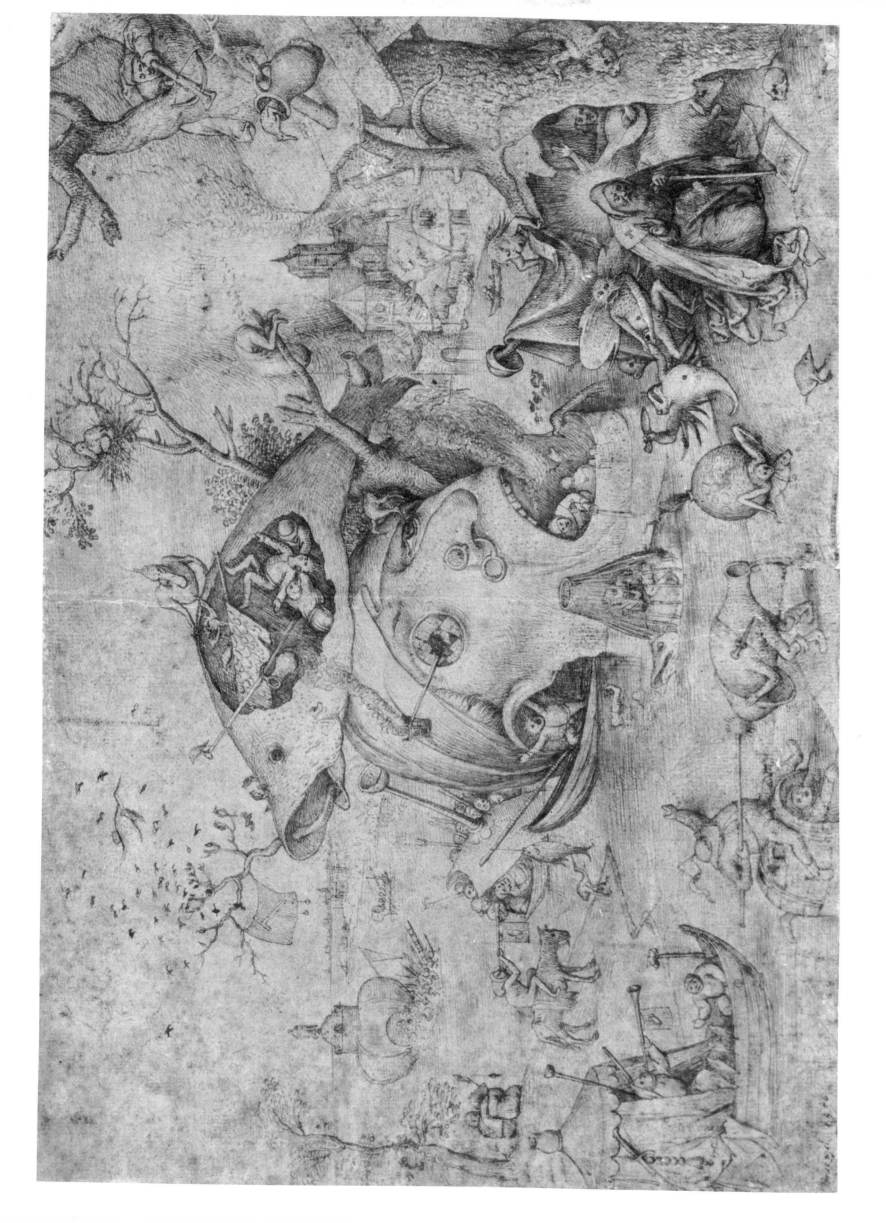

PIETER BRUEGEL THE ELDER

502 Rider and Two Horses

Pen and bistre over black chalk, 164 x 184 mm.

Color notes such as: *swart pert* (black horse), *rot pert* (red horse), *bruinockker* (brown-ochre colored), *licht bruinockker* (light brown-ochre colored); in addition: *nart leuen* (from life)

Vienna, Albertina (Inv. 7862)

LITERATURE

Schoenbrunner-Meder, No. 1029

Albertina Catalogue, II, No. 81

de Tolnay, No. 93, Pl. LIX

THIS, ALONG with a few other drawings of animals, shows how Bruegel was a master in characterizing animals as well as human beings. Here, the fact that a red and a black horse were together pulling a cart may have decided Bruegel's choice of sketching this couple instead of another one. The stance and carriage of the front horse and the seat of the rider are observed and rendered with equal mastery. This drawing was executed, according to de Tolnay, about 1559-63. See also the note to No. 504.

PIETER BRUEGEL THE ELDER

503 Peasant Seated, Holding a Basket

Pen and bistre over charcoal, 158 x 153 mm.

Color notes such as: *swardtte hoedt* (black hat), *grisse roock*
(gray jacket); in addition: *nar hedt leuen* (from life)

Vienna, Albertina (Inv. 7866)

LITERATURE

van Bastelaer and Hulin de Loo, No. 58

Albertina Catalogue, II, No. 82

de Tolnay, No. 108, Pl. LXVII

PIETER BRUEGEL THE ELDER

504 Crippled Beggar

Pen and brown ink over black chalk, 102 x 94 mm.

Color notes such as: *grisse rock* (gray coat), *witte kousen*
(white stockings)

Amsterdam, Rijksmuseum, Rijksprentenkabinet
(No. A. 1448)

LITERATURE

van Bastelaer and Hulin de Loo, No. 52

de Tolnay, No. 100, Pl. LXIII

EXECUTED, ACCORDING to de Tolnay, about 1566-67. See the note
to No. 504.

OVER FIFTY sketches of peasants by Pieter Bruegel have come down
to us. More than any other artist before him, and surpassed only by
Rembrandt, Bruegel sketched the socially low-ranking people from
life. In all these drawings the artist recorded the essential characteristics of the peasant of his time as he saw them. Bruegel did not wor-
ship the peasants as later generations would, nor did he criticize or
even pity them. He saw them as human beings, dressed in poor although often colorful clothes, living in their narrow world of daily
cares and sorrows, deprived of the benefits of culture, religion, or
physical care.

Bruegel stressed the fact that he sketched these peasants from
life by stating this on almost all the drawings, realizing the novelty
of this approach and being aware of the difference between a study
from life and a freely invented sketch. This difference was of great
importance for the sixteenth-century artist as well as the theoretician.
The creativity of the invention was estimated higher than the skill of
the "recorder." This is probably the reason that of the hundreds of
peasants in Bruegel's paintings, only two or three are based upon
drawings from life; all the others, although resembling the peasants
of the "naer het leven" drawings in character and general appearance,
owed their existence to Bruegel's creative mind and hand.

Bruegel sketched the peasants first with black chalk, occasionally
red chalk (see No. 505), and added notes about the colors of their
garments: then he finished the drawing, including the color notes
with the pen and brown ink.

This crippled beggar was drawn, according to de Tolnay, about
1564-66.

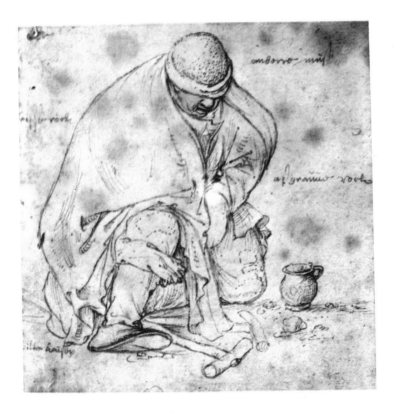

PIETER BRUEGEL THE ELDER

505 Three Peasants

Red chalk, pen and brown ink, 154 x 200 mm.

Color notes such as *wijtte grijse muts, ombere kousen, gelle broeck* (white-gray cap, umber-colored stockings, yellow pants)

Rotterdam, Museum Boymans-van Beuningen (No. P. Bruegel de Oude, 7)

PROVENANCE

F. J. O. Boymans

LITERATURE

de Tolnay, No. 105

OCCASIONALLY, BRUEGEL used red instead of black chalk in drawing peasants from life. The color of the chalk enhances the impression of immediacy and liveliness of this "naer het leven" study (see note to No. 504).

Executed, according to de Tolnay, about 1564-66.

PIETER BRUEGEL THE ELDER

506 Peasant Woman Seated

Pen and brown ink over black chalk, 138 x 99 mm.

Color notes such as: *grisse mus* (gray cap), *swardtte lerssen* (black boots), *ville witte lappen* (dirty white rags)

Berlin, Ehem. Staatliche Museen, Kupferstichkabinett (K.d.Z. 4948)

LITERATURE

Friedlaender, *Pieter Brueghel*, p. 18

Berlin Catalogue, p. 19, No. 4948, Pl. XVII

de Tolnay, No. 109, Pl. LXVIII

PIETER BRUEGEL THE ELDER

507 Studies of Three Peasants

Pen and brown ink over black chalk, 157 x 200 mm.

Color notes such as: *donckker groenne mus, witte veer* (dark green cap, white feather), *donckker purper broeck* (dark purple pants), *gelle lerre broeck* (yellow leather pants), *donckker omberre rock en met groen van binnen* (dark umber-colored jacket, green inside); in addition: *nart het leuen* (from life)

Berlin, Ehem. Staatliche Museen, Kupferstichkabinett (K.d.Z. 5539)

LITERATURE

van Bastelaer and de Loo, No. 74

Berlin Catalogue, p. 19, No. 5539

de Tolnay, No. 110, Pl. LXVIII

BRUEGEL'S COLOR notes enable us to imagine the woman's appearance: her skirt was ochre-brown, a green collar on top of it; over a black skirt she wore a brown apron. Her cap was gray, her boots were black.

Executed, according to de Tolnay, about 1566-67. See the note to No. 504.

BRUEGEL FIRST sketched the standing peasant in the center of the sheet, then he added the more elegantly dressed man at the left, then the peasant at the right, seated at a table.

See also the note to No. 504. Executed, according to de Tolnay, about 1566-67.

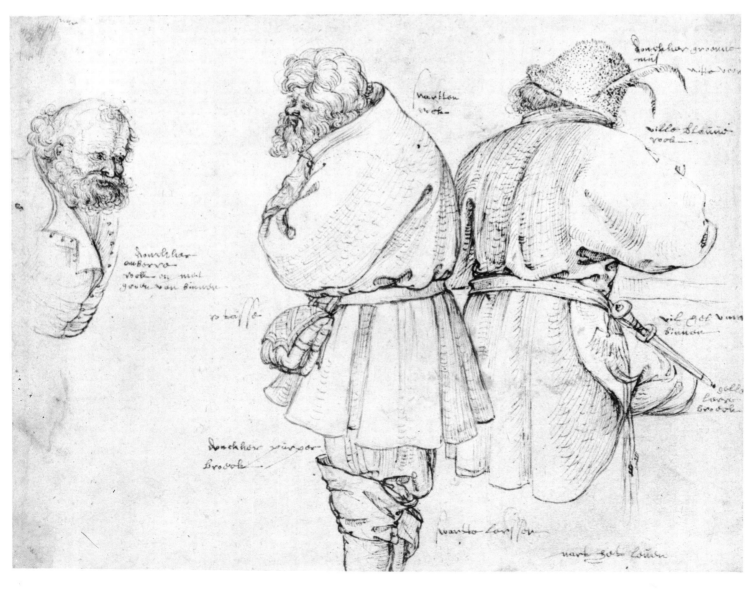

PIETER BRUEGEL THE ELDER

508 The Horse-Dealer

Pen and brown ink over black chalk, 195 x 146 mm.

Color notes such as: *swardtte mus* (black cap), *as grauwe rock* (ash-gray jacket), *groene bant* (green belt); in addition: *nar hedt leuen* (from life)

Frankfort-on-Main, Staedel Art Institute (No. 764)

LITERATURE

van Bastelaer and Hulin de Loo, No. 49

de Tolnay, No. 113, Pl. LXX

Bruegel characterized this figure as a shrewd man, sure of himself and pitiless when his purse is at stake. His well-rounded countenance points to his success. It is therefore no wonder that tradition sees in him a horse-dealer; he might well have been one.

At the left Bruegel sketched the head and shoulders of another man.

Executed, according to de Tolnay, about 1566-67. See also the note to No. 504.

PIETER BRUEGEL THE ELDER

509 **Two Seated Peasant Women**
Seen from the Back

Pen and brown ink over black chalk, 154 x 184 mm.

Color notes such as: *rosse mus* (rose-colored cap), *witte doeck* (white scarf), *ville lichtte ombere rock* (dirty light umber-colored jacket), *suart / groen / rot / blou* (black, green, red, blue), *suartte lerssen* (black boots); in addition: *nart het leuen* (from life)

Dresden, Staatliche Kunstsammlungen

LITERATURE

van Bastelaer and Hulin de Loo, No. 40

de Tolnay, No. 115, Pl. LXXI

Woermann, No. 124

EXECUTED, ACCORDING to de Tolnay, about 1568-69. See the note to No. 504.

PIETER BRUEGEL THE ELDER

510 Two Rabbis

Pen and brown ink over black chalk, 194 x 152 mm.

Color notes such as: *gris bondt* (gray fur), *witte doeck* (white scarf), *rode strepen* (red stripes), *purper...re rock* (purple dress); in addition: *nar hedt leuen* (from life)

Frankfort-on-Main, Staedel Art Institute (No. 765)

LITERATURE

Handzeichnungen alter Meister in Frankfurt-am-Main, I, No. 7

de Tolnay, No. 114, Pl. LXX

THIS IS ONE of the very few Bruegel drawings from nature in which two figures form a scene instead of being merely juxtaposed, and in which an element of activity is introduced.

Curiously enough, this activity, namely reading and bringing a book, only stresses the remoteness from life of these two figures. In an apparently cold interior, wrapped in their clothes and covered by fur hats, they are oblivious of everything else in the world except reading.

Executed, according to de Tolnay, about 1568-69. See also the note to No. 504.

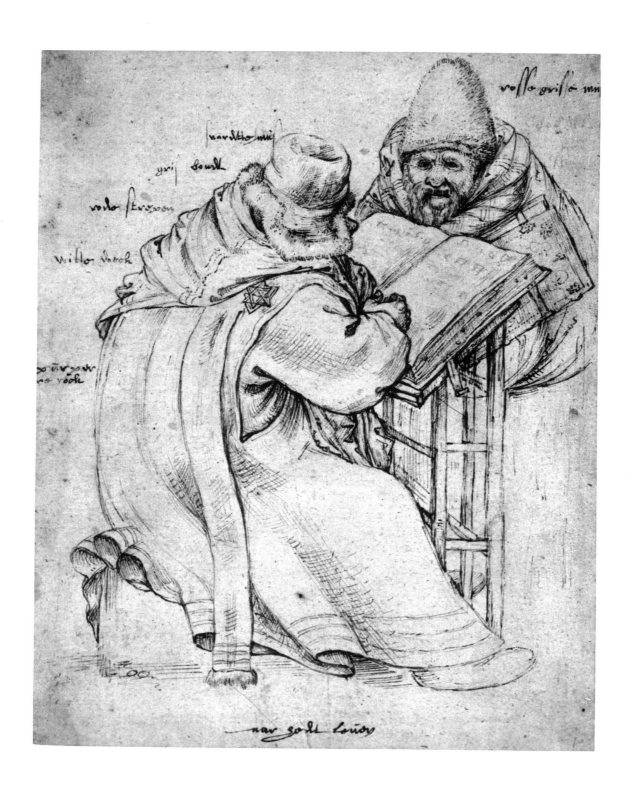

JAN BRUEGHEL THE ELDER
(1568-1625)

JAN BRUEGHEL THE ELDER *Born at Brussels. Son of Pieter Bruegel the Elder. Studied with Goetkint in Antwerp. Worked with Rubens and Hendrik van Balen. Died at Antwerp, 12 January 1625.*

511 Stormy Sea

Pen and brush with brown and blue ink, 195 x 232 mm.

Inscribed by the artist: *Brueghel fecit primo decembri 1614*

Berlin, Ehem. Staatliche Museen, Kupferstichkabinett (K.d.Z. 724)

LITERATURE

Berlin Catalogue, No. 724

Winkler, *Flaemische Zeichnungen*, p. 36, Fig. 19

THE STORMY weather at the shore, the strong wind tossing the small sailboats around, the moving water, and the people struggling against the wind have been rendered with a "plein air" feeling unusual for the time. Even within the *oeuvre* of Jan Brueghel, this drawing has no parallel. With simple means, a few pen lines and blue washes, the artist has suggested the cold and stormy atmosphere.

The fact that the artist himself indicated the year and date accurately, partly in Latin, partly in Italian, probably makes one believe that he, too, looked upon it as an exceptional drawing.

HENDRICK GOLTZIUS

(1558-1616)

HENDRICK GOLTZIUS *Painter and engraver. 1590-91 in Italy. Before 1600 exclusively an engraver. Died at Haarlem 1 January 1616.*

512 Portrait of a Man

Silverpoint, 171 x 133 mm.

Inscribed on top: *Anno 1591. AETAT SUAE 47*

Signed left: *H. Goltzius fecit*

Berlin, Ehem. Staatliche Museen, Kupferstichkabinett (K.d.Z. 5863)

PROVENANCE

von Beckerath

LITERATURE

Berlin Catalogue, p. 32, No. 5863, Pl. XXV

Reznicek, *Hendrick Goltzius Zeichnungen*, p. 378, No. 303, Fig. 204

HENDRICK GOLTZIUS was originally an engraver. He made a number of small, striking drawings of contemporaries executed in silverpoint and intended as preparatory studies for prints. In 1590, Goltzius left for Italy, returning to Haarlem in the fall of 1591. This drawing in large format was probably executed in Germany during his return trip. The subject represented here has a keen, intelligent face. He leans with his right arm on a table; the slightly opened mouth is visible under his drooping moustache.

In Italy, Goltzius made the acquaintance of portraitists such as Zuccaro and Giovanni Bologna. In technical facility and the ability to draw in all techniques he surpasses all his contemporaries. In spite of the strictly graphic manner of drawing, which evinces a relationship to the art of Dürer, the figure has been rendered in a vivid and pictorial fashion. It is clear that the portrait painting of Frans Hals of Haarlem must have found its origins here.

GOLTZIUS

513 Group of Trees in a Wood

Pen and brown ink with touches of color on blue-tinted
   paper, 284 x 200 mm.

Signed: *HG*

Hamburg, Kunsthalle (No. 21977)

PROVENANCE

Harzen

LITERATURE

Reznicek, No. 397, Fig. 347

THIS IS one of the earliest pure studies of trees or woodland scenes in Dutch art; it was executed around 1600.

Hendrick Goltzius, who must have become acquainted with the drawings and studies of landscapes of such artists as Barocci in Italy, where he resided in 1591 and 1592, achieved startling results with his chiaroscuro woodcuts in three colors; he has also produced a striking effect here with shades of blue, green, and yellow. The structure of beeches, branches, and leaves is indicated by thin pen- and brush-lines. The pictorial vision already proclaims Goltzius the painter. In 1600 his first painting was completed. Before that time he had been exclusively an engraver. His mode of drawing gained no following in the Netherlands, except that in the colored etchings of Hercules Seghers one finds related effects, which however appear less realistic than in Goltzius' case. A companion piece to this tree study is in the collection of Frits Lugt in Paris.

JACQUES DE GHEYN

(1565-1629)

JACQUES DE GHEYN *Born at Antwerp. Pupil of Goltzius. Trained also as an engraver. Died at The Hague 1629.*

514 Pietà

Pen and brown ink, 250 x 194 mm.

Signed: *JDGijn*

Amsterdam, Rijksmuseum, Rijksprentenkabinet (No. 05. 181)

LITERATURE

van Regteren Altena, *The Drawings of Jacques de Gheyn*, p. 68

THIS IS one of the most stirring and emotional drawings we know from the hand of Jacques de Gheyn, a pupil of Goltzius. This manner of drawing is uncommon in Holland in the sixteenth century, but in Italy, especially in Venice (Veronese, Palma Giovane), it is not unusual. Since Goltzius was in Venice in 1590-91 and even made a portrait of Palma Giovane, it is quite possible that de Gheyn learned this mode of drawing from him. Perhaps de Gheyn's representation is even based on an Italian composition. In any case, the strong verticalism and the parallel repetitions of Christ's attenuated body in the figures of Mary and John on the right are noteworthy. The enclosure of the scene at the left by the trunk of the cross gives this vertical element another emphatic accent. If our assumption is correct, this drawing could have been executed between 1591 and 1595.

GHEYN

515 Woman on Her Death-Bed

Pen and brown ink, 146 x 194 mm.

Amsterdam, Rijksmuseum, Rijksprentenkabinet
  (No. A3962)

PROVENANCE
Franken

LITERATURE
van Regteren Altena, p. 52

WITH NERVOUS yet precise lines, with equal attention for the rendering of blankets, costumes, hands, and the still face, the artist portrayed the dead with an accuracy that creates the impression of loving care rather than detachment. The drawing is indeed a study for a miniature on parchment, now in the British Museum in London, where a man standing near the bed and pointing to the woman probably is a self-portrait of the artist. In that case the woman was a relative of his, either his mother or his mother-in-law, Eva Stalpaert van der Wielen, as Professor van Regteren Altena suggests. The drawing certainly dates from 1601, the year Jacques de Gheyn painted the miniature.

GHEYN

516 The Birdcatcher

Pen and brown ink on gray paper, 165 x 130 mm.

Rotterdam, Museum Boymans-van Beuningen (No. H. 7)

PROVENANCE

Argoutinsky; Koenigs

LITERATURE

van Regteren Altena, p. 50

GHEYN

517 Four Heads of a Horse

Pen and brown ink, black chalk, 250 x 215 mm.

Berlin, Ehem. Staatliche Museen, Kupferstichkabinett
(K.d.Z. 2275)

LITERATURE

Berlin Catalogue, p. 31, No. 2275

THIS BOY with his trap was drawn by de Gheyn several times. Shortly after 1600 we begin to find more of de Gheyn's studies "after life," especially those of fishermen and intimate domestic scenes. These are the beginning of the so-called genre subjects that became popular in the seventeenth century. Daily life is discovered and the artists liberate themselves from the stereotyped world of religious and mythological representations. De Gheyn, together with Goltzius and Savery, were among the first to have an eye for landscape, animals, flowers, and plants, and especially for the events of man's daily existence.

DE GHEYN made a great number of studies of horses, lying down, grazing, trotting, etc. He also drew and engraved battles with cavalry regiments. In 1603 he even made a life-sized painting of the renowned stallion won by Lodewijk van Nassau from the Archduke and presented to Prince Maurice in 1600 (Amsterdam, Rijksmuseum).

Goltzius trained de Gheyn as an engraver. The swelling and diminishing engraver's lines and the technique of cross-hatching give this drawing a typically graphic character. Dots and diminutive lines suggest shadows and the gloss of the horse's hide. Particularly remarkable in this study is the utter gracefulness of the composition, which is typical of de Gheyn's work. The heads are distributed over the page in such a way that an elegant equilibrium is set up between the blank and filled areas of this almost square piece of paper. Thus this drawing, which was begun as a sketch from life, acquires an artistic unity. Moreover, the tender expression of the animal's eyes fills the drawing with a gentle melancholy.

ROELANDT SAVERY

(1576-1639)

ROELANDT SAVERY *Born Courtai. Studied with Jacob and Hans Bol. Worked in Prague and the Tyrol 1606-07. In Utrecht from 1619, where he died on 25 February 1639.*

518 A Young Monkey

Black, red, and yellow chalk and brush, 406 x 300 mm.

Signed: *R. Savry*

Amsterdam, Rijksmuseum, Rijksprentenkabinet

PROVENANCE

de Vos, Jr.

LITERATURE

Mols, *Oude teekeningen...in Amsterdam*, No. 71

van der Kellen, *Honderd teekeningen...in the Rijksprentenkabinet*, No 12

van Regteren Altena, in *Openbaar Kunstbezit*, II, 1958, No. 4

EARLY IN the seventeenth century, a number of draughtsmen in the Netherlands made animal drawings that adhered closely to nature. Among them were Goltzius (mainly dogs), de Gheyn (horses, mice, and insects) and Savery. The latter made studies of animals ranging in size from the smallest to enormous elephants. These include virtually all the animals with which he populated his representations of Paradise. He especially loved drawing deer, cranes, and camels. Monkeys occur less frequently.

In this example, now in the Print Room in Amsterdam, he surpasses all his contemporaries by the warm humaneness with which he has caught the melancholy features of this chained animal.

The monkey has no tail and is probably a specimen of the *macaca silvana*, which lives on the rock of Gibraltar. When and where the artist saw this monkey is difficult to say. Originally from Courtrai, Savery established himself at an early age in Haarlem. Thereafter he went to Prague (1604) to the Court of Emperor Rudolph II, who attracted many foreign artists. In 1612 he was in Amsterdam and in 1614 in Vienna in the service of Emperor Matthew, a brother of Rudolph II (d. 1612).

In 1615 he went to Salzburg and Munich, returning the following year to Amsterdam and then going to Tirol. After that (1618), he lived in Haarlem and from 1619 to 1639 in Utrecht. Dürer's work served as the main inspiration for his faithful imitation of nature. In turn, Savery became the most important forerunner of numerous Dutch animal painters.

ADRIAEN BROUWER

(1605/06-1638)

ADRIAEN BROUWER *Born at Oudenaerde in Flanders.
1621-26 at Antwerp and Amsterdam. Worked in Haarlem
1626-31. From 1631 worked at Antwerp, where he died 1
February 1638.*

519 Studies of Peasants

Pen and brown ink over pencil, 215 x 328 mm.

Berlin, Ehem. Staatliche Museen, Kuperstichkabinett
  (K.d.Z. 5391)

LITERATURE

Berlin Catalogue, p. 100, No. 5391, Pl. LXXV

OF THE many artists who painted peasant scenes in seventeenth-century Netherlands, Brouwer is the most profound intrepreter of that
segment of the population. Unlike other artists, such as Adriaen van
Ostade, he did not limit himself to depicting the outer appearance of
peasants, nor to telling the daily happenings or humorous anecdotes
of their lives. He tried to understand the poorest human beings,
deprived of everything and living the simplest of lives, who experi-
enced human emotions that were frightening in their starkness.

Only a very few drawings by Adriaen Brouwer have come down to
us. In these he sketched the essential features and characteristics very
rapidly, with only a few lines.

PETER PAUL RUBENS

(1577-1640)

PETER PAUL RUBENS *Born at Siegen 28 June 1577. Studied with the landscape painter Tobias Verhaegt in 1590. 1591-94 studied with Adam van Noort. Became guild member in 1598. 1600-08 in Italy. Traveled to Mantua, Venice, Rome, and Genoa. Visited Spain, Paris, and England. Died 30 May 1640 at Antwerp.*

520 Three Caryatids, after Primaticcio

Red chalk, largely worked over in red water color with a fine brush, heightened with white body-color, turned yellow, 269 x 253 mm.

Rotterdam, Museum Boymans-van Beuningen (No. V.6)

PROVENANCE

Happaert; Lankrink; Koenigs

LITERATURE

van Regteren Altena, in *Burlington Magazine*, LXXVI, 1940, p. 194

Burchard, *Loan Exhibition of Works by Peter Paul Rubens, Kt.*, 1950, No. 50

Held, *Rubens, Selected Drawings*, No. 166, Pl. CLXXII

RUBENS SKETCHED these caryatids after Primaticcio's drawings for sculpture. The figures very much resemble those of the stucco decorations that Primaticcio executed in the Château at Fontainebleau in the "Chambre à coucher de Mme. d'Estampes" (now "Escalier du Roi"). Rubens interpreted the Mannerist drawings, now lost, of the artist (died 1570) in his own way and gave the women a Rubensesque liveliness, although their stance is very close to the one that Primaticcio gave his caryatids.

The date of execution of this drawing is uncertain.

RUBENS

521 Study for the Figure of Christ

Charcoal, heightened with white chalk, on buff paper,
400 x 298 mm.

Cambridge, Massachusetts, Harvard University, Fogg Art
Museum (No. 1949.3), Meta and Paul J. Sachs Collection

PROVENANCE

de Wit (?); Boehm; Weisbach; Sachs

LITERATURE

Glueck and Haberditzl, *Die Handzeichnungen von Peter
Paul Rubens*, No. 61

Mongan-Sachs, *Fogg Catalogue*, No. 483, Fig. 249

Burchard and d'Hulst, (Catalogue of the Exhibition)
Tekeningen van P. P. Rubens, 1956, No. 34

In 1610-1611 Rubens painted the large triptych of the "Elevation of the Cross," now in the Cathedral at Antwerp. It was one of the most important commissions he had received so far; this is probably one of the reasons that so many preparatory drawings for this triptych are known.

In the drawing reproduced here Rubens sketched the figure of Christ as he intended him to be nailed on the cross, looking up to God the Father, who was originally represented over the painting. A second drawing for the same figure is also in the Fogg Art Museum.

RUBENS

522 Study of a Nude Male Torso

Charcoal (oiled), partly stumped, heightened with white
  chalk on rather rough, slightly discolored paper,
  315 x 367 mm.

Oxford, Ashmolean Museum

PROVENANCE

Lankrink; Chambers Hall

LITERATURE

Glueck and Haberditzl, No. 45

Ashmolean Catalogue, I, No. 200

Burchard and d'Hulst, No. 9

RUBENS TWICE made a sketch of a male figure bending backward in his effort to support or lower a heavy weight. Both studies, the one reproduced here and the one in the Boymans Museum, Rotterdam, must have been executed at the same time.

Since the artist incorporated a figure in this attitude in at least four paintings from 1602 through 1617, there is more than one answer to the question of when Rubens executed the drawing.

Stylistic similarities with drawings that Rubens made about 1610 for his "Elevation of the Cross" are in favor of the supposition that this drawing originated in connection with the same important commission. Later Rubens used the same figure, this time clothed, for a "Deposition," now in the Museum at Lille (ca. 1616-17).

Rubens probably made drawings such as the one reproduced here from nature, after having put a model in the required position. In sketching the figure the artist paid great attention to the shape and function of the muscles of the man's back and arm.

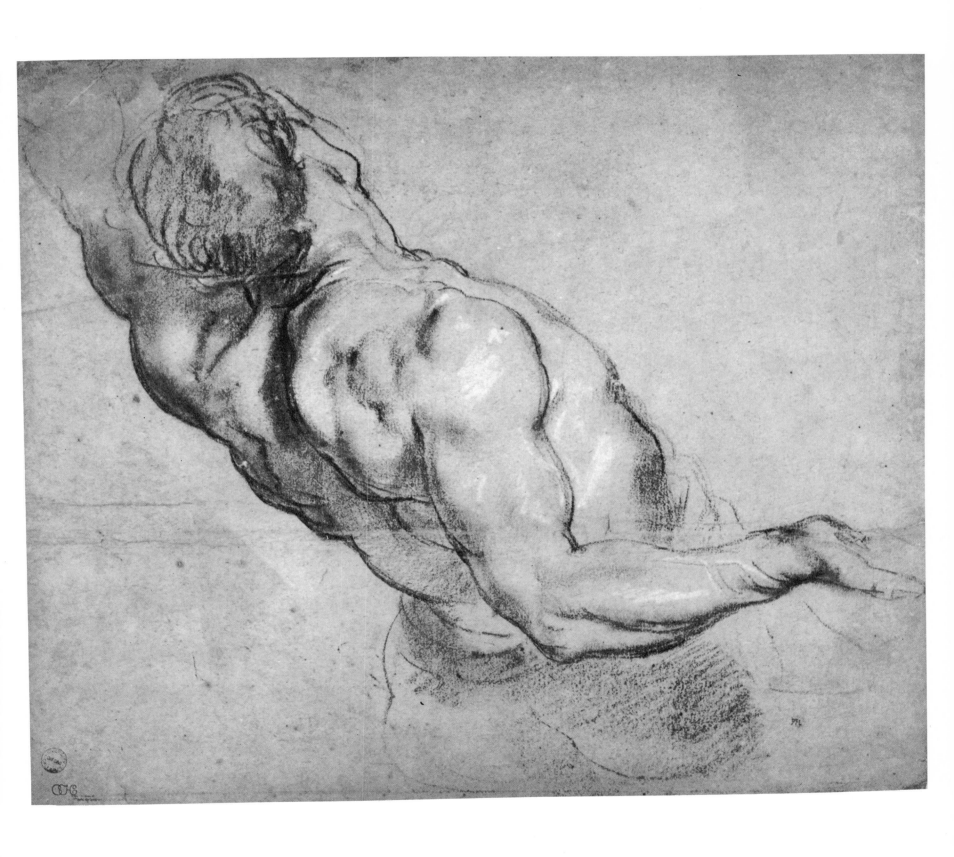

RUBENS

523 Study of a Male Figure, Seen from Behind

Charcoal, heightened with white, 375 x 285 mm.

Cambridge, Fitzwilliam Museum (No. 2177), Bequeathed
by C. H. Shannon, R.A., 1937

PROVENANCE

Ricketts and Shannon

LITERATURE

Glueck and Haberditzl, No. 59

THIS STUDY is probably connected with a boatman Rubens painted
as part of "The Miracle of St. Walpurga" (1610-11). The style of the
drawing is comparable to that of the "Study of a Male Nude Torso"
(see No. 522).

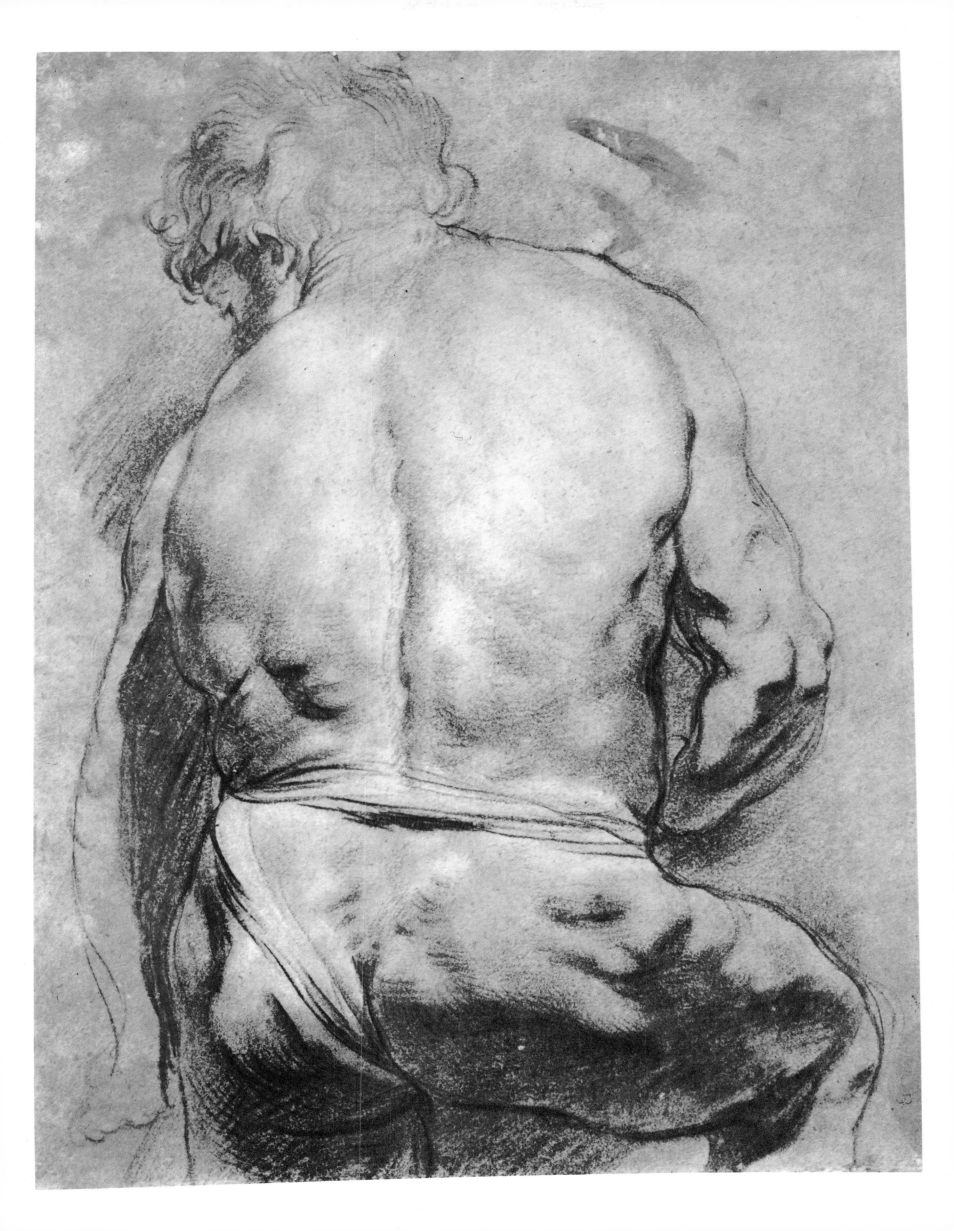

RUBENS

524 The Death of Adonis

Pen and brown wash, 217 x 153 mm.
London, British Museum

PROVENANCE
Morel de Vindé; Dijonval; Lawrence; Hawkins; Malcolm

LITERATURE
Hind, *British Museum Catalogue*, II, p. 58, No. 24
Evers, *Rubens und sein Werk*, pp. 135-136, Fig. 37
Held, No. 22, Pl. XXIII

THE BEAUTIFUL youth Adonis, mortally wounded by a boar, is dying in the arms of Venus, by whom he was beloved. Cupid is putting a bandage on the wound.

Rubens had painted the same subject previously, during his stay in Italy. In this drawing, and in two others that he did about the same time (ca. 1610-12), Rubens based his composition on the sculpture of Menelaus and Patroclus. In all the three drawings Rubens was looking for the most satisfactory attitude of the bodies, especially of the contrasting heads, one expressing the powerlessness of the dying young man, the other the desperate grief of Venus.

RUBENS

525 Studies for Apostles

Black chalk on grayish paper, 353 x 258 mm.

Cambridge, Massachusetts, Harvard University, Fogg Art Museum (No. 1936.123), Gift of the Honorable Mr. and Mrs. Robert Woods Bliss

PROVENANCE

Lankrink; Richardson, Sr.; Hudson; Reynolds; Lawrence; Bale; Oppenheimer

LITERATURE

Glueck and Haberditzl, No. 127

Mongan-Sachs, *Fogg Catalogue*, No. 484, Fig. 250

Burchard and d'Hulst, No. 54

RUBENS FIRST sketched these two young men looking up and subsequently added the head of the man at the left a second time at the bottom of the sheet in a slightly different attitude.

Rubens used this drawing for two apostles in his painting "The Assumption of the Virgin," which he executed in 1614-15 (now in the Museum in Vienna). There the apostles are looking up at the Virgin. It is likely that Rubens made the drawing in preparation for the painting.

RUBENS

526 Study for a St. Mary Magdalen

Black chalk, heightened with white, 332 x 242 mm.
London, British Museum (No. 1912-12-14-5)

PROVENANCE
Crozat; Lawrence; Heseltine

LITERATURE
Hind, *British Museum Catalogue*, II, p. 11, No. 16

THE ATTITUDE of the figure, her hands crossed against her bosom, her head bowed, suggests a repentant Magdalen. This was noted by Hind, who thought that the drawing might have been a study from life done for the figure of St. Mary Magdalen in the painting "Christ and the Four Penitents" at Munich.

RUBENS

527 Study for Daniel in the Lion's Den

Black chalk, heightened with white, on pale gray paper,
505 x 302 mm.

New York, The Pierpont Morgan Library

PROVENANCE

Bates; Fairfax Murray

LITERATURE

Glueck and Haberditzl, No. 97

Jaffé, in *Bulletin van het Rijksmuseum*, III, 1955, pp. 64-66

Held, No. 85, Pl. XCV

RUBENS MADE this large study of a seated youth clasping his hands in prayer for the figure of Daniel in a painting representing Daniel between the lions. It is likely that Rubens sketched the figure from a model he had put in the position required for the figure of Daniel. For such studies from life, intended for use in compositions, Rubens generally used black chalk and white chalk heightenings. This drawing is a particularly brilliant example of such studies.

For the same painting Rubens also made studies of lions (see following number).

RUBENS

528 Study of a Lion

Black chalk, brush and brown ink, heightened with white,
283 x 429 mm.

London, British Museum

PROVENANCE

Richard Payne Knight

LITERATURE

Hind, *British Museum Catalogue*, II, p. 36, No. 117

Glueck and Haberditzl, No. 98

RUBENS SKETCHED a number of lions and lionesses, partly from nature. He used the present study for one of the animals in his "Daniel in the Lions' Den." In this drawing the artist stressed both the latent ferocity of the animal and, in the richly flowing mane, the majestic grandeur of the king of beasts.

RUBENS

529 Study of a River God

Black chalk, heightened with white, 454 x 445 mm.
London, Victoria and Albert Museum (No. D.903-1900)

PROVENANCE
Versteegh; Lawrence; Dalton

LITERATURE
Parker, in *Old Master Drawings*, IV, 1929/30, p. 20, Pl. XXV

THIS RECLINING nude is a study for the figure representing the River Nile. This allegorical figure stands for the Continent Africa and was painted by Rubens in his "The Four Quarters of the Globe," now in the Museum at Vienna (ca. 1615). The figure in the painting differs only slightly from the one of this study; in the painting he reclines a little more and leans heavier against the vase at the left. In the drawing Rubens concentrated on the nude figure and indicated with a few lines the vase and the drapery, which covers the man's legs only.

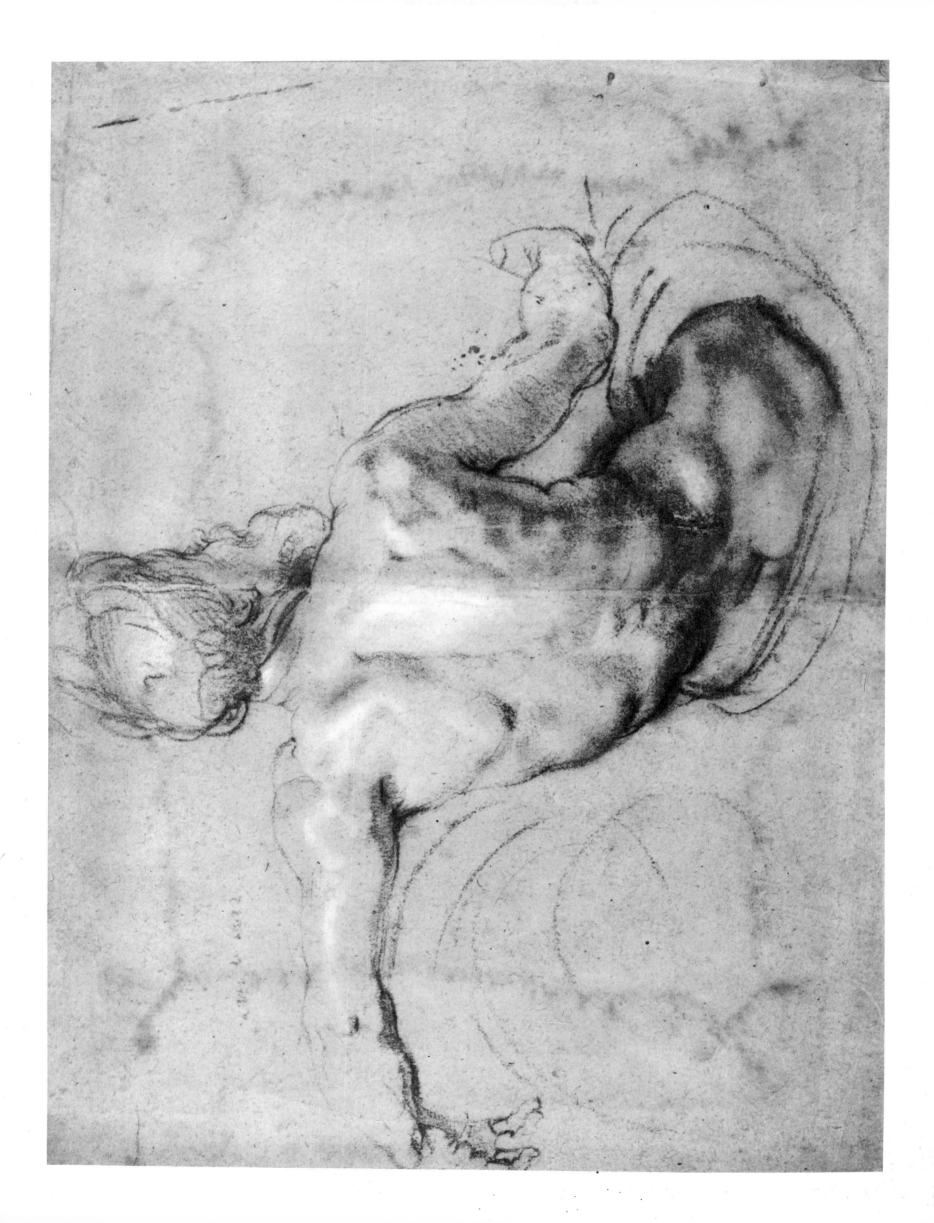

RUBENS

530 Three Robed Men

Black chalk, heightened with white, 281 x 314 mm.

Copenhagen, Royal Museum of Fine Arts (No. 13235),
    Gift of the Ny Carlsberg Foundation

PROVENANCE

Anatole France; Dubaut

LITERATURE

Sthyr, in *Kunstmuseets Aarsskrift*, XXIII, 1936, p. 50 ff.

Held, No. 36, Pl. XXXVII

THE FIGURES at the left and at the right both represent St. Andrew with his X-shaped cross. They differ in attitude, drapery, and even in facial expression, and show how Rubens changed and even remodeled a figure in his search for the most satisfactory representation of a particular personage. The figure at the right was used by Rubens in his triptych representing the "Miraculous Drought of Fishes," in Mechlin, painted in 1618/19. However, it is probable that the drawing was executed earlier.

The old man in the center was drawn previous to the addition of the two versions of St. Andrew. He served Rubens as a model for his Melchizedek in the painting of "Abraham and Melchizedek" in Caen.

RUBENS

531 Study for a St. Mary Magdalen

Black chalk, heightened with white, on brown paper,
262 x 402 mm.

Cambridge, Fitzwilliam Museum (No. 2182), Bequeathed
by C. H. Shannon, R.A., 1937

PROVENANCE

Lankrink; Robinson; Ricketts and Shannon

LITERATURE

Glueck and Haberditzl, No. 119

THIS SKETCH for a St. Mary Magdalen, kneeling and holding the
nails with which Christ had been fastened on the cross, was made by
Rubens for his painting "The Lamentations over the Dead Christ" in
the Museum at Brussels (ca. 1620). In this drawing Rubens paid special attention to the shape of the skirt and to the light and shade of its
folds.

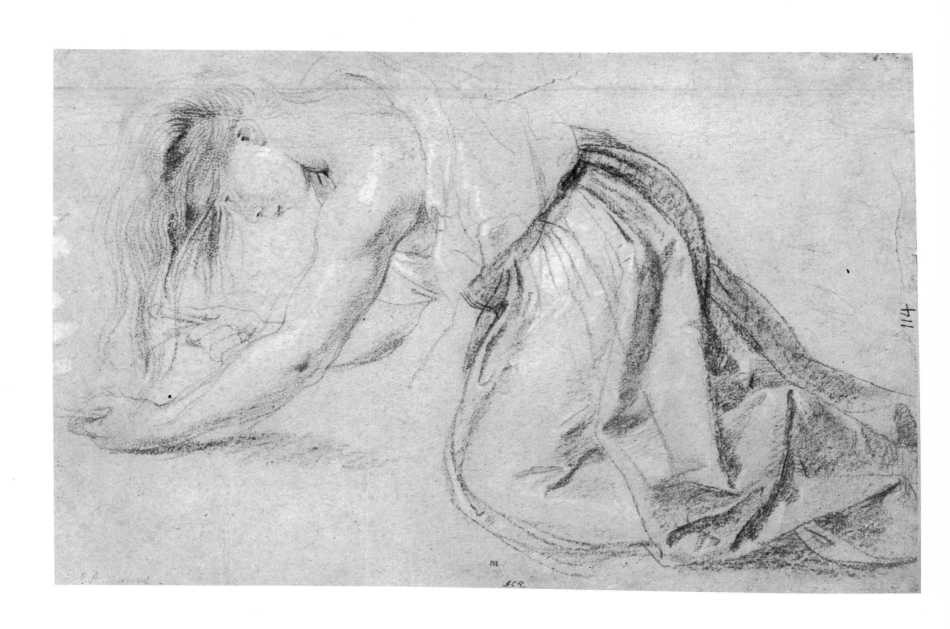

RUBENS

532 Studies of Cows

Pen and brush and brown ink, 340 x 522 mm.

London, British Museum (No. 1895-9-15-1046)

PROVENANCE

Versteegh; Lawrence; King William II; Leembruggen; Malcolm

LITERATURE

Glueck and Haberditzl, No. 136

Held, p. 12

It is probably this sheet that served for a print by Paul Pontius in a "Drawing-book," meant as a collection of examples for young artists who wanted to learn to draw. Rubens himself used two of the cows, the large one at the left and the small one at the top right corner, for his painting "Landscape with Cows," executed about 1618-20 (Munich).

In contrast to studies of cows by his Dutch or French contemporaries, Rubens paid more attention to the muscular structure of the animals. In sketching the cows Rubens was aware of the structure and position of the muscles, just as he was when making studies of the human body. The academic tradition of studying the nude has been applied, to a certain extent, to these animals.

A drawing very similar to this one is in the Devonshire collection, Chatsworth. The relationship between the two needs clarification, as does the question of whether Rubens made both, one, or none of these drawings.

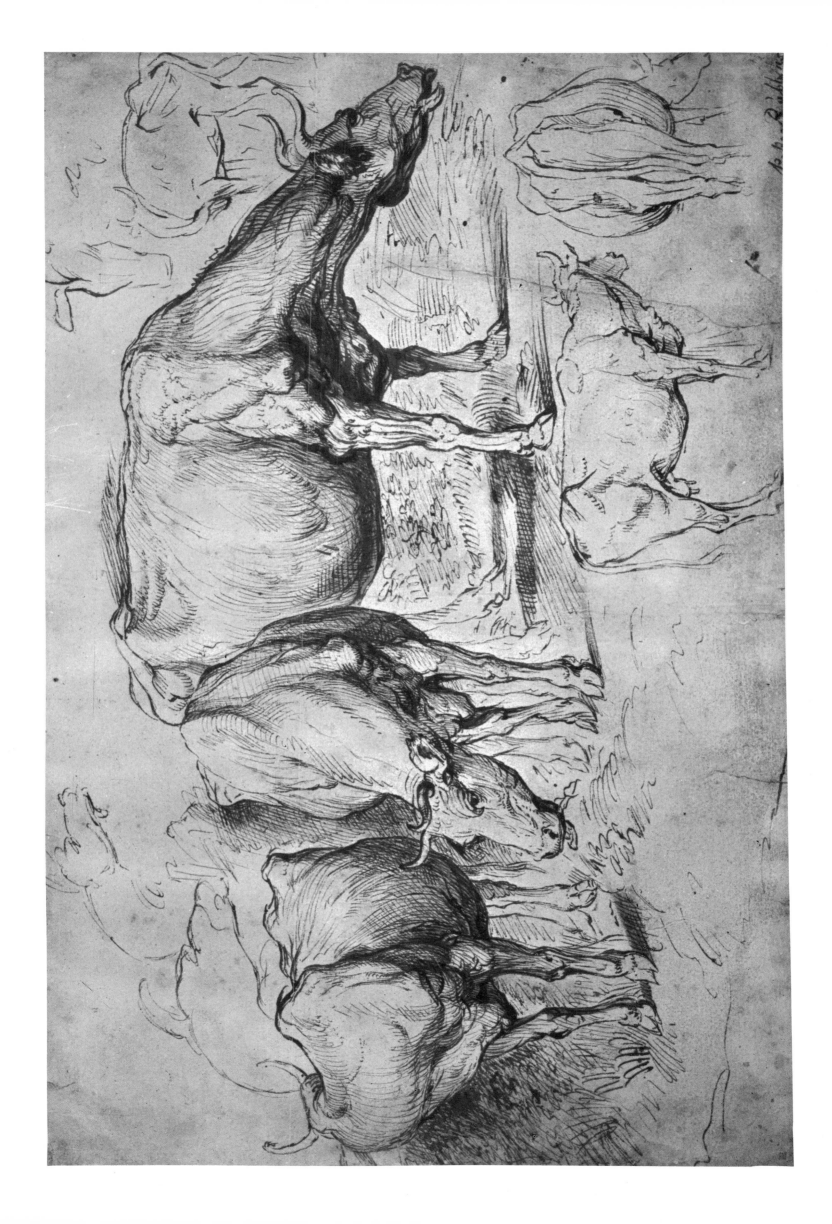

RUBENS

533 Two Farm Wagons

Black chalk, heightened with white, and brown pen, colored
chalks, 224 x 375 mm.

Berlin, Ehem. Staatliche Museen, Kupferstichkabinett
(K.d.Z. 3237)

PROVENANCE

Hone; Suermondt

LITERATURE

Berlin Catalogue, p. 253, No. 3237, Pl. CLXXXV

Glueck and Haberditzl, No. 95

Held, No. 133, Pl. CXLII

RUBENS USED the wagon at the left in his painting "Return from the
Harvest" (Pitti, Florence).

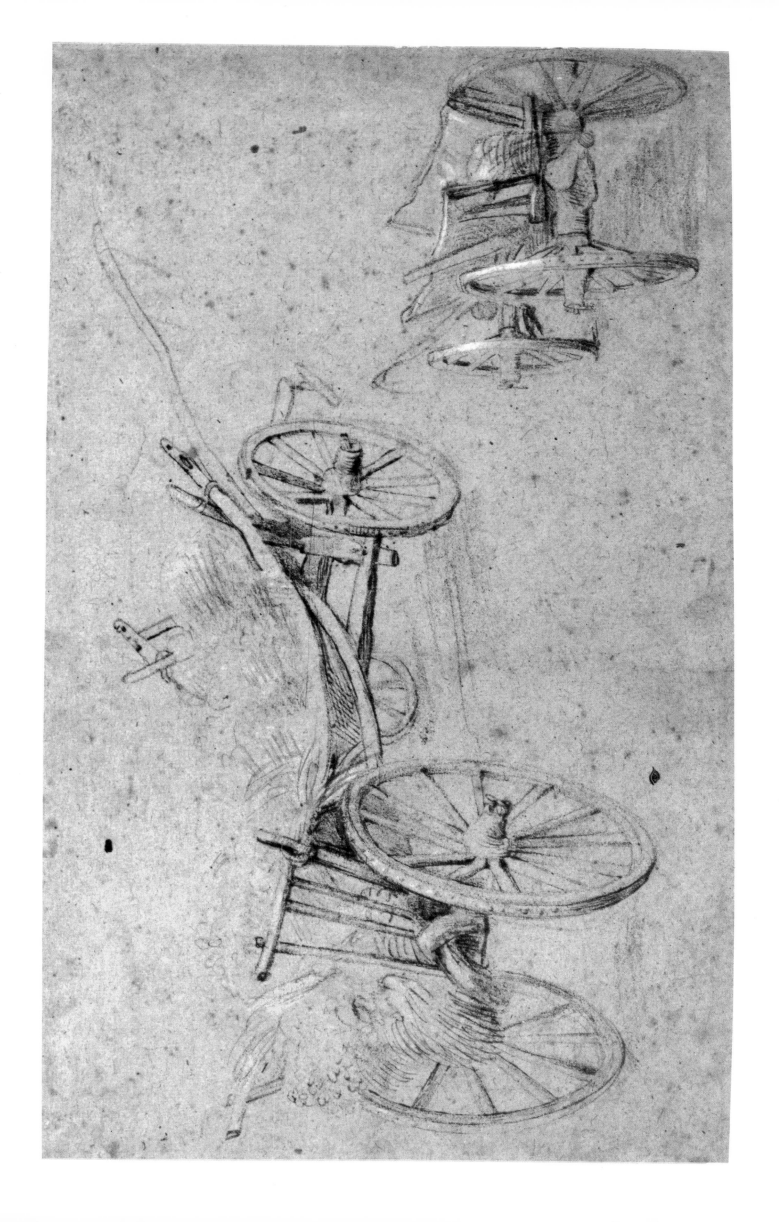

RUBENS

534 Portrait of Isabella Brant

Black, red, and white chalk, 381 x 292 mm.

London, British Museum (No. 1893-7-31-21)

PROVENANCE

Lankrink; Richardson; Thornhill; Lord Clive;
Spencer; Holford

LITERATURE

Hind, *British Museum Catalogue*, II, No. 92

Glueck and Haberditzl, No. 160

Held, No. 103, Pl. CXV

PROBABLY EXECUTED about 1622, this drawing is one of the most immediate and lively portraits of Isabella Brant, Rubens' first wife. Numerous portraits of her painted by Rubens and his school have come down to us; comparatively few drawings, however, are known. Isabella Brant died in 1626.

RUBENS

535 Portrait of Marie de' Medici

Black and red chalk, heightened with white, 356 x 278 mm.

At the right a strip of paper added by another hand. Annotated: *Rubens* and *Reyne mere*

Paris, Louvre, Cabinet des Dessins (No. 20224)

PROVENANCE

Crozat; Tessin; Count Nils Barck

LITERATURE

Rooses, *L'Oeuvre de P. P. Rubens*, No. 1514

Glueck and Haberditzl, No. 150

Lugt, II, No. 1020

IN THE years 1622 to 1625 Rubens painted for Marie de' Medici (1573-1642) a series of twenty-five paintings representing scenes from her life. The queen, mother and regent of Louis XIII, gave Rubens the commission in order to decorate the Palais du Luxembourg, built for her by Salomon Brosse.

This series of paintings, now in the Louvre, is one of the most important commissions Rubens ever received and, likewise, one of the most significant baroque works of art. The artist prepared the paintings in consultation with the queen, making many drawings and oil sketches. He also portrayed the queen a number of times in drawings that subsequently were used for her portraits in the paintings.

The drawing here reproduced served for the portrait of the queen in the painting representing "The Prosperous Government." It is the most finished of all the portraits Rubens made of Marie de' Medici when he was in Paris, in 1622. The portrait leaves no doubt about the queen's inherited passion for power.

The artist used, with great skill and flexibility, black, red, and white chalk, a combination first employed in Italy and subsequently brought to the Netherlands by Hendrick Goltzius. France was the country where this technique "à trois crayons," later in the eighteenth century, would be used in the most delicate and sensitive way by such artists as Antoine Watteau and Honoré Fragonard.

RUBENS

536 Young Woman with an Ostrich Fan

Black and red chalk, heightened with white, 538 x 347 mm.
Paris, Louvre, Cabinet des Dessins (No. 20.196)

PROVENANCE
Barnard

LITERATURE
Glueck and Haberditzl, No. 204
Held, No. 118, Pl. CXXX and Frontispiece
Lugt, No. 1023, Pl. XXIII

SHORTLY AFTER 1630 Rubens completed a large painting, "The Garden of Love" or, as it was called in Rubens' estate, "The Conversation of Young Ladies." This painting, bought by Philip IV after the death of the artist and now in the Prado in Madrid, represents a variation of a theme treated often before and after Rubens, Watteau having given the best-known later interpretation of the subject. The painting expresses better than any other by Rubens his joy of life and his rapture at youth and elegance.

For no other painting by Rubens have so many large figure studies been preserved: nine in total. In these studies, brilliantly executed in red, black, and white chalk, the same gaiety is expressed as in the painting. The youth of the figures, the richness of their dresses, and the elegance of their movements have been rendered with a profound love and a great mastery.

The figure reproduced here is a study for a young lady at the extreme right of the painting.

RUBENS

537 Young Woman with Crossed Hands

Black and red chalk, heightened with white, 470 x 358 mm.
Rotterdam, Museum Boymans-van Beuningen (No. V.81)

PROVENANCE
Lankrink; Boehler; Koenigs

LITERATURE
Glueck and Haberditzl, No. 207
Held, No. 110, Pl. CXXI

THIS DRAWING was probably executed about the time Rubens was preparing his "Garden of Love," since it is similar in style and use of black, red, and white chalk to the preparatory drawings for the painting. It is undoubtedly one of the most delicate and tender portraits Rubens made. Not only the face, but also the hands, were drawn with great concentration and care.

RUBENS

538 Portrait of Thomas Howard, Earl of Arundel

Sepia wash and oil, 460 x 355 mm.

Williamstown, Massachusetts, Sterling and Francine Clark
   Art Institute

PROVENANCE
Hudson; Private Collection, London

LITERATURE
Glueck and Haberditzl, No. 178

THOMAS HOWARD, Second Earl of Arundel (1585/86-1646), owes his fame mainly to his patronage of arts and learning. He was the first in England to make a magnificent collection of works of art, including antique sculptures—now partly at Oxford—and paintings by his contemporaries. He employed many artists, among whom van Dyck and Rubens are the most outstanding.

Rubens painted a portrait of the Earl in the 1630's, which is now in the Isabella Stewart Gardner Museum in Boston. The Earl is represented in armor, holding a baton. Although Thomas Howard did not become a general until 1638, he had been Earl Marshal since 1621, and it is likely that the painted portrait was executed before 1638.

The majestic drawing reproduced here is a study immediately preceding the painting; in the painted portrait Rubens changed the composition only in minor details.

RUBENS

539 The Feast of Herod

Pen and brown ink, with black and red chalk,
273 x 473 mm.

Cleveland, Ohio, The Cleveland Museum of Art
(No. 54.2), Delia E. and L. E. Holden Funds

PROVENANCE

Unidentified Viennese (?) collection about 1800 (Lugt 622)

LITERATURE

Burchard, in *The Burlington Magazine*,
XCV, 1953, pp. 383-387

Burchard and d'Hulst, No. 131

Francis, in *The Bulletin of The Cleveland Museum of Art*,
XLI, June, 1954, pp. 124-126

Held, No. 67, Pl. LXXVII

SALOME HAS brought in the salver with St. John the Baptist's head and lifts the cover; Herod, seated at the right, is horrified, while Herodias points with her fork to St. John's tongue.

Rubens made this drawing late in his life in preparation for a painting that is now in the Lady Lever Art Gallery at Port Sunlight. It is only one of the stages in the development of this composition; as it is now, the painting shows about twice as many figures as the drawing. Rubens repeatedly made quick studies for the compositions of paintings, first with chalk and subsequently with the pen.

On the other side of this sheet Rubens made a sketch of "Tomyris and the Head of Cyrus," also a scene in which a hero's head is being mocked after a tragic death.

RUBENS

540 A Country Lane

Bistre, pen, wash, and pencil, 313 x 403 mm.

Cambridge, Fitzwilliam Museum (No. 2178), Bequeathed
by C. H. Shannon, R.A., 1937

PROVENANCE

Kerrick; Ricketts and Shannon

LITERATURE

Glueck and Haberditzl, No. 137

Held, No. 130, Pl. CXLIII

IN CONTRAST to most of the landscapes or trees Rubens drew, here
he sketched a well-kept country lane with fences and flower borders.
It is possible that the drawing was originally larger at the left, and
that the lane was more in the center of the composition, thus adding
to the impression of order and neatness. This lane does not recur in
paintings by Rubens or in other drawings, and it is a matter of dis-
pute when he sketched it.

RUBENS

541 Tree with Brambles

Pen and brown ink over black chalk with a few touches in
  red chalk and in blue, 352 x 298 mm.

Chatsworth, Devonshire Collections (No. 1008)

PROVENANCE

Flinck (?)

LITERATURE

Vasari Society, 2d Series, VI, 1925, No. 12

Glueck and Haberditzl, No. 135

THIS IS one of the few landscape drawings by Rubens, undoubtedly
drawn from nature. Here he chose a rather wild spot with brambles
growing over a tree, interlaced with dead branches. After having
sketched the tree and the brambles, Rubens went over it with the
pen, especially indicating the brambles and the dark areas between
the branches and the leaves.

RUBENS

542 Woodland Scene

Oiled charcoal, touched with red and white chalk, on stone
  colored paper, 383 x 499 mm.

Oxford, Ashmolean Museum

PROVENANCE

Lankrink; Chambers Hall

LITERATURE

Glueck and Haberditzl, No. 170

Ashmolean Catalogue, I, No. 201

Held, No. 137, Pl. CXLVI

AT THE end of his life Rubens painted and sketched more landscapes
than ever before. Particularly after he had acquired the Castle Steen,
in the Brussels surroundings, the artist often chose landscape as the
main subject for his paintings. In this drawing Rubens seems to have
been interested particularly in the rendering of the light of the distant
sky visible through the trees.

ANTHONY VAN DYCK

(1599-1641)

ANTHONY VAN DYCK *Born at Antwerp 22 March 1599. 1609 apprenticed to Hendrik van Balen. Pupil and assistant of Rubens. 1620-21 worked in England. 1621-27 in Italy. 1627-28 in Holland. Died at London, 9 December 1641.*

543 The Entombment

Pen and brush with brown ink, washed in dark lilac, red, and greenish tints, corrected with white body color and touched with red chalk, 256 x 218 mm.

Chatsworth, Devonshire Collection (No. 856)

PROVENANCE

Flinck

LITERATURE

Vasari Society, VI, No. 19

Vey, *Van-Dyck-Studien*, pp. 36 ff.

IN THIS and in another similar drawing now in the Teyler Museum, Haarlem, the young van Dyck created a highly dramatic representation of "Christ's Entombment." The elaborate washes, the vehemence of pen lines and brush strokes, the dark and heavy colors are all expressive of a somber mood, or even a state of affliction, as in the figure of Mary supported by St. John at the right. It is not known whether this drawing was intended as a study for a composition that van Dyck planned to paint but then apparently never executed. If such is the case, the drawing could be considered in its function and execution as an oil sketch.

DYCK

544 Christ Falling under the Cross

Brush and wash in sepia over black pencil, 155 x 202 mm.

Turin, Biblioteca Reale (No. 16366)

LITERATURE

Bertini, *Disegni di maestri stranieri della Biblioteca Reale di Torino*, No. 103, Fig. 14

Vey, pp. 11 ff.

d'Hulst and Vey, (Catalogue of the Exhibition) *Antoon van Dyck, Tekeningen en olieverfschetsen*, 1960, No. 7

DYCK

545 Christ Falling under the Cross

Pen and wash on white paper, 160 x 205 mm.

Lille, Palais des Beaux-Arts, Musée Wicar (No. 960)

PROVENANCE

Thane; Roupell; Thibaudeau; Wicar

LITERATURE

Pinchart, p. 215, No. 960

Vey, pp. 11 ff.

d'Hulst and Vey, No. 8

VAN DYCK was only about seventeen or eighteen years old when he was asked to join the most renowned artists of his time in painting a series of fifteen paintings representing scenes from the life of Christ and the Virgin Mary. It must have been a great honor for the young artist to paint one of these, the ninth in a series. Rubens and Jordaens were among the other artists participating. The series of paintings representing the "Mysteries of the Rosary" are still in the church for which they were made: the former Dominican Church, now St. Paul's Church, in Antwerp.

The large number of preparatory studies that van Dyck made for his painting, "Christ Falling Under the Cross," is evidence of the importance he attached to the commission. In the drawing reproduced here Christ, moving to the left, has fallen and looks back at His Mother, who stands at the extreme right. The meeting of the Virgin and her Son replaces the more usual Veronica scene. In the painting, as it was finally executed, the composition was reversed. All the important elements of this earlier sketch, however, remained present (see the note to the following drawing).

IN CONTRAST to the previously executed drawing, reproduced above, van Dyck reversed the composition here. It would remain this way, and in the painting for which both drawings are preparatory studies, Christ is directed to the right. See the note to the preceding drawing.

DYCK

546 The Mystic Marriage of St. Catherine

Pen and brush in brown, 158 x 237 mm.

New York, The Pierpont Morgan Library

PROVENANCE

Lawrence; Norblen; Morant; Roupell; Fairfax Murray

LITERATURE

Vey, pp. 83 ff.

d'Hulst and Vey, No. 28, Pl. XV

THE CHRIST Child, seated on the Virgin's lap, puts the wedding ring on the finger of St. Catherine. They are surrounded by Saints: St. George (in the middle) and St. Anthony (behind St. Catherine) can be recognized.

The composition of this drawing as well as of the painting with the same subject for which it is a preparatory sketch (now in the Prado, Madrid) is reminiscent of Venetian prototypes. The style of the drawing, however, leaves no doubt about its being executed before van Dyck went to Italy.

Subsequent to this drawing van Dyck made a more carefully and elaborately designed "modello" for the same painting; the composition, however, remained the same as in the more sketchily handled drawing here reproduced.

DYCK

547 The Descent of the Holy Ghost

Pen and brush in brown, 207 x 280 mm.

Retouched with darker brown ink, probably by
    another hand

Paris, Louvre, Cabinet des Dessins (No. RF .00661)

PROVENANCE

Houlditch; Rogers; His de la Salle

LITERATURE

Tauzia, *Dessins His de la Salle*, No. 177

Lugt, I, No. 588, Pl. LIV

Vey, pp. 99 ff.

ABOUT THE middle of the first Antwerp period, van Dyck painted a "Descent of the Holy Ghost" which was formerly at Potsdam (lost in 1945). While preparing the composition of that painting, the artist also sketched the present drawing which, however, is not directly connected with the painting but rather a separate study based upon Rubens' rendering of the same subject (St. Gudule, Brussels).

DYCK

548 Diana and Endymion

Pen and brush in brown, heightened with white, on blue-gray paper, 190 x 229 mm.

New York, The Pierpont Morgan Library

PROVENANCE

Lawrence; de Vos; Seymour Haden; Fairfax Murray

LITERATURE

The Pierpont Morgan Library, *Illustrated Catalogue of an Exhibition Held on the Occasion of the New York World's Fair*, No. 79

Great Master Drawings of Seven Centuries, 1959, No. 45

ENDYMION, THE most beautiful of men, was thrown into a perpetual sleep, to be visited and embraced every night by the goddess of the moon. On this sheet, van Dyck sketched twice the swiftly descending goddess approaching the sleeping shepherd. With a nervous touch, sketching hastily, the artist tried to find the most adequate rendering of the legend. In one study Diana is looking at the youth; in the other, she is kissing him.

DYCK

549 The Martyrdom of St. Catherine

Black chalk, pen and brown ink; yellow, lilac, and red
   water color, 285 x 210 mm.

Paris, Ecole Nationale Supérieure des Beaux-Arts

PROVENANCE

Schneider; Armand; Valton

LITERATURE

Guiffrey, *Antoine van Dyck, sa vie et son oeuvre*, pp. 29, 32

Vey, pp. 78 ff.

d'Hulst and Vey, No. 30

AN ANGEL is coming down to crown the Saint while she is martyred
on a wheel (top left). The angel, while putting the crown on St.
Catherine's head, points with the other hand to the heavenly light
in which Christ is appearing. The executioners, some on horseback,
are struck by the appearance of the light and run away in confusion.
One executioner is being trampled by a horse, another falls from
his horse.

Van Dyck made this sketch about the middle of his first Antwerp
period. Here too, as in other drawings from this time, violent action
and dramatic contrasts between light and dark are expressed by
swiftly applied broad washes and abruptly bending pen lines.

DYCK

550 Study for Christ Crowned with Thorns

Black chalk with touches of red and white chalk (retouched, probably by a later hand, with some red and black chalk and gray wash), 370 x 270 mm.

Oxford, Ashmolean Museum

PROVENANCE

Lankrink; Richardson; Hudson; Reynolds; Chambers Hall

LITERATURE

Ashmolean Catalogue, I, No. 129, Pl. XXVI

Vey, pp. 115 ff.

d'Hulst and Vey, No. 38, Pl. XXII

TOWARD 1620, van Dyck painted a "Christ Crowned with Thorns" (formerly in Berlin, destroyed 1945) for which he made a large number of preparatory drawings. In his search for the most satisfactory composition, van Dyck changed the scene from one with a violent action into a more quiet, rather devotional representation. At first, the body of Christ was turned more sharply to the right, while his left arm was stretched across his body in the opposite direction. In the present drawing, however, Christ's position has become more upright and his arms are crossed on his lap, expressive of quiet resignation. Van Dyck did not change it much when he finally painted the scene; he only added the cuffs around the wrists and covered the lowered legs. In the painting Christ is surrounded by mocking figures, one of whom is putting the crown of thorns on his head, while another pulls Christ's hair; the hand of the latter figure is already indicated in the drawing.

DYCK

551 Studies for Sleeping Disciples

Brush and brown ink, 160 x 246 mm.

Berlin, Ehem. Staatliche Museen, Kupferstichkabinett
(K.d.Z. 5683)

PROVENANCE

von Beckerath

LITERATURE

Berlin Catalogue, No. 5683

Vey, pp. 178 ff.

Stechow, in *The Minneapolis Institute of Art Bulletin*,
1960, p. 7 ff.

TWICE VAN Dyck sketched a group of two sleeping disciples on this sheet of paper. He thought of incorporating these in a representation of the "Betrayal of Christ," first combining the scene of "Christ Visiting the Sleeping Disciples" with that of the "Betrayal," and subsequently merging the two scenes into the one of Christ being betrayed while the disciples are still sleeping. Later, van Dyck abandoned this idea and substituted the scene of the sleeping disciples with the group of Petrus and Malchus. Thus, he represented the "Betrayal" in the drawing reproduced under the following number.

DYCK

552 The Betrayal of Christ

Black chalk with red and pen with black wash over,
   533 x 403 mm.

Hamburg, Kunsthalle (No. 21882)

PROVENANCE

Harzen

LITERATURE

Pauli, No. 7

Vey, pp. 178 ff.

d'Hulst and Vey, No. 44

Stechow, op. cit.

JUDAS HAS grabbed Christ's hand and is bending slightly to kiss Him. At the left, soldiers are rushing forward to capture Christ. Petrus has thrown Malchus on the ground; he hopelessly tries to defend himself.

This drawing is the "modello" for a painting that Rubens owned at his death, which probably was painted for van Dyck's teacher. The painting differs slightly from the sketch, the most notable change introduced by van Dyck being the alteration of the group of Petrus and Malchus. In the painting, they face toward the center of the composition, instead of outward as in the drawing. The drawing was squared by the artist to facilitate the transfer of the composition to the larger canvas.

The style of the drawing, angular and sweeping lines, and the vehement movements of figures are characteristic of van Dyck in the latter half of his first Antwerp period (in 1621 van Dyck left Antwerp for Italy). The composition is based on a drawing by Maerten de Vos.

DYCK

553 Studies of a Woman Sleeping

Black chalk, heightened with white (retouched with red
chalk and washes by a later hand), 310 x 378 mm.

Inscribed, perhaps by Van Dyck: *AVDÿck 1620*

Madrid, Biblioteca Nacional

PROVENANCE

Carderera

LITERATURE

Barcia, No. 8692

Glueck, in *Pantheon*, V, 1930, p. 201

d'Hulst and Vey, No. 47

VAN DYCK undoubtedly sketched this figure from life. After she
had changed the position of her head slightly, he repeated the upper
part of her body on the same sheet of paper.

This figure does not recur in van Dyck's paintings; it is therefore
not certain whether van Dyck, in sketching the model, thought of
a figure in a representation of a scene such as "Nymphs Resting."

The drawing was probably executed in or around 1620.

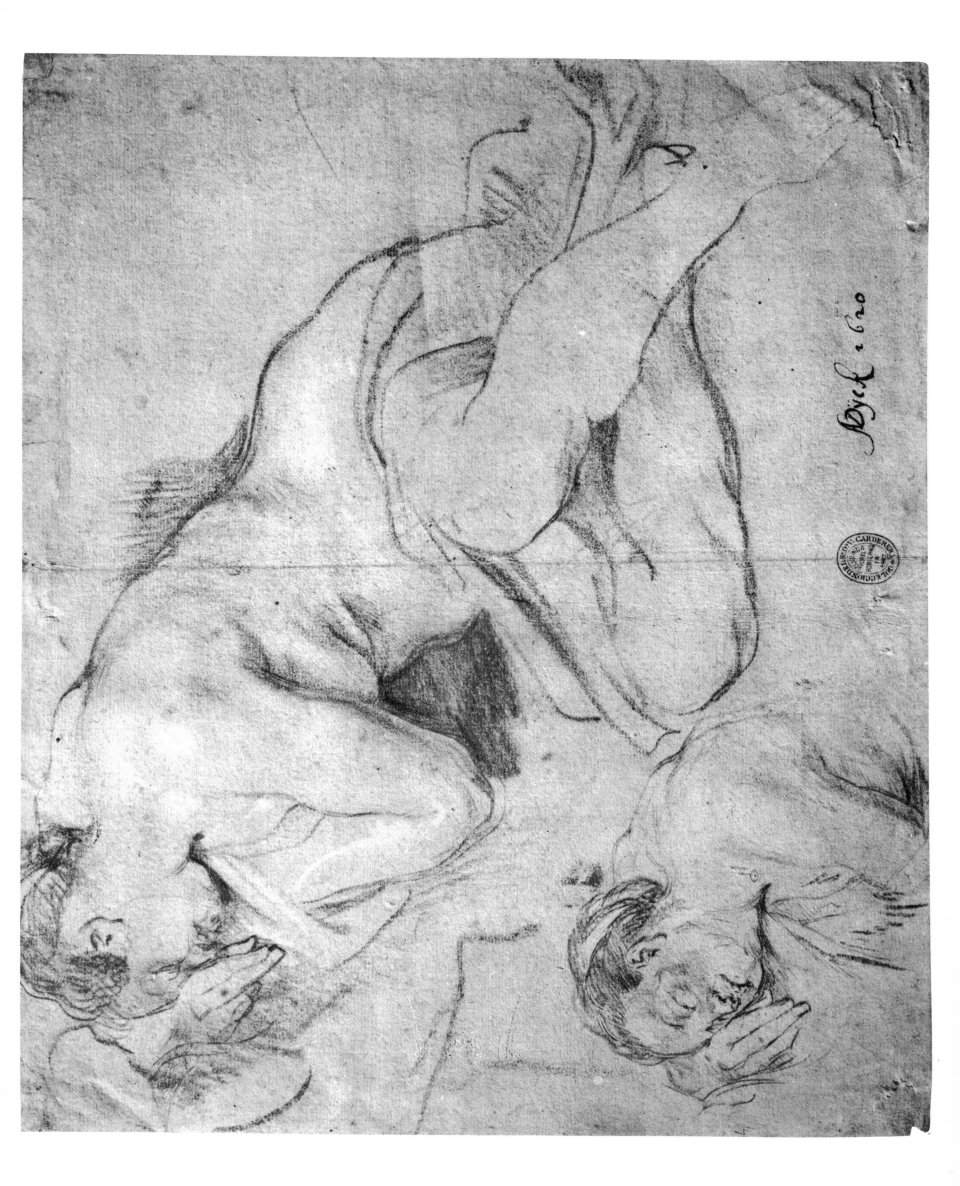

DYCK

554 Studies of the Head of a Horse and of a Man on Horseback

Pen and brush in brown, 264 x 165 mm.

Color notes by the artist: *wit / der neuse incarnatie / half farmilioenachtich / grau*

Amsterdam, Rijksmuseum, Rijksprentenkabinet
  (No. A.302)

PROVENANCE

de Vos

LITERATURE

Moes, *Les Dessins, Mémorial, Trésor de l'Art belge aux XVIIe siècle*, p. 52, Pl. XIV

d'Hulst and Vey, No. 48, Pl. XXX

THE MAN on horseback, wearing a helmet and carrying a shield and a lance, is probably a St. George. In that case, both he and the horse turn toward the dragon he is fighting.

The vividly sketched heads of horses could be free sketches. The nervous tension of the animals, who open wide their eyes and nostrils, is expressed in vibrant lines and shades contrasting with the white of the paper.

DYCK

555 Portrait of Hendrik van Balen

Black chalk, 243 x 198 mm.

Chatsworth, Devonshire Collections (No. 998)

PROVENANCE
Flinck

LITERATURE
Vasari Society, IV, 1908-09, Fig. 23
d'Hulst and Vey, No. 78, Fig. 50

THE LONG tradition of series of portraits was taken up and renewed by van Dyck. During his lifetime, eighty portraits of statesmen, artists, noblemen, and others were etched and engraved by a number of Flemish artists after drawings by van Dyck. Almost all the sitters of this "Iconography" were contemporaries of the artist. By omitting the texts, which were customary, and especially by giving the sitter his individuality and liveliness, van Dyck's portraits differ considerably from those of the older similar series.

Hendrik van Balen, one of the painters represented in the "Iconography," belonged to an older generation than van Dyck himself (he was probably born in 1573 and died in 1632); he painted religious and especially mythological scenes. Van Dyck expressed van Balen's love for classical antiquity by letting his right hand rest on an antique bust.

DYCK

556 View of Rye

Pen and brown ink, 202 x 294 mm.

Inscribed by the artist: *Rie del naturale li 27 d'Aug^{to}
1633-A vand . . .*

New York, The Pierpont Morgan Library

PROVENANCE

Richardson; van Rijmsdyck; Fairfax Murray

LITERATURE

Burchard, "A View of Rye by Anthonie van Dyck,"
in *Old Master Drawings*, 1938, pp. 47-48, Fig. 51

d'Hulst and Vey, No. 100, Fig. 61

RYE, SITUATED in Sussex, near Hastings, was an important harbor until the end of the sixteenth century, especially for traffic and transport between England and France. The city, built on a hill and surrounded in van Dyck's time by water, now by marshes, has always attracted artists. Van Dyck sketched it a number of times, in this drawing from the northeast. The houses on the slopes of the hill are dominated by St. Mary's Church.

Only a few landscape drawings by van Dyck have come down to us, and all these seem to have been done from nature. In his later life the artist especially seems to have been drawn to nature and found the rest and concentration to record some views that interested him.

JACOB JORDAENS

(1593-1678)

JACOB JORDAENS Born at Antwerp 19 May 1593. Student of Adam van Noort. Member of the guild in 1615. Worked in Antwerp. Died there 18 October 1678.

557 The Entombment of Christ

Pen in brown and sepia wash, 118 x 197 mm.

Antwerp, Stedelyk Prentenkabinet (No. 106)

PROVENANCE

Koester; Gaa

LITERATURE

d'Hulst, *De tekeningen van Jakob Jordaens*, No. 3, Fig. 27

IN THIS drawing, executed shortly before 1618, the youthful Jordaens is highly indebted to his teacher Rubens. The way of drawing with the pen, repeating lines until they were sufficiently satisfactory, subsequently applying bold washes, is entirely derived from Rubens. Likewise, the theme of the man holding with his teeth the cloth on which Christ's body is lying was borrowed from Rubens. It is not surprising, therefore, that this drawing for some time was considered as being from the hand of Rubens.

JORDAENS

558 Head of an Old Man Drinking
(Portrait of Adam van Noort)

Black and red chalk, heightened with white, 187 x 136 mm.

Cambridge, Fitzwilliam Museum (No. 2083), Bequeathed
by C. A. Shannon, R.A., 1937

PROVENANCE

Ricketts and Shannon

LITERATURE

Delen, *Jacob Jordaens*, pp. 7, 13

d'Hulst, No. 77, Fig. 126

JORDAENS MADE this study from life for the figure of the King in
his painting, "The King Drinks" (Museum, Brussels). Jordaens often
used people from his immediate surroundings as models for figures
in his paintings and drawings. In this case, Jordaens' father-in-law,
Adam van Noort, also a painter, was the model for the drawing and
consequently for the king in the painting.

JORDAENS

559 Venus Sleeping

Brush and brown ink, water color and red chalk
  over black chalk, 173 x 267 mm.

Lille, Palais des Beaux-Arts, Musée Wicar (No. 970)

PROVENANCE

Wicar

LITERATURE

d'Hulst, No. 130, Fig. 167

IN A technique that Jordaens often used, employing chalks as well as different water colors, the artist sketched "Venus Asleep," accompanied by two resting nymphs and a standing Amor. The composition, based upon Rubens' painting representing "Cimon and Iphigenia," served Jordaens for his painting, now in the museum at Antwerp, also representing "Venus Asleep."

JORDAENS

560 A Study of a Seated Man

Brush in brown and gray over black chalk, 285 x 267 mm.

Los Angeles, California, Los Angeles County Museum
(No. P.234.54-1)

THE ARTIST sketched the man freely and boldly, creating the impression that we look down upon the figure. The eyes of the figure are closed, the mouth is slightly opened, the left arm seems to be completely relaxed. The figure perhaps was thought of as one of the apostles sleeping in Gethsemane.

LUCAS VAN UDEN

(1595-1672)

L UCAS VAN U DEN *Born at Antwerp 18 October 1595.*
Student of his father Artus van Uden. 1626-27 member of
the guild. Died at Antwerp 4 November 1672.

561 Woodland with Monastic Buildings

Pen and brown ink, gray wash and body-colors,
   221 x 310 mm.

New York, The Pierpont Morgan Library

PROVENANCE

Fairfax Murray

LITERATURE

Stampfle, *Landscape Drawings and Watercolors,*
  1953, No. 57

L UCAS VAN Uden, one of the foremost landscape painters in Antwerp
in the seventeenth century, was often called upon by Rubens, Jordaens, and Teniers to add landscapes to figure scenes painted by them.
His landscapes have a greater restfulness than those of Rubens; his
interpretation of nature is less joyful than that of his great contemporary. His paintings, often small in size and unpretentious, show
a great sensitivity for the qualities of light and space. Especially in
his colored drawings we learn to appreciate him as a landscape artist
who paid attention to detail and loved accuracy, yet knew how to
convey the impression of the greatness of nature.

The present drawing was finished as if it were supposed to be a
complete work of art; nevertheless, Lucas van Uden used it himself
as a starting point for a painting (now in the Museum at Basel).

FRANS SNYDERS

(1579-1657)

FRANS SNYDERS Born at Antwerp 11 November 1579. Studied with Pieter Brueghel the Younger and Hendrik van Balen. 1602 member of the guild. 1608-09 in Italy. Influenced by Rubens. Worked in Antwerp. Died there 19 August 1657.

562/563 Studies of a Boar's Head

Pen in brown and brown wash, 102 x 145 mm.
  and 128 x 185 mm.

London, British Museum (Nos. 0010-130 and 0010-131)

PROVENANCE

Knight

LITERATURE

Hind, *British Museum Catalogue*, II, p. 35,
  Nos. 113 and 114

THESE TWO studies of the same head of a boar, seen from two different points of view, were formerly attributed to Rubens. It is more likely, however, that Frans Snyders, who was often asked by Rubens to paint as "specialist in animals" some of the dogs, boar, deer, or other animals in paintings of his, must be considered as the artist who made these studies.

PIETER JANSZOON SAENREDAM

(1597-1665)

PIETER JANSZOON SAENREDAM *Born at Assendelft 9 June 1597. Student of P. de Grebber. Worked in Haarlem. Died there 31 May 1665.*

564 The Nave and Side Aisles of the Cathedral at Utrecht

Pen and brown ink, colored chalks and water colors, on blue paper, 385 x 525 mm.

Inscribed by the artist: *den 15en September int jaar 1636 Pieter Saenredam geteykent Ste Maertens Domskerck binnen uÿttrecht*

Utrecht, Gemeente Archief

PROVENANCE

Munnincks van Cleef

LITERATURE

Hofstede de Groot, *Utrechtsche kerken*, p. 5, Pl. III

Swillens, *Pieter Janszoon Saenredam, Schilder van Haarlem*, No. 124, Fig. 155

Catalogue Exhibition Dutch Drawings, 1958-59, No. 54, illustration of detail on cover

Catalogue Exhibition Saenredam, 1961, No. 119

SAENREDAM, DEDICATED himself almost exclusively to the portrayal of architecture. In his paintings as well as in his drawings he combined a sensitive and poetic feeling for the large interior spaces and their interrelationship, and for the light tempered by the stained glass windows, with an interest in detail and an accuracy in rendering architectural features worthy of an archaeologist or architectural historian.

The drawing here reproduced represents the nave and side aisles of the cathedral at Utrecht seen from behind the crossing near the south transept. Since the nave collapsed in 1674 and was demolished afterward, the drawing is a precious document of the original appearance of the Gothic nave. The artist, however, gave more than a mere document: he translated the pews, the chandeliers, and organs with the background of pillars, windows, and vaults into an intricate pattern of forms and lines.

The artist used such drawings as this one, sketched on the spot, as the first stage in the preparation of his paintings. The next step was a measured drawing of the size of the painting to be executed. This measured drawing subsequently was transferred to the panel, then the artist started to paint the subject. Of the drawing here reproduced no measured drawing or painted version has come down to us.

De Ste: Catryne kerck,
Binnen Muytrecht.

SAENREDAM

565 Interior of St. Catherine's Church at Utrecht

Black chalk and pen in brown, 302 x 393 mm.

Inscribed by the artist: *P. Saenredam / De Ste Catrÿne
kerck, / binnen-uÿttrecht*, and near the vanishing point:
6 voet

Utrecht, Gemeente Archief

LITERATURE

Swillens, No. 132, Fig. 179

Catalogue Exhibition Saenredam, 1961, No. 133

ALTHOUGH SAENREDAM often included in his compositions elements from outside his field of vision, the perspective construction is always accurate. His sense for documentation made him often write on the drawing not only the year in which he executed it but also the day, or even the span of time it took him to finish it. In the drawing here reproduced the artist indicated the vanishing point within a circle, and made a note about the distance between the vanishing point and the floor as being six feet. We can conclude that he made the drawing while standing.

As in most churches in Holland in the seventeenth century the walls in St. Catherine's Church were whitewashed. Saenredam had a sensitive eye for the delicate graduations of white and gray tones caused by the cool light falling on the smooth yet lightly textured walls.

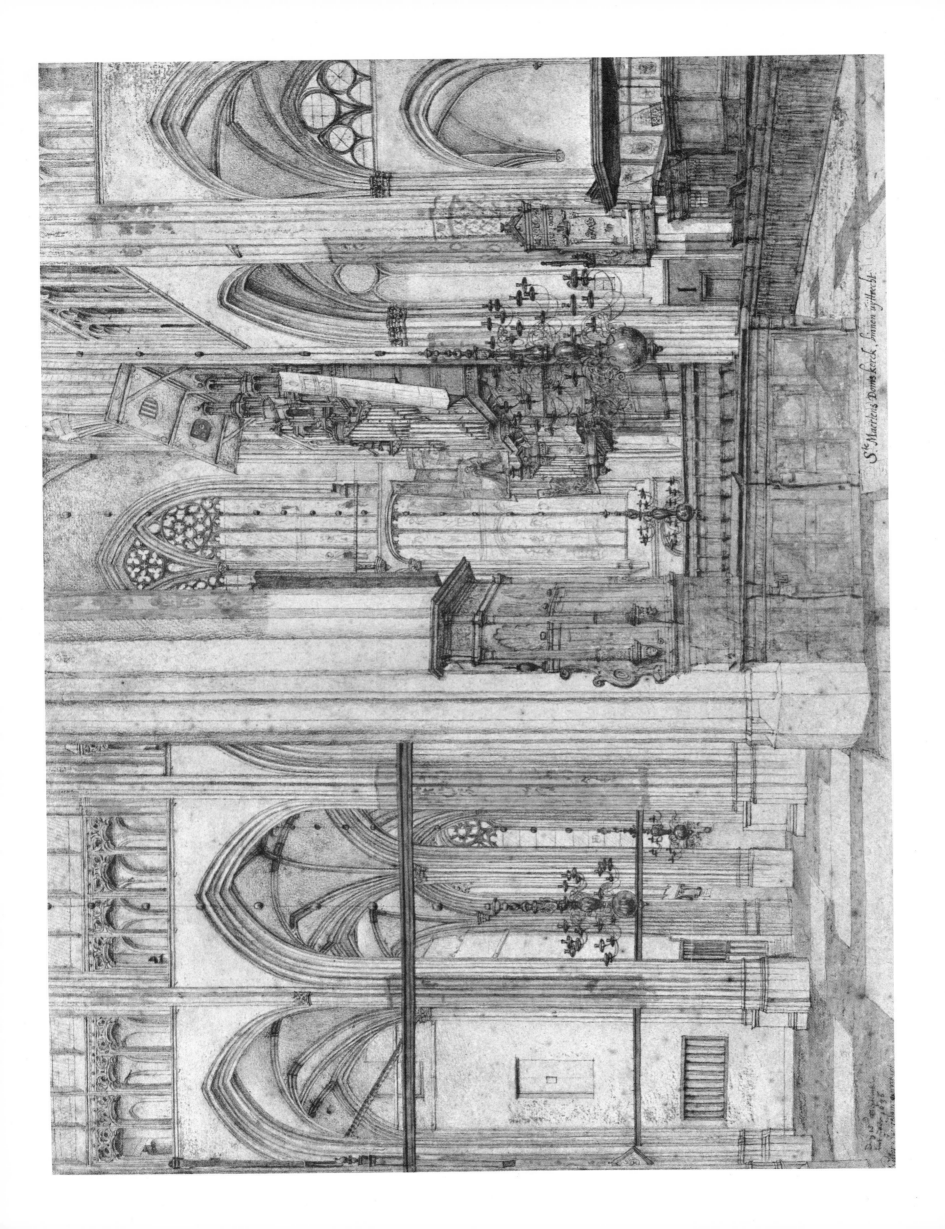

S.te Maaritens Domkerck, innen uijtheecht.

REMBRANDT HARMENSZ. VAN RIJN

(1606-1669)

REMBRANDT HARMENSZ. VAN RIJN *Born Leyden 15 July 1606. Student of Jacob van Swanenburg in Leyden and of Pieter Lastman in Amsterdam. Worked in Leyden; in Amsterdam from 1631. Died there 8 October 1669.*

566 The Reading

Sepia brush, 173 x 190 mm.

Bayonne, Musée Bonnat (No. 1447/641)

PROVENANCE

Woodburn

LITERATURE

Hofstede de Groot, No. 682

van Regteren Altena, *Hollaendische Meisterzeichnungen*, No. 19

Benesch, *The Drawings of Rembrandt*, 1954, I, No. 52, Fig. 56

REMBRANDT

567 Self-Portrait

Pen and brown ink, brush and India ink, 127 x 95 mm.

London, British Museum

PROVENANCE

Cracherode

LITERATURE

Benesch, 1954, I, No. 53, Fig. 60

THIS DRAWING is one of Rembrandt's youthful works. To judge by the woman's costume (note the collar), he probably made it between 1628 and 1630. It is not quite clear what the drawing is meant to represent. Until now it has been regarded as a family scene by candle-light, in which the woman perhaps represented Rembrandt's sister Lisbeth and the young man Rembrandt himself. The bearded man on the right, wearing a high cap, may be a rabbi. He is reading to them. In this connection "The Presentation in the Temple" also comes to mind.

According to van Regteren Altena, however, the woman is looking into a mirror. If that is the case, it seems likely that two different drawings were combined on one page. The light of the candle throws flickering shadows on the walls and unites the two drawings.

The quick, passionate way of drawing or sketching with the brush, also noticeable in the self-portrait (following plate) is typical of Rembrandt's later works during the years in Leyden (1628-29) when, after the spell of strong impulses, he again and again seeks renewed concentration.

REMBRANDT'S UNREMITTING need for self-analysis is manifested in the first years of his independent development in a number of painted and etched self-portraits. From this period (before 1630) there exist only two drawings. Yet these very two drawings, in Amsterdam and London (the latter reproduced here), embody so many essential elements that they may be said to equal or even surpass in significance the more finished portraits in painting and etching.

In these youthful works, Rembrandt records the changing facial expressions that correspond to all kinds of emotions and seeks to represent them through strong contrasts—in the present instance by seemingly arbitrary brush strokes and pen lines, which serve to suggest rather than to define. The free, spontaneous mode of drawing that Rembrandt uses here was not unknown in Europe at this time, but it had not previously been employed to express deeper human feelings. The face, looking out at the world in surprise and slight dismay, and with a lock of hair falling over the forehead, resembles the early painted self-portrait in the Mauritshuis at The Hague. There are several similar etched self-portraits; none of them, however, derives directly from this drawing, which may be dated to 1628 or a little before.

REMBRANDT

568 Old Man Seated in an Armchair

Red and black chalk, 225 x 145 mm.

Monogram and date: *RHL 1631*

Haarlem, Teyler Museum (No. O.50)

LITERATURE

Hofstede de Groot, No. 1332

Teyler Museum Catalogue, No. 50

van Borsum Buisman, *Teyler Museum, Handzeichnungen,*
    No. 13

Benesch, 1954, I, No. 40, Fig. 43

Exhibition Rembrandt Drawings, 1956, No. 16, Fig. 3

DURING 1630 and 1631 Rembrandt repeatedly drew the same old man. The artist, employing a technique also customary at this time in Italy (Guercino), used red chalk for nearly all these drawings. Sporadically, until after 1640, Rembrandt continued to draw with red chalk. Generally, however, he rendered better the delicate variations of light and the direct expression of what he observed when he used pencil and brush.

A number of study-portraits of this very old man became the model for etchings and paintings of Saints (Paul, Peter) and of prophets (Jeremiah). Once again in 1637 this same seated old man returns in a painting and an etching, i.e., Joseph telling his dreams. This reveals how Rembrandt must have remained captivated by this picturesque figure.

This drawing from Haarlem was not conceived as a direct preparatory study. Rembrandt, then twenty-five years old, was gripped here by the very idea of old age, which crumbles away like a ruin. The figure rises against the barely defined background, isolated in and fused with its heavy cloak. The tattered robe hangs over the nearly formless feet.

In this almost extinguished body life exists deeply and compassionately only in the gaze of the eyes and in the grip of the two old hands.

REMBRANDT

569 The Lamentation for Christ

Pen and bistre, the paper cut down at the top,
   the upper corners restored, 171 x 154 mm.

Berlin, Ehem. Staatliche Museen, Kupferstichkabinett
   (K.d.Z. 2312)

LITERATURE

Hofstede de Groot, No. 73

Valentiner, *Rembrandt, Handzeichnungen*, I, No. 494

Berlin Catalogue, P. 228, No. 2312, Pl. CLXXVII

Benesch, 1954, I, No. 100, Fig. 107

REMBRANDT

570 Study for Jacob Lamenting

Pen, brown ink, and wash, 172 x 155 mm.

Berlin, Ehem. Staatliche Museen, Kupferstichkabinett
   (K.d.Z. 5213)

PROVENANCE

Richardson, Jr.; Reynolds; von Beckerath

LITERATURE

Hofstede de Groot, No. 29

Valentiner, I, No. 97

Berlin Catalogue, p. 222, No. 5213, Pl. CXLIV

Benesch, 1954, I, No. 95, Fig. 102

AROUND 1635 Rembrandt made a number of pen drawings dominated by a clearly emotional character. Whether or not this is related to experiences in his personal life is difficult to determine. The series "Representation of Passion," made in 1633 and in the following years and commissioned by the Stadholder Prince Frederik Hendrik, might have induced him to sketch compositions like the one reproduced here. Even though he takes up the subject time and again, "The Lamentation for Christ" does not, in the last analysis, belong to this series.

As Benesch was the first to remark, the composition of this drawing, in which Mary clings to Christ's body in anguish, is inspired by fifteenth-century representation of Rogier van der Weyden and his school.

Originally the lower portion of the drawing was larger. The highly emotional pen strokes are concentrated in the facial expressions of the bystanders. The artist has intensified the deeply grieved expression of Mary by putting the figure of John in a similar stooping posture. The ladder and the upright part of the cross re-emphasize the tragic significance of the moment portrayed. On the right Nicodemus and Simon of Nazareth bend over this deeply moving group and effectively complete the composition by their huge size and power.

THIS DRAWING was also made around 1635. The brushstrokes that give a dark silhouette to the figure on the left (one of Jacob's wives) heighten the dramatic effect. The figure of Jacob, who throws himself backward in his chair, is enclosed in a slightly lighter shade. Being not yet satisfied with the expression on Jacob's face, Rembrandt drew a variant of it in the upper right corner. Here Jacob looks up to God and turns away from the bystanders.

This subject of Jacob lamenting the death of Joseph, whose bloody coat he sees, was treated earlier by Rembrandt. Between 1630 and 1633 he made an etching of this very subject. The head in profile at the top is a study for the man who shows the bloody coat to Jacob. More than the rest of the drawing, this study resembles the earlier version.

REMBRANDT

571 Self-Portrait

Red crayon, 129 x 119 mm.

Washington, D. C., National Gallery of Art,
    Rosenwald Collection (No. B.9409)

PROVENANCE

Valerius Roever; C. F. U. Meek

LITERATURE

Hind, *Vasari Society*, 2d Series, I, 1920, No. 8

Valentiner, II, No. 662

Benesch, *Rembrandt, Selected Drawings*, 1947, No. 81

Van Gelder, in *The Burlington Magazine*, XCI, 1949, p. 207

Benesch, 1954, II, No. 437, Figs. 494 and 495

Exhibition Rembrandt Drawings, 1956, No. 70

*Exhibition Rembrandt Drawings from American
    Collections*, 1960, No. 28, Pl. XXII

THIS IS one of the most elaborate self-portraits in red crayon. It may be dated to the year 1637, because the image corresponds to that in the painted self-portrait of 1637 in the Louvre, Paris (Bredius, No. 29) and to that in the etched "Self-Portrait" of 1638 (Bredius, No. 20). Moreover, two fragmentary sketches for a "Deposition" or "Lamentation" are drawn on the verso. They were perhaps used for one of the paintings in the series of "Representation of the Passion," commissioned by Prince Frederik Hendrik, which Rembrandt was working on during these years. If this generally accepted date is correct, Rembrandt was then thirty-one years old, in the full bloom of his life and inspired by an indomitable energy, which unmistakably radiates from this portrait.

REMBRANDT

572 The Crucifixion

Pen and wash, corrections with bistre and white,
   165 x 239 mm.

Frankfort-on-Main, Staedel Art Institute (No. 861)

LITERATURE

Hofstede de Groot, No. 332

Valentiner, I, No. 487

Benesch, 1947, No. 158

Benesch, 1954, III, No. 586, Fig. 716

IN THIS masterly composition, original in all its details, Rembrandt places the staff with the sponge soaked in vinegar in the foreground so as both to link the two groups of bystanders on the left and the right and at the same time to separate them from the figure of Christ on the cross, which is placed just slightly off center.

Meanwhile Mary, who is supported by two women, faints at the right; behind the cross Mary Magdalen falls to her knees and at the left, the anguished John leans against a rock. The city in the background is indicated by a few slight lines.

The drawing was made shortly after 1654; Benesch dates it around 1647. It carries on the theme of Christ on the cross, which begins with an etching in oval (Bredius, No. 79) around 1644 and concludes with "The Three Crosses," an etching of 1653 in which Christ was also depicted frontally.

REMBRANDT

573 Saskia Seated by a Window

Pen and wash, 172 x 125 mm.

Paris, Frits Lugt

PROVENANCE

Lawrence; Esdaile; Locker-Lampson

LITERATURE

Valentiner, II, No. 677

Benesch, 1947, No. 40

Benesch, 1954, II, No. 253

SITTING IN front of an open window, this young woman was drawn with sweeping pen lines. She peers at the outside world as her elbow rests on the windowsill and her right hand supports her head.

Broad brushstrokes on the wall behind her and on the upper part of her body barely suggest the space in the background. Thus the figure seems unattached and the melancholy pose in front of the window is even more striking.

It is not certain whether this figure represents Saskia. On the strength of the style of drawing, it is datable at 1634 and 1635.

REMBRANDT

574 Study of Two Women, Each with a Baby

Pen, bistre wash, 165 x 164 mm.

Stockholm, Nationalmuseum (No. 2039/1863)

PROVENANCE

Jan van de Cappelle (?); Crozat; Tessin

LITERATURE

Hofstede de Groot, No. 1596

Kruse and Neumann, *Die Zeichnungen Rembrandts...
im National Museum zu Stockholm*, IV, No. 7

Benesch, 1954, III, No. 708, Fig. 850

REMBRANDT SKETCHED three more drawings of women with children in the same format. Benesch dates these studies about 1646. If one assumes that Titus was depicted in one of these, the date must be put back to about 1642, as he was born in 1641. However, between 1634 and 1640 Rembrandt also drew children and babies repeatedly. These children were not his own children, since all died one or two months after birth. Later on, one hundred thirty-five of these drawings were assembled in a portfolio entitled "The Life of Women and Children," which was in the 1680 inventory of the marine painter Jan van de Cappelle.

It is hard to decide whether the second woman on this drawing is a nurse or a mother. Unlike the earlier child studies, this sheet was sketched with an unprecedented certainty of hand, with powerful strokes and heavy shading. A few heavier lines, used as contours or accents, serve to indicate the essential movement, poses and expressions. A typical example is the half-circle which delineates the arm of the suckling child.

1840.

REMBRANDT

575 Woman Carrying a Child Downstairs

Pen and brown ink, and brown wash, 187 x 133 mm.

New York, The Pierpont Morgan Library

PROVENANCE

Fairfax Murray

LITERATURE

Valentiner, II, No. 675

Fairfax Murray Publication, I, No. 191

Benesch, 1947, No. 79

Benesch, 1954, II, No. 313, Fig. 347

van Gelder, *Dutch Drawings and Prints,* No. 60

Exhibition Rembrandt Drawings from American Collections, 1960, No. 23

To JUDGE from the style of this drawing (see No. 573), it was made about 1636. The presumption that the woman is Saskia with her son Rumbartus (b. December 15, 1635) is untenable, because Rumbartus died two months after his birth and this struggling boy being carried down a staircase is plainly older. The drawing belongs to the series entitled, "The Life of Women and Children" (see the preceding drawing).

Typical of Rembrandt's style of drawing is his ability to suggest by means of repeated curved lines the movement made in descending steps. In the same fashion, he accentuates with a few bold curved pen strokes the struggling movement of the child. The two opposing actions are kept in balance by the woman's bag, which hangs on a long cord. With ineffable tenderness, the young woman (perhaps an older sister) holds her face against the cheek of the fretful little boy. By placing the figures against a blank background, while on the right a dark wash indicates a scarcely recognizable wall, the artist intensifies this radiant tenderness and involuntarily enhances the intimacy of this companionship.

REMBRANDT

576 Woman in North-Holland Costume, Seen from the Back

Pen and brown ink and wash, 220 x 150 mm.

Haarlem, Teyler Museum (No. O.51)

PROVENANCE

Richardson, Sr.; West; Lawrence; Esdaile; Mendes de Leon;
    Verstolk van Soelen; Leembruggen

LITERATURE

Hofstede de Groot, No. 1327

Valentiner, II, No. 704

Borsum Buisman, No. 14

Benesch, 1954, II, No. 315, Fig. 357

REMBRANDT

577 The Naughty Boy

Pen in brown ink, wash, heightened with white,
    206 x 143 mm.

Berlin, Ehem. Staatliche Museen, Kupferstichkabinett
    (K.d.Z. 2611/13771)

PROVENANCE

van Wessem; de Vos, Sr.; de Vos, Jr.; van Hillegom

LITERATURE

Hofstede de Groot, No. 140

Valentiner, II, No. 781

Benesch, 1947, No. 67

Benesch, 1954, II, No. 401, Fig. 459

THE WOMAN seen from the back, leans against a table. The tablecloth is turned back so that the leg of the table is visible. Behind the table sits a lad. On the right there is an indication of an arch resting on a pillar. We know the front of the woman's costume from a drawing of the same person; it is now in the British Museum, London.

Legend has it that the woman is Geertgen Dircx, the nurse of Titus. If this is so, the drawing should be dated after 1641-42, at least six years later than is warranted by its style.

Precisely in 1635-36 Rembrandt was able to refine his way of applying wash by very subtle shading. He concentrates everything on the essential points by leaving out all superfluous details and the execution is controlled and rapid: not one line is redundant.

MADE AROUND 1635, this drawing of a popular subject was soon copied (Budapest, Hamburg). The struggling lad resembles the boy being carried down a staircase (see No. 575). The boy also reminds one of Cupid, painted by Rembrandt in 1634 (Collection Thijssen, Lugano) and especially of the Ganymede, who bears the same features and is also depicted crying (1635, Dresden).

In this drawing, the little boy loses his right shoe; the older woman in the background, who may be a nurse, lifts her left hand in an admonishing gesture and holds an object, which may be a toy, in her right hand. In the doorway two children look on with keen interest.

The walls and the staircase on the left are indicated sketchily and tersely, but the shadows create the illusion of space. Without doubt this drawing also belongs to the series of one hundred thirty-five sketches, later assembled in a portfolio entitled "The Life of Women and Children."

REMBRANDT

578 An Elephant

Black chalk, 233 x 354 mm.

Vienna, Albertina (Inv. 17558)

LITERATURE

Hofstede de Groot, No. 1469

Benesch, 1947, No. 83

Benesch, 1954, II, No. 457

WE KNOW of four drawings with studies of elephants by Rembrandt. Two are in Vienna, one in London, and one in New York, The Pierpont Morgan Library. There were probably more of them, as this elephant appears again in 1638 in a different pose, in the background of an etching with Adam and Eve. On another drawing three elephants appear. Probably it is the same animal portrayed in three different positions.

Little is known about this elephant, which must have toured the Netherlands as a spectacle in 1637, except that Roelandt Savery (Utrecht) also drew a similar animal several times. Studies of flowers and plants, although they may occasionally appear in paintings, are not known by Rembrandt's hand, but animal studies (birds of paradise, horses, pigs, dromedaries, lions) are numerous. Of these, the elephant studies are the most characteristic. A few lines of shadings suggest the wrinkled skin and the movement of the trunk and the heavy feet are depicted with quick strokes. It was only rarely that Rembrandt signed and dated his drawings; apparently the excitement of this spectacle caused him to record it by a date.

REMBRANDT

579 Portrait of Saskia in a Turban

Black chalk and brown wash, on grayish paper,
195 x 140 mm.

Bayonne, Musée Bonnat (No. 1450/644)

PROVENANCE

Diaz; Bonnat

LITERATURE

Benesch, 1954, IV, No. 761, Fig. 912

REMBRANDT

580 Two Studies of Saskia Asleep

Pen and brush in brown ink, 130 x 171 mm.

New York, The Pierpont Morgan Library

PROVENANCE

van Rijmsdyck; Tighe; Fairfax Murray

LITERATURE

Fairfax Murray Publication I, No. 180

Valentiner, II, No. 690

Benesch, 1954, II, No. 189, Fig. 319

Exhibition Rembrandt Drawings from American Collections, 1960, No. 24

THIS STUDY for a portrait of a woman with a beret and ostrich feather, about 1641-43, is a good example of Rembrandt's complex manner of drawing. The first step was to sketch in thin chalk lines the foreground, the figure itself, and a suggestion of the niche in the background. In the next phase Rembrandt takes brush and bistre and with broad strokes indicates the shadow within the niche. Then, still using the brush, he applies spots of brown ink here and there upon the drawing. The background barely dry, the draughtsman now takes a heavier black chalk: the beret is firmly outlined and then the mantle and sleeves of the subject; with only a few lines a curtain is hung at the right. Miraculously enough, there now emerges from this diversified maze of lines a perceptible unity; the figure has taken on relief and has come into being, as it were, out of almost indefinable suggestions.

No painted portrait is known after this drawing. Between 1640 and 1643, however, Rembrandt painted a number of portraits behind balustrades or in niches, and some also in fancy dress. Rembrandt found the prototype for them in Venetian paintings of the early sixteenth century and in Raphael's portrait of Castiglione, which was sold at auction in Amsterdam in 1639.

THESE STUDIES were made in 1635-37. The upper one was undoubtedly drawn first and it resembles Saskia most. In the second (lower) study, Saskia has moved a little, she has sunk deeper in her pillow, and slightly shifted her hand; her mouth is now open and her sleep is rendered so directly and vividly that one seems to hear her breathing or even snoring slightly. The pillow and the cover are indicated with a few lines. The difference between a somewhat lighter and a heavier sleeper is brilliantly observed and typified.

Between 1635 and 1641 four children were born to Saskia and she spent much time confined to her room. Rembrandt was often in the bedroom, observing and drawing the intimate atmosphere of sleeping, resting, and nursing.

REMBRANDT

581 Panorama of London, with Old St. Paul's (Seen from the North)

Pen and brown ink, heightened with white, 164 x 318 mm.

Berlin, Ehem. Staatliche Museen, Kupferstichkabinett (K.d.Z. 1150)

LITERATURE

Hofstede de Groot, No. 170

Benesch, 1947, No. 112

Rosenberg, *Great Draughtsmen from Pisanello to Picasso*, p. 79, Fig. 151

Benesch, 1954, IV, No. 788, Fig. 935

Berlin Catalogue, p. 237, No. 1150, Pl. CLXXIV

MOST AUTHORS agree that this drawing must have been made around 1640. A second, less spontaneously drawn view of London is now in Vienna. Two other drawings, executed at the same time and stylistically comparable to this view of London, bear the date of 1640 and are signed. They represent St. Alban's Cathedral and Windsor Castle. Lugt considers the signatures false and attributes the drawings to Govert Flinck or some other disciple of Rembrandt; Benesch, Hind, Rosenberg, and others believe them to be Rembrandt's, executed however after prints or other graphic models. Hofstede de Groot surmised that Rembrandt took a trip to London, but this assumption has been proved untenable.

All authors agree that the drawing reproduced here is the most beautiful of the series, not only because of its interplay of contrasts and sensitive touch, but also because, to quote Rosenberg: "there are subtle transitions and at no point is the sequence of planes interrupted; in the bright and hazy distance the building (St. Paul's) retains its structural clarity and is bathed in a beautiful sunlight."

The use of motifs such as this view quite agrees in general with Rembrandt's tendency, shortly before and after 1640, to make use in his paintings of architectonic elements that derive from old cathedrals, castles, and similar structures, which the artist had not necessarily seen in actuality. The manner of drawing, which is distinguished by a loose system of lines and rather reminds one of crude brushstrokes, is anything but characteristic of Rembrandt's work. However, the way in which space is suggested and the handling of the luminous effects speaks for Rembrandt.

REMBRANDT

582 Lion Resting

Pen and brush in brown ink, 138 x 207 mm.

Paris, Louvre, Cabinet des Dessins (No. RF 4.721)

PROVENANCE

Reveley; Roupell; Bonnat

LITERATURE

Hofstede de Groot, No. 751

Neumann, *Rembrandt Handzeichnungen*, Pl. XVII

Demonts, Pl. XXXIV

Lugt, III, No. 1190

van Regteren Altena, *Hollaendische Meisterzeichnungen*, No. 23

Benesch, 1954, V, No. 1214, Fig. 1438

REMBRANDT DREW a number of studies of lions, all certainly after life. The date of these studies is not altogether certain. Lugt suspects that they were made around 1641-42. Benesch, however, divides them into various groups and dates this particular drawing 1651-52. The nuances of the texture of the skin, the build of the animal, and the powerful tail, which could start lashing at any moment, are first set down with the brush and then accentuated with forceful pen lines.

This example from the Louvre belongs to a set of exceptionally beautiful studies that Rembrandt once kept in a book entitled *Beesten nae(r) 't leven* (animals after life), according to the inventory (1656) of his collection.

REMBRANDT

583 Study in Reverse for the "Hundred Guilder Print"

Pen and brown ink, wash, heightened with white,
    144 x 184 mm.

Berlin, Ehem. Staatliche Museen, Kupferstichkabinett
    (K.d.Z. 2695)

PROVENANCE

E. Durand(?); Th. Rousseau; Posonyi

LITERATURE

Hofstede de Groot, No. 56

Valentiner, I, No. 409

Neumann, *Aus der Werkstatt Rembrandts*, p. 92, Fig. 27

Benesch, 1954, I, No. 188, Fig. 200

Berlin Catalogue, p. 225, No. 2695, Pl. CLII

THE "HUNDRED Guilder Print" is an etching on which Rembrandt worked for many years. After making many changes, he completed the complicated composition around 1648-49. It represents Christ healing the sick and blessing the children while apostles and scribes surround him and the rich youth approaches him. The content of the representation is based on the text of Matthew 19.

It is now generally accepted that the first sketches for this composition, to which the one from Berlin reproduced here also belongs, were designed around 1642-43. (Benesch assumed it to be as early as 1639-40.)

In this drawing Rembrandt has made a study of a group of sick people. The figures in the foreground and the woman making an imploring gesture will reappear in the etching in a more elaborate form. The heavy lines with which the figures seen from the back are constructed and the thicker pen lines around the arm and the feet of the prostrate woman were drawn last of all, in order to give the group plasticity.

The drawing is a marvelous example of Rembrandt's vivid imagination and inventiveness.

REMBRANDT

584 The Return of the Prodigal Son

Pen and brown ink, wash and corrections with white body-
color, 209 x 227 mm.

Haarlem, Teyler Museum (No. O.48)

PROVENANCE

de Vos, Jr.

LITERATURE

Hofstede de Groot, No. 1318

Valentiner, I, No. 388

Borsum Buisman, No. 12

Benesch, 1954, III, No. 519, Fig. 641

"THE RETURN of the Prodigal Son" was first depicted by Rembrandt in an etching of 1636. He repeated the theme in this drawing of about 1642 and again, shortly before his death, he treated the same subject in a painting.

As Luke 15:20 says of the prodigal, ". . . But when he was yet a great way off, his father saw him, and had compassion, and ran, and fell on his neck, and kissed him." Rembrandt depicted here the emotion and the quiet but poignant joy of the father and the son reunited after the latter has said, "I am no more worthy to be called thy son."

In the etching of 1636 Rembrandt strongly emphasizes the boorish character of the Prodigal Son. In the drawing, however, the depiction of the profound moment itself becomes all-important. The work has been set down with pathos and the lines are so charged with emotion that they communicate to us the inner feelings of the two figures. This suggestive manner of drawing asks us to supplement what we do not see. By repeating the lines enclosing the arms of the two figures, Rembrandt suggests their gestures, because every line indicates a movement that reveals a different phase of the violent emotions they feel. This is a painter's drawing. The uncertain play of light and dark creates contrasts that correspond marvelously to the changing moods. But these very contrasts also create a feeling of space and set our imagination to work. This principle of mobility, which at the same time represents a human emotion, is one of the fundamentals of the seventeenth-century European art.

REMBRANDT

585 Cottage near the Entrance of a Wood

Pen and ink, sepia wash, 286 x 439 mm.

New York, Robert Lehman

PROVENANCE

Richardson, Sr.; Pond; Barnard; West; Esdaile; Lawrence;
Baron Grahame; Heseltine; Gutekunst; Hirsch

LITERATURE

Hofstede de Groot, No. 1049

Benesch, 1947, No. 64

Benesch, 1954, IV, No. 815, Fig. 965

Exhibition Rembrandt Drawings from American Collections, 1960, No. 40

THIS IS the largest landscape drawing from Rembrandt's hand. He seldom drew in this large format and the very fact that this drawing is signed and bears a date proves the importance that Rembrandt himself attached to it.

Chance would have it that his pupil, Lambert Doomer, drew the same farmhouse. The water-butt and the window on the right next to the door are missing in his drawing. Nor is there any indication of a wood on the left. Yet it seems likely that Doomer, who was in his last year of apprenticeship, was on the spot at the same time as Rembrandt.

In 1645 Doomer left for France. In view of Doomer's character, one can take for granted the topographical accuracy of his drawing. One can then conclude that Rembrandt added a strongly dramatic accent to the scene by including the country road on the left, the dark group of trees, and details such as the poultry in the lower right corner. The foreground is enlivened by vigorous pen lines.

The irregular contours, the surprising play of light and shade, and the unmonumental romantic motif correspond to Rembrandt's conceptions, which are essentially unclassical.

REMBRANDT

587 Standing Male Nude

Pen and brown ink, wash, heightened with white,
  252 x 193 mm.

London, British Museum

PROVENANCE

Cracherode; Payne Knight

LITERATURE

Hofstede de Groot, No. 933

Hofstede de Groot, *Bredius bundel*, p. 93

Benesch, 1947, No. 148

Benesch, 1954, IV, No. 710, Fig. 853

THIS DRAWING introduces us to Rembrandt's atelier where a nude model is posing. We know from other drawings made in Rembrandt's studio that the pupils worked sitting in a wide circle around the subject. The master stood behind them, giving advice and making corrections. At least three more drawings of this same young man exist, each of them drawn from a different angle. And, in an etching of about 1646 (Bartsch, No. 194), Rembrandt depicted this very model in almost the same fashion.

The subject stands in front of a curtain and leans with his left arm on a pillow. Possibly the drawing reproduced here was originally the work of a pupil, whose hand can barely be recognized beneath the master's authoritative corrections.

REMBRANDT

588 The Liberation of St. Peter from Prison

Pen and ink, sepia wash, 195 x 220 mm.

Frankfort-on-Main, Staedel Art Institute (No. 858)

LITERATURE

Hofstede de Groot, No. 333

Valentiner, II, No. 547

Benesch, 1954, III, No. 616, Fig. 747

THE LIBERATION of Peter is described in *Acts*, Chap. XII. During the night before Herod was to bring Peter to the tribunal of the people, Peter slept in captivity between two soldiers, while in front of the door the warden guarded the prison. The Bible does not mention that the soldiers slept. It only says: "And behold, the angel of the Lord came upon him, and a light shined in the prison; and he smote Peter on the side, and raised him up, saying, Arise up quickly. And his chains fell off from his hands."

Rembrandt chose for this drawing the moment of Peter's awakening. The light shining in the prison is indicated by a few strokes. The heavy strokes on the right and in the left foreground accentuate the space. The solid form of the sleeping soldier suggests his deep rest and concentrates our attention on the miraculous apparition of the Angel, whose outspread wings effectively complete the composition. The drawing was made around 1648.

REMBRANDT

589 Nurse and Eating Child

Black chalk, 165 x 130 mm.

Vienna, Albertina (Inv. 17755)

LITERATURE

Hofstede de Groot, No. 1455

Benesch, 1954, II, No. 276, Fig. 303

THIS DRAWING was made around 1635. The artist sketched the figure of the woman in a few quickly executed chalk lines. These lines serve to give a vague indication of the shape of the woman rather than a clear contour. All attention is concentrated on the face of the nurse as she carefully follows the movements of the child, who is totally absorbed in eating a fruit (?). The halo over the child's head is very curious. It could not merely be the beams of a burning candle (as Benesch believes), because the shadows would then fall in a different way. Probably Rembrandt, while making the drawing, thought of Mary with the child Christ or of Anne with the young Mary. The latter representation does not occur elsewhere in Rembrandt's work.

REMBRANDT

590 A Farm on a Country Road

Pen in brown ink, wash, arched at top, 128 x 200 mm.

Chatsworth, Devonshire Collections (No. 1037)

PROVENANCE

Flinck

LITERATURE

Hofstede de Groot, No. 851

Benesch, 1954, VI, No. 1233, Fig. 1460

REMBRANDT

591 A Farm on the Waterfront

Pen in brown ink, wash, and white body-color,
128 x 204 mm.

Chatsworth, Devonshire Collections (No. 1033)

PROVENANCE

Flinck

LITERATURE

Hofstede de Groot, No. 847

Lugt, *Mit Rembrandt in Amsterdam*, p. 125, Fig. 78

Benesch, 1954, VI, No. 1232, Fig. 1459

LANDSCAPE DRAWINGS of Amsterdam and surroundings by Rembrandt were in the possession of the son of Govert Flinck and were acquired in 1723 by the Duke of Devonshire. Most of these drawings were made between 1645 and 1655. It can be assumed that the example reproduced here was executed in 1648-49, during one of the many walks that Rembrandt used to take from Amsterdam.

All these sketches are distinguished by their clarity, balance, sense of space, and atmosphere. Details such as the dovecote hanging on the farmhouse, the haystack, and the sunken road never distract our attention from the unity of the whole. The artist constantly discovers the countryside afresh and then records it in its full richness and in all its essential elements.

SEE THE notes to the preceding plate.

This is one of the very beautiful sketches from the series once in Flinck's possession. The farmhouse is located in a picturesque spot at the water's edge, near Ouderkerk on the Amstel River. Lugt suggests that the view is taken on the Bullewijk looking toward its church tower, which is in the background.

The rowboat in the middle of the foreground not only creates a sense of space and depth in the composition, but also gives it a serene peace that pervades the atmosphere. The drawing was executed around 1650.

REMBRANDT

592 Cottage beside a Canal

Reed pen, washed in bistre, 149 x 248 mm.

Chicago, Illinois, The Art Institute (No. 53.37), The Clarence Buckingham Collection

PROVENANCE

Zoomer; Verstolk van Soelen; de Vos; Seymour
Haden; Stroelin

LITERATURE

Hofstede de Groot, No. 954

Lugt, *Mit Rembrandt in Amsterdam*, Fig. 3

Benesch, 1954, VI, No. 1297, Fig. 1527

Exhibition Rembrandt Drawings from American Collections, 1960, No. 52, Fig. 44

REMBRANDT MADE a number of sketches of this thatched cottage, each from a different point of view. Two are in Chatsworth, one is in the Lugt collection, Paris, and one is in the Print Room in Copenhagen. The relaxed manner of drawing indicates a late date of execution. It is generally accepted that the drawing was made between 1652 and 1655. Two rowboats lie in the foreground in the canal. On the right, beside the farmhouse, three fishing nets are hung up to dry. In front of the house two persons are seated at a table. Behind them stands a tall pole holding a stork's nest. In spite of the complicated assemblage of buildings and trees, this quick sketch maintains a remarkable unity.

REMBRANDT

593 The Prodigal Son among the Swine

Pen and brown ink, 159 x 235 mm.

London, British Museum (No. 1910-2-12-179)

PROVENANCE

James; Salting

LITERATURE

Hofstede de Groot, No. 1119

Valentiner, I, No. 387

Benesch, 1954, III, No. 601, Fig. 732

REMBRANDT

594 The Raising of the Daughter of Jairus

Pen and brown ink, and wash, 144 x 193 mm.

Copenhagen, Royal Museum of Fine Arts (No. 18008),
   Gift of the Ny Carlsberg Foundation

PROVENANCE

von Frey; Falck

LITERATURE

Valentiner, II, No. 824

Fischer and Sthyr, *Seks Aarhundreders europaeisk
   Tegnekunst*, p. 109, Pl. LIII

Benesch, 1954, V, No. 1002, Fig. 1217

THE THEME of the Prodigal Son is one that Rembrandt took up again and again. In this case it was perhaps chosen after he had seen an engraving of the same subject by Dürer. The emaciated Prodigal Son kneels, leaning on a stick by a trough from which swine are eating. On the right is a sow, a suckling pig beneath her. There are three known studies of pigs by Rembrandt. These drawings form the basis of this composition, which renders only the bare essentials of pose and expression with the utmost economy of means. This sober style of drawing is characteristic for the years 1646-50.

IT IS not altogether clear what subject the artist intended to represent here. It is possible that it shows Christ healing a sick person or perhaps raising the daughter of Jairus, a theme already treated by Rembrandt earlier.

The drawing was executed around 1655-57. After 1650 Rembrandt tried to approach the essence of events, often taken from the Bible, by minimizing the use of lines in order to indicate movement and suggest volume.

The brushstrokes help to intensify the atmosphere. The parallel shadings, on the right and over the bed, give one a lively sensation of space and movement.

REMBRANDT

595 The Baptism of Christ

Pen and brown ink, wash, 165 x 252 mm.
Dresden, Staatliche Kunstsammlungen (No. C.1312)

LITERATURE
Holfstede de Groot, No. 214
Valentiner, I, No. 350
Benesch, 1954, VI, No. A86, Fig. 1680

THIS DRAWING was constructed with strong, heavy, and angular lines and then provided with parallel shadings. It shows all the peculiarities of Rembrandt's late style of drawing. It belongs, however, to a group that ought perhaps be lifted as a whole out of Rembrandt's *oeuvre* and attributed to an unknown pupil of his. Whether this remarkable pupil might be Aert de Gelder is not certain.

Most of the drawings of this group are distinguished by a clear and well-organized composition. The rays of light falling upon Christ or issuing from him are mostly indicated by lines, as is done here. The drawing was probably executed around 1660 or later.

REMBRANDT

596 The Carrying of the Cross

Pen and brown ink, wash, and corrections
   in white body-color, 174 x 273 mm.

Haarlem, Teyler Museum (No. O.62.A)

PROVENANCE

von Fries; de Bailleul (?); Marignane; de Groot

LITERATURE

Valentiner, II, No. 482

Borsum Buisman, No. 15

Benesch, 1947, No. 197

Benesch, 1954, V, No. 923, Fig. 1134

REMBRANDT MADE three different drawings of this scene but never made use of them for an etching or a painting. This drawing is the latest known version, dated by Benesch in 1653 and by van Regteren Altena in 1659-60 on account of the similarity to "The Capture of Christ" of that very period (Stockholm), which likewise has a repoussoir at the left.

The figures are barely indicated in outline, except for the main group with the figure of Christ falling beneath the weight of the cross and Mary, kneeling beside him to wipe off his brow. The procession has come to a stop; the soldiers at right are engaged in a violent discussion. The heavy shading in the middle lends added emphasis to the collapse of Christ. The emotional content of the scene finds its reflection in the broad strokes of the reed pen at the left, which have a remarkable freedom and suggest in every detail the terror and tragedy of the drama.

REMBRANDT

597 Noah's Ark

Reed pen and brown ink and brush, 199 x 243 mm.

Chicago, Illinois, The Art Institute (No. 53.36), The
   Clarence Buckingham Collection

PROVENANCE

de Villenave; van den Zande; de Biron; Mathey; Stroelin

LITERATURE

Valentiner, I, No. 6

Benesch, 1954, V, No. 1045, Fig. 1261

*Exhibition Rembrandt Drawings from American Collec-
   tions*, 1960, No. 75, Fig. 68

REMBRANDT

598 Christ Walking on the Waves

Pen and brown ink, 190 x 290 mm.

London, British Museum (No. 1910-2-12-180)

PROVENANCE

Lawrence; Esdaile; Salting

LITERATURE

Hofstede de Groot, No. 1120

Valentiner, I, No. 426

Benesch, 1947, No. 272

Benesch, 1954, V, No. 1043, Fig. 1259

THIS UNUSUALLY broad reed pen drawing, executed with angular lines, is a typical example of Rembrandt's late style of draughtsmanship. Unlike works of previous years this drawing possesses a picturesque diffuseness and for all its sturdy vigor, aims at tonality. There are other reasons why this drawing is original. The ark is the artist's own invention and breaks with every traditional conception. Moreover, it is nearly always the moment when the animals enter the vessel two by two that is depicted; Rembrandt, however, chose the text of *Genesis* 7:7: "Noah went in, and his sons, and his wife, and his sons' wives with him." Only after that do the animals enter. The figure seen from the back on the left is probably Noah himself, showing the ark to his wife. The drawing was executed around 1660 or shortly afterward. No painting of this scene by Rembrandt is known.

THIS DRAWING was executed around 1660. Even more strongly than in No. 596, the artist strove here for simplification. The drawing is based on the text of *Matthew* 14, verses 22-32, which is the passage where Peter, who has already left the boat on Christ's command, walks toward Jesus on the waves, but being seized with fear starts to sink and exclaims "Lord, save me." Then the Bible says: "And immediately, Jesus stretched forth his hand, and caught him, and said unto him, 'O thou of little faith, wherefore didst thou doubt?' " This is the exact moment Rembrandt chose to portray.

He has isolated the two main figures by placing them within a blank triangular space, indicating the light with a few beams. The stem and stern of the ship in the second plane are separated by this triangle. The disciples, some working, others looking on intently, are clustered around the mast in the bow of the ship. The ship and the waves are indicated sketchily and there is a suggestion of the warning of the storm. The main accent falls, however, on the reassuring gesture of Christ.

REMBRANDT

599 Female Nude Sitting on a Stool

Pen and brown ink, washed in sepia, 211 x 174 mm.

Chicago, Illinois, The Art Institute (No. 53.38),
   The Clarence Buckingham Collection

PROVENANCE

Corot; Stroelin

LITERATURE

Benesch, 1954, V, No. 1122, Fig. 1344

Exhibition Rembrandt Drawings from American Collections, 1960, No. 74, Fig. 66

BETWEEN 1658 and 1661 Rembrandt drew a series of female nudes. Seven etchings of nudes were also completed in these years. One of these etchings, dated 1658, is related to this study and bears the inscription "For the Surgeon's guild." It is therefore possible that Rembrandt found his models in hospitals during these years.

The artist has established the contours of his subject with a minimum of pen lines, sometimes drawing sets of almost parallel strokes. For the most part the modeling is indicated with the brush and with a few light touches of shading. The structure of the brush strokes of the background, dark on the left and with rays of light flowing in from the right and from the top, lends an intense animation to the space. Rembrandt's main purpose here was to capture the numerous delicate nuances produced by the shadows, which at the same time establish a unity between the figure and its surroundings.

Rembrandt did not pursue a classical ideal of beauty. His models simply offered him the opportunity to study the light effects and to approximate reality.

REMBRANDT

600 Parable of the Wicked Servant

Reed pen and brown ink, 100 x 140 mm.

Leningrad, Hermitage (No. 21584), Acquired by the
Hermitage in 1925

PROVENANCE

Prince Youssoupoff

LITERATURE

Benesch, 1954, V, No. 1055

Kuznetsof, in *Trudy Gosudarstvennogo Ermitazha,
Zapadnoevropevskoe Iskusstvo*, VI, 1961, p. 71

WITH THE utmost brevity Rembrandt sketched four standing figures, characterizing all persons clearly as to their action and their relationships to each other notwithstanding the bold simplicity of lines and forms. The standing man wearing a tall hat is clearly dominating the scene while he is addressing himself with conviction and authority to the obsequiously bowing figure. The man at the very right accompanies the latter and expresses concern and interest, while the figure at the left seems rather an onlooker than an actively engaged participant of the scene. Style and technique leave no doubt as to the time when Rembrandt made the drawing; it certainly is one of his late studies, executed ca. 1660-65.

The subject represented in this drawing, traditionally interpreted as the "Parable of the Laborers in the Vineyard," is more likely another parable, as has been suggested by Kuznetsof, namely the "Parable of the Wicked Servant." Probably the end of the parable is illustrated, according to which "then his lord, after that he had called him, said unto him, O thou wicked servant, I forgave thee all that debt, because thou desiredst me: Shouldest not thou also have had compassion on thy fellowservant, even as I had pity on thee? And his lord was wroth, and delivered him to the tormentors, till he should pay all that was due unto him" (*Matthew* 18:32-34).

JAN LIEVENS

(1607-1674)

JAN LIEVENS *Born at Leyden 24 October 1607. Student of Joris van Schooten at Leyden and of P. Lastman in Amsterdam 1617-19. Worked in Leyden, England, Antwerp (1634-43), The Hague (1661), and from 1643 in Amsterdam, where he died 8 June 1674.*

601 Portrait of the Clergyman Caspar Streso (1603-1644)

Black chalk, 232 x 193 mm.

Paris, Frits Lugt

PROVENANCE

Schaak; Ploos van Amstel; Kerr Lawson

LITERATURE

Henkel, *Le Dessin hollandais des origines au XVIIe siècle,* Pl. LXXIV

Schneider, *Jan Lievens,* No. 272

THE REVERSE side of this drawing bears an inscription of about 1700, mentioning that "Domine Strso" (sic) was a clergyman in The Hague. This drawing, then, must have been executed after Lievens' return from Antwerp, which took place around 1641.

The firm draughtsmanship recalls the style of the Flemish masters, who intended their portrait drawings to be engraved. Lievens in fact made an etching after this portrait (Dutuit, No. 67).

The draughtsman has here liberated himself altogether from the influence of Rembrandt's graphic technique. In Antwerp, in the circle of the great portrait painters, he followed the International portrait style, which imitated nature faithfully down to the smallest detail. Especially in the face one can observe a high degree of refinement, which might indicate a rather late date of execution. Since Lievens established himself in The Hague in 1661, Henkel places the drawing between 1661 and 1664. If that is correct, there may be a connection with the style of Jan de Bray and Cornelis Visscher.

JAN VAN GOYEN

(1596-1656)

Jan van Goyen Born at Leyden 13 January 1596. Studied with van Schilperoort, van Swanenburg and Esaias van de Velde in Haarlem and in The Hague. Worked from 1631 in Leyden. From 1634 in The Hague, where he died 30 April 1656.

602 Landscape near a River

Black chalk, wash, 110 x 195 mm.

Signed and dated: *VG 1631*

Berlin, Ehem. Staatliche Museen, Kupferstichkabinett (K.d.Z. 12259)

PROVENANCE

von Savigny

LITERATURE

Berlin Catalogue, p. 140, No. 12259

JAN VAN GOYEN

603 River Bank

Black chalk, brush in gray ink, wash, 172 x 272 mm.

Signed and dated: *VG 1653*

Paris, Louvre, Cabinet des Dessins (No. RF.00841)

PROVENANCE

His de la Salle

LITERATURE

Tauzia, No. 184

Lugt, I, No. 306, Pl. LIV

THIS IS a typical Dutch scene in the environs of Leyden. The sky is overcast and strong gusts of wind herald the beginning of the storm. On the right is a church tower and a country road with a bridge. Three men in a rowboat battle with the wind on the choppy water. On the left, a man walks with lowered head toward a barn, in front of which stands a tree, which is also bowed down by the storm. In the left foreground, drawn in darker shades, two women are conversing. Their skirts are blown to the right, as are the reeds along the bank.

This manner of drawing is typical of Jan van Goyen's style after about 1630. By means of a few indications he seeks to evoke an atmosphere to which even the figures are subordinated. Every detail—in short, every line—tends with remarkable consistency to strengthen the force of the wind that rages over this landscape. The diagonal lines in the sky also contribute significantly to this effect.

OVER A thousand drawings, made in rapid succession during his travels through the country, testify to the industrious life of Jan van Goyen. Especially during the years after 1640 his facility was such that he could find seemingly simple solutions for the most complicated motifs and compositions. He knew how to create a unified atmosphere by means of a refined brush technique and a very sparing use of chalk. His grasp of essentials is so sure that even the slightest detail is clearly "readable."

In the distance on the right is a church tower and a little nearer a chalk oven. In the foreground are two men in a boat carrying a large fish-basket. On the left, in front of the farm, fish are being sorted. Over shades of gray first set down with the brush, the artist has indicated the tree trunks and the leaves with small strokes and curlicues.

ALBERT CUYP

(1620-1691)

ALBERT CUYP *Born at Dordrecht in October 1620. Studied with his father Jacob Gerritsz. Cuyp. Influenced by van Goyen and Dirck van Hoogstraten. Died 7 November 1691.*

604 Study of Trees

Black chalk, with washes of greenish brown, yellow, and blue, 191 x 310 mm.

New York, The Metropolitan Museum of Art

LITERATURE

Tietze, *European Master Drawings in the United States,* No. 77

A SECOND drawing of trees and a fence, in the same format and executed in the same technique, was formerly in the Oppenheimer (*Sale Catalogue,* July, 1936, No. 227) and Larsen collections. Both were probably made around 1650.

The black chalk lines repeat the structure of the yellow drawing, in which the initial framework of the trees and landscape had first been accurately rendered. Thus a curious double effect comes into being. It is as though the wind were rustling through the leaves and branches. The old fence in the middle of the composition is the only thing to remind us of people in the wide solitude of untouched nature.

ADRIAEN VAN OSTADE

(1610-1684)

ADRIAEN VAN OSTADE *Born at Haarlem 10 December 1610. Student of Frans Hals, Brouwer, and in 1640 came under the influence of Rembrandt. Worked at Haarlem, where he died 2 May 1684.*

605 Peasants Dancing

Black chalk, pen and brush with brown ink, 208 x 163 mm.

Signed and dated: *AVostade 1636*

Haarlem, Teyler Museum (No. P.74)

PROVENANCE

van Gogh; Pitcairn Knowles

LITERATURE

Scholten, *Catalogue Teyler Museum*, p. 148, No. 74

Trautscholdt, *Ueber Adriaen van Ostade als Zeichner*,
    p. 283

THIS IS one of the earliest drawings of Adriaen van Ostade. It is dated 1636. The influence of Adriaen Brouwer is clearly perceptible in the representation and characterization of the figures. Brouwer had also lived in Haarlem shortly before 1630. However, Brouwer's drawings are sharper and more impassioned; van Ostade lacks his sarcasm and remains more genial.

The dancing peasant in the foreground, who is so beautifully characterized, conceals the source of light that shines upon the figures carousing at the table. The fiddler standing on a bench still catches this light, which is dispersed in nuances in the barn behind him. The subtle varied shades of brown impart a somewhat clearer structure to the rather flimsy lines describing the construction and the details of the setting. The pen lines that delineate the figures, however, are short and savage and their staccato abruptness lends a rather rough character to the scene.

OSTADE

606 Group of People Leaning over a Rail

Brush, bistre, and wash in India ink, 188 x 297 mm.
Frankfort-on-Main, Staedel Art Institute (No. 905)

THE FIGURES are probably spectators standing behind a wooden rail, watching and discussing a game of skittles in the garden of a tavern. The drawing was probably made around 1640-45. It is executed with sharp, irascible pen lines and angular accents. The deliberate way in which the shading of the figures is applied in a grayish brown wash gives the group a lively and varied character. Yet the animated facial expression and the striking way in which each individual's pose is caught give every figure its own personality. The man at the extreme left is filling his pipe, and next to him is a peasant holding a glass of beer. The middle figure in the background likewise has a glass in his hand.

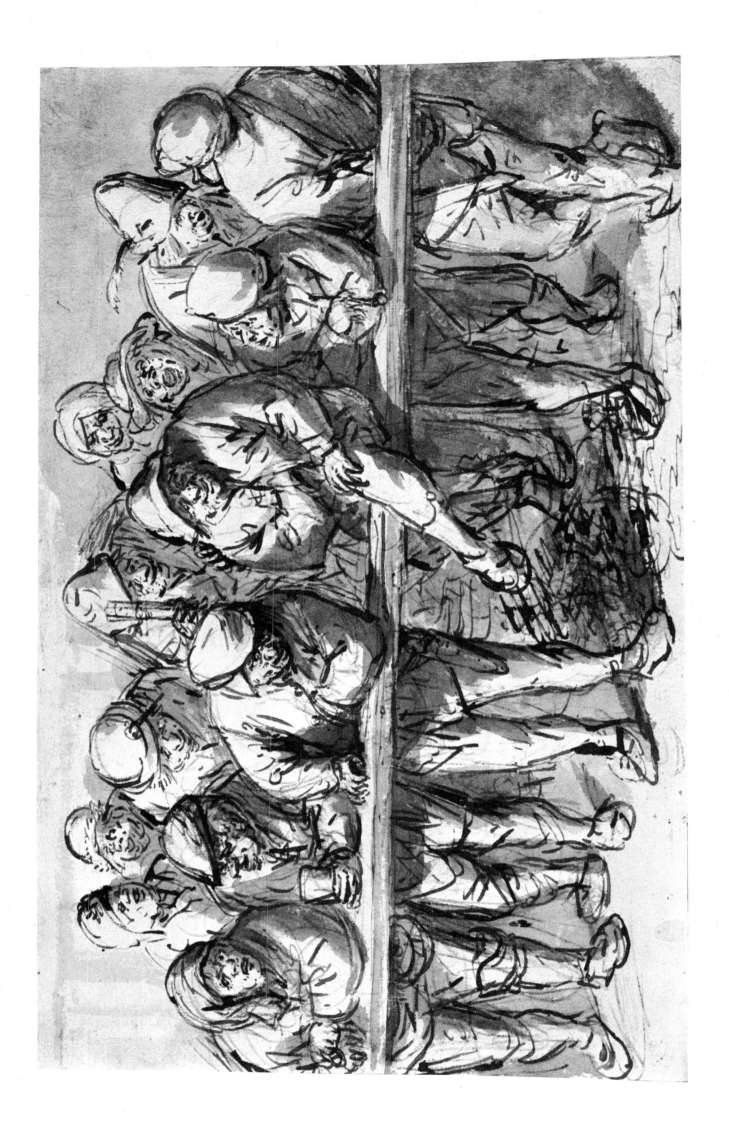

OSTADE

607 The Letter (Les Harangueurs)

Bistre, pen and ink over black chalk and wash on dark
  bluish paper, 217 x 190 mm.

Berlin, Ehem. Staatliche Museen, Kupferstichkabinett
  (K.d.Z. 16533)

PROVENANCE

Oppenheimer

LITERATURE

Godefroy, *L'oeuvre gravé de Adriaen van Ostade*, No. 19

Trautscholdt, p. 296

THIS DRAWING is the first study for an etching (Bartsch, No. 19). A painting was made of the same subject, in reverse (Collection Hengel, Paris, Hofstede de Groot, No. 65). The Berlin Kupferstichkabinett has a second drawing, which is connected even more closely with the etching. The luminous effect arises from the candle held by a man in front of the mullion of the window. The radiance creates contrasts of light and dark that are especially elaborated on the right side of the drawing, whereas on the left side they have not yet been fully developed. The etching is dated around 1667. Godefroy assumes that the painting served as the model for the etching. But it is more likely that the etching was based only on preliminary drawings and that the painting originated independently, although based on this drawing which had been the model for a later state of the etching.

In the painting there are vine leaves over the window, which make their appearance only in the later state of the etching. The etching and the painting show only four figures unlike the drawings, which have in the one case seven and in the other six. The persons are, as Heppner demonstrates (*Journal of the Warburg and Courtauld Institutes*, III, 1939-40, p. 29) "Rederijkers" ("Rhetoricians") of the Haarlem chapter "De Wijngaardtrancken," whose motto was "Love above all."

OSTADE

608 Study for the Van Ostade Family Portrait

Pen and chalk, washed with bistre and India ink,
126 x 214 mm.

Paris, Frits Lugt

PROVENANCE

Paert; Warwick

LITERATURE

Trautscholdt, p. 293

WE KNOW of three drawings (all in the Lugt collection) that were made as studies for the family portrait, dated 1654, which is in the Louvre in Paris (Cat. 1922, No. 2495). It has always been known as the portrait of the van Ostade family. In the painting the group has been completely rearranged and the children seem to be one or two years older; Adriaen van Ostade is seated at 'the extreme left and the young man is standing behind him. No children are placed between the father and mother; the girl, here on the left, is moved to the right, and so on.

In the painting as well as in the two other studies, which are variations of the one reproduced here, ten figures are represented, while there are eleven here.

All three drawings were first sketched very lightly in chalk. After that, the figures were delineated with a few pen lines. Then the shadows were added in order to give the figures relief and to suggest space. The numerous compositions of large family groups of the sixteenth century (Floris, Hoefnagel) find their final expression in the "Conversation Pieces" of the nineteenth century.

OSTADE

609 Seated Man Seen from the Back

Black chalk, heightened with white, on brown-gray paper,
124 x 110 mm.

Frankfort-on-Main, Staedel Art Institute (No. 3182)

OSTADE

610 Study of a Pig

Pen and chalk on brown paper, 180 x 223 mm.

Dated on reverse: *den 25 februari 1674*

Rotterdam, Museum Boymans-van Beuningen (No. H.153)

PROVENANCE

Koenigs

LITERATURE

Trautscholdt, p. 298

VAN OSTADE studied man in his everyday attitude, sketching him incessantly during his occupations, his having a good time or, as in this drawing, while he had a rest. The artist used some of his drawings for his paintings and his etchings; many, however, he did simply for the sake of sketching, for capturing the momentary aspect of a figure. The present drawing seems to belong to the latter category.

VAN OSTADE worked in Haarlem and was a younger contemporary of Frans Hals. His interests were mainly directed toward the intimate life of peasants and simple artisans. Relying on his drawings, he sought, as a painter, to catch the atmosphere of his subjects, down to the smallest details. Not only men but animals held his attention. He remained fascinated by this world until he grew older, portraying it again and again with obvious tenderness.

Numerous studies of pigs have been preserved by painters such as Rembrandt and Paulus Potter. In this work, van Ostade has made two careful sketches in chalk of a pig just before it is to be slaughtered. Even though it is merely an animal study, one has the sensation that it was conceived in connection with its rural surroundings. Thus this simple subject is, as it were, transported into a world in which man and animal are mutually dependent and are in constant touch with each other through the harsh conditions of peasant life.

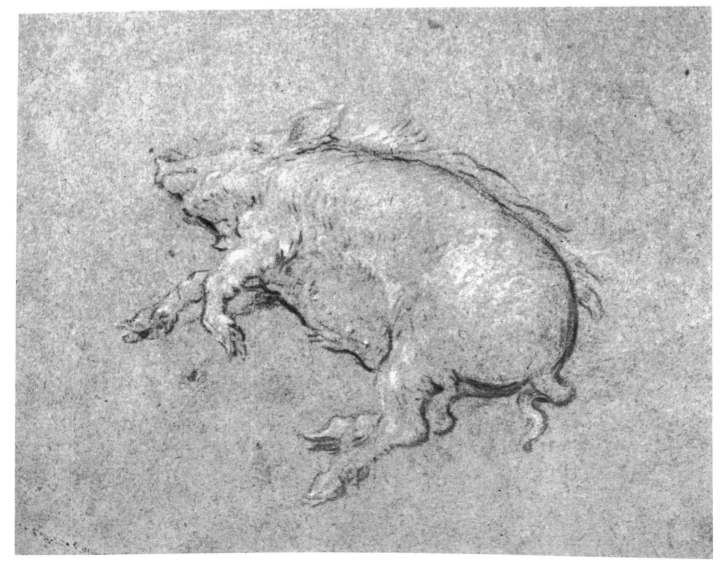

JACOB VAN RUISDAEL

(1629-1682)

JACOB VAN RUISDAEL *Born at Haarlem. Studied with his father Isack and his uncle Salomon van Ruisdael. 1648 member of the Haarlem guild. 1657 at Amsterdam. Died 14 March 1682 at Haarlem.*

611 Landscape with a Stone Bridge

Black chalk and brush in gray, 165 x 205 mm.

Leningrad, Hermitage (No. 5535), Acquired by the Hermitage before 1797

LITERATURE

Rosenberg, *Jacob van Ruisdael*, pp. 18, 114, No. Z39, Fig. 17

Dobroklonsky, *Gosudarstvennyi Ermitazh, Grafika*, Pl. LXXI

RUISDAEL WAS apparently fascinated by the light that came under the bridge from the other side of it, and that contrasted with the shadowy banks and the water in front of them. The trees, silhouetting against the sky, are dissolved into a lively pattern of innumerable small light areas and dark lines and dots. This interest in the vibrating light and the "clair-obscur" in nature comes in this drawing, executed shortly before 1650, at an early moment in Ruisdael's career. It is only later that the contrasts between light and dark in his paintings become more dramatic, even there where nature did not provide them.

RUISDAEL

612 View of Haarlem

Black chalk, brush with gray ink, 164 x 239 mm.
Paris, Louvre, Cabinet des Dessins (No. 23.017)

LITERATURE
Rosenberg, No. 59 (catalogue of drawings)
Lugt, II, No. 670, Pl. XXX

ON THE horizon at the right, the Cathedral of St. Bavo in Haarlem stands out against the sky. On the left can be seen a row of dunes, and in the foreground are others with shrubs, drawn in a slightly darker shade of gray than the cloudy sky. The birds seem to be harbingers of threatening weather. Yet the sun is still shining and the farms and trees, in the middle of the composition, stand out sharply in its light. The illumination, which is full of contrasts, gives a dramatic effect to the vista contemplated by two men at the right. After a first, barely recognizable sketch, the composition was tinted with the brush. The drawing that is now visible forms the last stage. In this final drawing, which contains indications rather than contours, the picturesque effect is strengthened by means of short strokes and seemingly disconnected scrawls.

The suggestion of spaciousness, atmosphere, and mood is made all the stronger by this technique. According to Lugt, the drawing was executed between 1654 and 1655, Ruisdael's first creative years. The artist was then not yet twenty-five years of age.

PHILIPS KONINCK

(1619-1688)

PHILIPS KONINCK *Born at Amsterdam 5 November 1619. Studied with his brother Jacob Koninck and with Rembrandt. Worked in Rotterdam and Amsterdam, where he died in 1688.*

613 Landscape with Houses amidst Trees

Pen and brown ink, brown and gray wash, heightened with white, 250 x 290 mm.

Inscribed: *p. Konin.*

Leningrad, Hermitage (No. 15121), Acquired by the Hermitage in 1924

PROVENANCE

Betzky; Academy of Fine Arts, Leningrad

LITERATURE

Dobroklonsky, *Dessins des maîtres anciens*, No. 139

Gerson, *Philips Koninck*, No. Z45

Agafonova, in *Trudy Gosudarstvennogo Ermitazha*, I, 1956, p. 159, Fig. 1

IN THIS drawing Philips Koninck, one of Rembrandt's pupils, combined a view of houses under trees, seen from a high point, with a distant view over trees and houses. At the left a woman is laying out linen sheets on a bleach-field. Since most of the bleach-fields in Holland were situated at the foot of the dunes near Haarlem, this view may have been sketched from those dunes.

By judiciously using simple means, a pen, a brush, brown and gray ink, and some white body-color, the artist created a spacious, sunny landscape, colorful notwithstanding the few tones employed. The preponderance of linear elements in the trees, as well as the tone of the colors and the horizon placed high are found in drawings by Philips Koninck that date from the 1640's and 1650's. This drawing therefore probably dates from the same time.

KONINCK

614 Landscape with Boathouse

Pen and brown ink, with water color, 156 x 224 mm.

New York, Harry G. Sperling

PROVENANCE

Zoomer; Roever; Goll van Franckenstein; Esdaile; Holford

LITERATURE

Reproduced in print by Ploos van Amstel (as Rembrandt)

Josi, *Collection d'imitations de dessins d'après les principaux maîtres hollandais et flamands* (as Rembrandt)

Smith, *A Catalogue Raisonné...Rembrandt*, VII, p. 200, No. 20

Waagen, *Treasures of Art in Great Britain*, II, p. 204

Lugt, *Les Marques de Collections*, 1921, p. 560

THIS LANDSCAPE, which passed through the hands of five of the most discerning collectors, always has been considered as a drawing done by Rembrandt. It is only recently that it has been recognized as one of the most impressive and accomplished drawings by Philips Koninck. In composition as well as technique it has all the characteristics of this pupil of Rembrandt's. The distant view combined with trees and buildings—in the middle distance a watermill can be distinguished—the combination of the water color with ink, and the specific forms of foliage and trees, of houses and other objects, as well as of the lonely man standing near the boat house recur in other drawings by the artist. Notwithstanding the high horizon and the predominance of brown, characteristics one finds in Koninck's early drawings, this landscape probably has to be considered as a comparatively late work, executed in the 1660's or 1670's because of the considerable freedom of draughtsmanship and delicate nuances in the colors (compare, for example, the landscape drawings in the Musée Condé, Chantilly, and in the Teyler Museum, Haarlem).

ABRAHAM FURNERIUS

(Ca. 1628-1654)

ABRAHAM FURNERIUS *Born perhaps at Amsterdam. Pupil of Rembrandt. Brother-in-law of Koninck. Died at Rotterdam in 1654.*

615 Landscape with a Bridge

Pen and brown ink and brown wash, heightened with
    white, 100 x 170 mm.

Inscribed: *a furnerius fecit*

Leningrad, Hermitage, Acquired by the Hermitage
    before 1797

FURNERIUS WAS one of Rembrandt's gifted pupils who studied with him about 1640-1645. No paintings by him are known; he therefore seems to have specialized in landscape drawings. It is not surprising that these drawings often resemble closely those by Philips Koninck since the latter was likewise a pupil of Rembrandt's and in addition a brother-in-law of Furnerius.

The drawing here reproduced shows the strong contrasts between light and dark, so characteristic for many of the landscapes of this gifted artist. The subject of the drawing is a mixture of fantasy and reality: the bridge and the houses, likewise the trees, are either a faithful rendering of such motifs in Amsterdam or another Dutch city such as Rotterdam, or a fantasy based upon this reality; the mountains in the background, however, are entirely un-Dutch. Such a transfer of a familiar view into fantastic surroundings was a device common with many a seventeenth-century Dutch landscape artist.

PAULUS POTTER
(1625-1654)

PAULUS POTTER *Born 20 November 1625. Studied with his father Pieter Simonsz. Potter in Amsterdam and with Jac. de Wet in Haarlem. 1645 worked in Delft. 1649 in The Hague. 1652 in Amsterdam, where he died 17 January 1654.*

616 Two Pigs

Black chalk, 81 x 128 mm.
Paris, Louvre, Cabinet des Dessins (No. 22.826)
LITERATURE
Galichon, *Gazette des Beaux-Arts*, I, 1866, p. 393
Lugt, II, No. 560, Pl. XVI

PAULUS POTTER

617 Study of a Bull

Black pencil, 126 x 155 mm.
Signed: *P. Potter f.*
Turin, Biblioteca Reale (No. 16535)
LITERATURE
Bertini, No. 64, Fig. 17

THESE ARE probably two studies of the same animal. Potter's studies of pigs, lying down, standing, in profile, etc., have been preserved in great numbers. The artist, who died at the age of twenty-nine, also left us a number of beautiful studies of horses, goats, deer, cows, and dogs. All of them are striking for their characteristic poses and simplicity of means. Marc de Bije etched this drawing in the seventeenth century.

THIS IS one of many autograph animal studies by this gifted painter of animals and landscapes. This same bull also occurs in paintings between 1648 and 1652, sometimes in a slightly different pose. The technique of wash applied with the brush makes for an intense radiance emanating from the animal. The same effect is also reached in his paintings after 1647. This drawing was probably executed shortly after that year.

GERARD TER BORCH

(1617-1681)

GERARD TER BORCH *Born at Zwolle. Influenced by Frans Hals. 1635 master of the Haarlem guild. Traveled and worked in England, Rome, Muenster and Spain. 1650-54 in Zwolle. From 1654 worked at Deventer, where he died 8 December 1681.*

618 Two Men on Horseback

Pencil, black chalk and pen in brown, 191 x 305 mm.

At the right numbered *10* (changed into *13*)

Amsterdam, Rijksmuseum, Rijksprentenkabinet
(No. A.1209)

SUCH STUDIES of men on horseback one generally does not associate immediately with the painter known primarily for his elegant interiors with women and cavaliers, and for his quiet and noble portraits of distinguished men and ladies. In his youth, however, Ter Borch was interested in cavalry and the life of the soldier, and in the 1630's he painted a number of scenes including men on horseback, engaged in fighting as well as resting. This drawing belongs to a series of studies of similar subjects and dates from that same period.

GERARD TER BORCH THE ELDER

(1584-1662)

GERARD TER BORCH THE ELDER *Father of a large family. Four of his children became artists also: Gerard the Younger, Gesina, Moses, and Harmen. Traveled to Italy 1607-11.*

619 Young Girl Reading a Book

Pen and wash in gray and brown, red chalk, 97 x 89 mm.

Amsterdam, Rijksmuseum, Rijksprentenkabinet
  (No. A.764)

PROVENANCE

Terborch the Elder, Family archives; Zebinden

LITERATURE

van Regteren Altena, *Hollaendische Meisterzeichnungen,*
  III, p. 9, figure frontispiece

THE TER BORCH possessions remained in the family until they were auctioned in 1886. The Rijksprentenkabinet in Amsterdam acquired nearly all the drawings and documents.

The drawing of the young girl reading a book might represent one of his children, perhaps Gesina. It was executed after his trip to Italy (1607-11), when he revealed himself to be a gifted topographical draughtsman. Once back in Holland he must have been deeply touched by the sober, intimate everyday life that so many Dutch artists of the seventeenth century attempted to represent. The young girl pictured here is a typical example of this earnest feeling.

To judge from the costume, the drawing was executed around 1630-35. The modesty of expression and the simplicity of observation anticipate related motifs which were later to impress **Vermeer of Delft.**

WILLEM VAN DE VELDE
(1633-1707)

WILLEM VAN DE VELDE *Born at Leyden 18 December 1633. Studied with his father Willem, and with Simon de Vlieger. Worked in Amsterdam and Greenwich, where he died 6 April 1707.*

620 Ships Saluting in a Calm

Pen and brown ink, wash, over black chalk, 143 x 335 mm.
Signed: *W.V.V.*
Lille, Palais des Beaux-Arts, Musée Wicar (No. 1047)

WILLEM VAN DE VELDE, marine painter and draughtsman as his father, was the naval reporter of his time. In thousands of drawings he recorded the battles between the Dutch and British fleets, and portrayed ships of all makes and years. First he was employed by the Dutch; later, after 1673, by the English.

In the present drawing ships salute while an important person, or persons, with their entourage are brought in smaller boats to some of the ships. With great ease and an unequaled understanding for ships, their riggings, and the behavior of sails and flags the artist sketched the scene, starting as he always did by drawing the horizon with a ruler and subsequently arranging the ships on the surface of the water. It remains to be established whether the waves on the water in this drawing were added by Willem van de Velde himself or by another hand.

JAN VAN HUYSUM

(1682-1749)

Jan van Huysum Born at Amsterdam 15 April 1682. Studied with his father Justus van Huysum. Worked in Amsterdam, where he died 7 February 1749.

621 Flower Piece

Pen and brown ink, charcoal and water color,
    408 x 318 mm.
Signed: *Jan van Huysum fecit*
Shawnee Mission, Kansas, Mr. and Mrs. Milton McGreevy

Although Jan van Huysum came late in the tradition of Dutch still-life painting, his paintings do not represent a last flowering or decadence of this art that the Dutch seventeenth-century painters had brought to a high level. On the contrary, he added to the art of still-life painting an element of lively sophistication and decorative elegance, retaining the thorough meticulousness of his predecessors. Not only as a painter but also as a draughtsman Jan van Huysum was a most accomplished artist. In contrast to his seventeenth-century predecessors, who rarely made still-life drawings, he sketched them frequently, sometimes as studies for his paintings, in other instances as finished works of art which in their turn could provide him the composition for a painting. The drawing, here reproduced, probably has to be considered as a finished drawing. Whether it also served as a study for a painting, however, has not been established.

JOHAN BARTHOLD JONGKIND

(1819-1891)

JOHAN BARTHOLD JONGKIND *Born at Latrop. 1846 settled in France. Died at Côte Saint-André in 1891.*

622 Windmills

Water color over black chalk, 263 x 450 mm.

Signed and dated: *Jongkind / Rotterdam 3 Sept 67*

Cambridge, Massachusetts, Harvard University, Fogg Art Museum, Granville L. Winthrop Bequest

PROVENANCE

Schoeller; Mme Klatz; Winthrop

JONGKIND LEFT Holland, as van Gogh did, and established himself in France (1846), where he was more appreciated in his lifetime than in his native country. In France he changed his romantic style and proceeded gradually to a new interpretation, which would have a profound influence on Impressionism. First in his water colors, subsequently in his paintings Jongkind achieved a rendering of light in bright, freely applied colors, which impressed Monet, who knew Jongkind's work well, and other impressionists.

The "Windmills" of this water color were sketched by Jongkind on one of his trips to Holland. The light on the mills as well as on the dike and the polders cannot be understood without supposing that Jongkind's love for the French light and his experiences in rendering it influenced him even when representing a subject as Dutch as windmills.

In the same year he painted the same subject (Private Collection in Holland, exhibited Rotterdam, 1955, No. 198, Fig. 186). The row of mills resembles those still standing near the village of Kinderdijk, south of Dordrecht, and consequently the painting just mentioned is supposed to represent those. This identification, however, needs further support.

VINCENT VAN GOGH

(1853-1890)

VINCENT VAN GOGH *Born at Groot Zundert 30 March 1853. 1869 became apprentice at Goupil's in The Hague. 1873 transferred to Goupil's in London. In May 1875 settled in Paris. 1876 taught in boarding school in Ramsgate, England. 1879-80 at the Borinage, Belgium. 1881 at The Hague. 1883 at Drenthe in northeastern Netherlands. Moved to Antwerp to become student at the Academy. 1886-88 in Paris. 1888 moved to Arles. Entered Asylum St. Paul at St. Rémy-en-Provence. 1890 moved to Auvers-sur-Oise. 27 July 1890 attempted to end his life. Died on 29 July 1890.*

623 Weeping Woman

Black chalk, brush in gray and black, heightened
   with white, 490 x 305 mm.

Chicago, Illinois, The Art Institute (No. 47.23),
   Given in Memory of Tiffany Blake

PROVENANCE

Gerstenberg; Heinemann

LITERATURE

de la Faille, *L'Oeuvre de Vincent van Gogh*, No. 1069

THE SOMBER years in The Hague, from December 1881 to September 1883, were for Vincent van Gogh one constant struggle, a struggle for existence as well as for the mastery of drawing the human figure and expressing the hardships under which his models were suffering. These models were the poor men and women in almshouses, the woman with her child whom he had decided he should try to rescue and protect, and people he met in the streets.

The drawing here reproduced, probably done in March-April 1883, exemplifies the mood of most of his sitters during these years. The attitude of the woman as well as the way she and her surroundings are drawn, the heavy contrasts between light and dark and the angularity of lines and forms, enhance the expression of sadness and sorrow.

VAN GOGH

624 View of Arles

Reed pen and India ink, 430 x 547 mm.

Signed: *Vue d'Arles / Vincent*

Providence, Rhode Island, Rhode Island School of Design,
Museum of Art, Gift of Mrs. Murray S. Danforth

PROVENANCE

Cassirer; Freudenberg; Danforth

LITERATURE

du Quesne-van Gogh, *Vincent van Gogh, herinneringen
aan haar broeder*

de la Faille, No. 1416

Rhode Island School of Design, *Museum Notes*, April, 1946

Tietze, *European Master Drawings in the United States*,
No. 152

Shoolman and Slatkin, *Six Centuries of French Master
Drawings in America*, Pl. CXXII

VINCENT VAN GOGH sketched this view of the city seen across meadows in May, 1888. About the oil painting of the same view he did at the time he wrote to his brother Theo: "A meadow full of very yellow buttercups—a ditch with Irises with green leaves and purple flowers—the town in the background—some gray willows—a strip of blue sky." The small sketch that accompanies these words in the letter is of the same composition as the drawing here reproduced.

With the obliquely placed rows of irises in the foreground, this composition is dynamic and restful at the same time. Van Gogh paid special attention to it and was concerned about achieving a satisfactory result: ". . . I'd like to do this study again, for the subject was very beautiful, and I had some trouble getting the composition."

In the drawing the colors of the trees and flowers have been translated into lines and dots of varying shape and intensity. Thus the "meadow full of very yellow buttercups" became a field of dots, light because of the white paper visible everywhere between them; the purple irises with their green leaves in the foreground are rendered with heavy strokes, the gay willows in the distance with thin and delicate parallel lines. The motif excited van Gogh: "A little town surrounded by fields all covered with yellow and purple flowers; exactly—can't you see it?—a Japanese dream."

VAN GOGH

625 The Blue Cart

Reed pen and bistre ink over black chalk, with red and
blue chalks, malachite green and mustard-yellow
water color, and white and pale blue gouache on
tan paper, 394 x 521 mm.

Cambridge, Massachusetts, Harvard University, Fogg Art
Museum (No. 1943.279), Grenville L. Winthrop Bequest

PROVENANCE

Seligmann; Schall; Galerie Artz and Du Bois, The Hague;
Haniel; Winthrop

LITERATURE

Meier-Graefe, *Vincent van Gogh*, Pl. XLIV

de la Faille, No. 1484

Huyghe, *Les dessins de van Gogh*, Pl. XV

Cooper, *Van Gogh, Drawings and Watercolors*, No. 22

"I HAVE a new subject in hand, fields green and yellow as far as the
eye reaches. I have drawn it twice already and am now starting it
again as a painting, absolutely like a Salomon (Philips) Koninck—
Rembrandt's pupil, you know, who did immense flat plains. Or else it
is like something of Michel, or Jules Dupré, anyhow it differs altogether from the rose gardens." This van Gogh wrote to his brother
Theo in June, 1888.

It is not sure whether the drawing here reproduced is one of the
two van Goghs mentioned, since four drawings of the same subject
exist in addition to a painting. In two drawings (Faille, Nos. 1485 and
1486) the plain with the ruins of Montmajour in the distance is seen
from the same point of view as in the painting (Faille, No. 412); in a
water color drawing (Faille, No. 1483) it is seen from the same direction but from a point a little farther down the slope on which the
artist was seated when he painted the picture. The drawing here reproduced shows the plain from a point a little more to the right, is
therefore not directly related with the painting and must have been
done separately.

Van Gogh's reference to Philips Koninck is entirely appropriate.
He likewise painted and sketched views of valleys and plains seen
from an elevated point, with rows of trees and dwellings here and
.there, and bordered in the distance by mountains. In contrast to the
seventeenth-century artist, however, van Gogh connected foreground
and background into one continuous stretch of land. Van Gogh's
handling of the pen is, furthermore, entirely different, tense instead
of relaxed and expressive instead of descriptive.

VAN GOGH

626 Peasant of the Camargue

Quill and reed pen and ink over soft graphite pencil on
  white paper, 494 x 380 mm.

Signed at lower left: *Vincent*

Cambridge, Massachusetts, Harvard University, Fogg Art
  Museum (No. 1943.515), Grenville L. Winthrop Bequest

PROVENANCE

Thorsten Laurin; Klaus Fahraeus; Winthrop

LITERATURE

Mercure de France, VIII, 1893, p. 313

Meier-Graefe, Pl. XLVII

de la Faille, No. 1460

Fels, *Vincent van Gogh,* p. 37

George, *Le dessin français de David à Cézanne,* Pl. LXXVI

Huyghe, Pl. XIX

Nordenfalk, *Van Gogh,* Fig. 39

Mongan, *One Hundred Master Drawings,* p. 192

Goldwater, *Vincent van Gogh,* Pl. XXIX

van Gelder, *De schoonheld van ons land, Prenten en
  tekeningen,* Pl. CXCV

Heise, *Grosse Zeichner des XIX Jahrhunderts,* p. 144,
  No. 14

"JUST AS I'm writing to you, the poor peasant, who has a caricature-like resemblance to our father, is entering the café," Vincent wrote to his brother in September 1888 (letter 534). "Anyhow, the resemblance is terrible. The evasive, and the tiredness and the vagueness of the mouth above all. It continuously seems a pity to me that I have not been able to catch it." The drawing here reproduced van Gogh had made about a month earlier after the painting he had just finished. He sent the drawing to his brother and would send the painting later: "Shortly you will make the acquaintance with Master Patience Escalier, kind of man with a hoe, formerly cowherd of the Camargue, at present gardener at a house in the Crau."

Van Gogh writes at length about the painting, about its "sun-steeped, sunburned quality, browned by the grand sun and grand air." He imagined the man "in the midst of the furnace of the harvest, in the very south," under the brilliant sun of which he says in the same letter: "Ah! those who do not believe in our sun here are real infidels."

As many of the large, finished drawings that van Gogh made in the south of France, this one was done after the painting, now in the Museum at Cologne. The drawing is, however, more than a mere recording; it has become an independent work of art. With a highly personal and expressive use of the reed pen the artist has been able to reflect the structure of the brush strokes and to translate the painted colors and their intensity into gradations of black or brown as well as to express volume, textures, and above all to penetrate behind the surface and to express the character of the poor man for whom he felt compassion.

Vincent

VAN GOGH

627 Bridge at Arles

Reed pen and brown ink, 242 x 318 mm.

Los Angeles, California, Los Angeles County Museum
(No. L.2100.49-188), Mr. and Mrs. George Gard
de Sylva Collection

PROVENANCE

Durieux-Cassirer; Paret; Seligmann; Gard de Sylva

LITERATURE

de la Faille, No. 1471

Catalogue Exhibition Vincent van Gogh, 1935-36, No. 115

Shoolman and Slatkin, *Six Centuries of French Master
Drawings in America*, Pl. CXXI

THE DRAWBRIDGE at Arles, known as "Pont de l'Anglais," was a
motif van Gogh sketched and painted various times in 1888 and
in the following year. He was especially attracted by the silhouette
of the double drawbridge against the blue sky, the cypresses near one
end of the bridge, the people and the carriages slowly moving across
it, and the women doing their laundry. The motif reminded him of
Japanese prints.

This drawing, coming late in the sequence of studies of the subject,
shows an increased and intensified simplification in composition and
motifs. Both banks, the bridge, and the body of water are in balance
with each other; the boats, present in earlier versions, have been
eliminated; the group of washerwomen has been reduced to one small
figure at the left near the bridge. The painted version of this drawing,
now in the Wallraf-Richartz Museum at Cologne, differs from it only
in minor details.

VAN GOGH

628 The Iron Bridge at Trinquetaille on the Rhône

Pen and brown ink on tan paper, 242 x 312 mm.

New York, Robert Lehman

LITERATURE

Meier-Graefe, p. 76

de la Faille, No. 1507

VINCENT WROTE in June 1888 to Theo, his brother: "I have a view of the Rhône—the iron bridge of Trinquetaille, where the sky and the stream are the color of absinth, the quays a shade of lilac, the figures leaning over the parapet blackish, the iron bridge an intense blue, with a note of vivid orange in the blue distance and a note of intense emerald green . . ."

In the drawing here reproduced the artist sketched the scene with bold strokes, transforming the parapet and the sloping side of the quay as well as the bridge and the pillars on which it rests into groups of parallel lines, dynamic even there where they render static forms. The bridge contrasting against the sky, the figures clustered together at one side of the open space, the interplay of light and line convey the mood expressed in the painting: ". . . I am trying to get at something utterly compelling and therefore irresistible."

VAN GOGH

629 Tree in a Meadow

Reed pen and India ink over charcoal, 488 x 613 mm.

Chicago, Illinois, The Art Institute (No. 45.31),
    Gift of Tiffany and Margaret Blake

PROVENANCE

van Gogh-Bonger; Jan Veth; Christine Veth

LITERATURE

de la Faille, No. 1468 (as "Coin de Parc à Arles")

Catalogue Exhibition Vincent van Gogh, 1935-36, No. 114

Tietze, *European Master Drawings in the United States*,
    No. 153

IN THIS drawing the ink has retained its original black color unusually well. In most other drawings of the Arles period and of a later date the ink, which in most cases originally was black, has turned dark or even a light tone of brown, thus giving a different impression from that intended by the artist.

Van Gogh made the drawing either at the very end of his stay in Arles or soon after he moved to St. Rémy. In the latter case the tree was sketched in the garden of the hospital. The drawing, called by the artist himself "L'arbre pleureur dans l'herbe" and therefore in English sometimes "Weeping Tree in Grass" expresses van Gogh's "subjective longing for the objective nature, a longing which was insatiable since nature meant for van Gogh the very substance of life. . . . Every detail of a tree, of a plant, became 'van Gogh,' because he made it into part of himself, thus elevating it without wanting to do so above the surrounding world" (A. M. Hammacher, 1953). Furthermore, the drawing is an early instance of van Gogh's expressing his feelings of solitude through rendering nature; later in St. Rémy and finally in Auvers-sur-Oise his landscapes will convey the same feelings with an ever increasing intensity until nature does not provide a place for the artist any more.

VAN GOGH

630 A Grove of Cypresses

Reed pen and brown ink over pencil, 626 x 465 mm.

Chicago, Illinois, The Art Institute (No. 27.543),
  Gift of Robert Allerton

PROVENANCE

Mrs. van Gogh-Bonger; Fahraeus; Olson; Eisenloeffel;
  Wacker; Thannhauser; Allerton

LITERATURE

Elzevier's Geillustreerd Maandschrift, XXX, 1905, p. 421

Meier-Graefe, Pl. XXIII

de la Faille, No. 1524

Catalogue Exhibition Vincent van Gogh, 1935-36, No. 118

Huyghe and Jaccottet, *Le dessin français au XIVe siècle*,
  Pl. CXXII

Shoolman and Slatkin, *Six Centuries of French Master
  Drawings in America*, Pl. CXXIV

AFTER HIS mental and physical collapse in the spring of 1889 van Gogh was brought to the Saint Paul de Mausole Monastery, an asylum in St. Rémy near Arles. Soon he painted more passionately than ever, feverishly making one landscape after another. In June he painted the first version of "Cypresses," which he changed later, in February 1890. The drawing here reproduced corresponds with the first version of that painting, since the two figures that van Gogh added to the painting are absent. The cypresses, energetically and quickly drawn with round, decided strokes, dominate the entire composition. They have become flames rather than trees, soaring in the strong sunlight, detaching themselves from the ground and assuming the shape of weightless nervous energy. These characteristics are more apparent in the drawing than in the painting, where the cypresses with "that difficult bottle-green shade," as the artist called their color, make a heavier and more massive impression.